Corruption in the American Political System

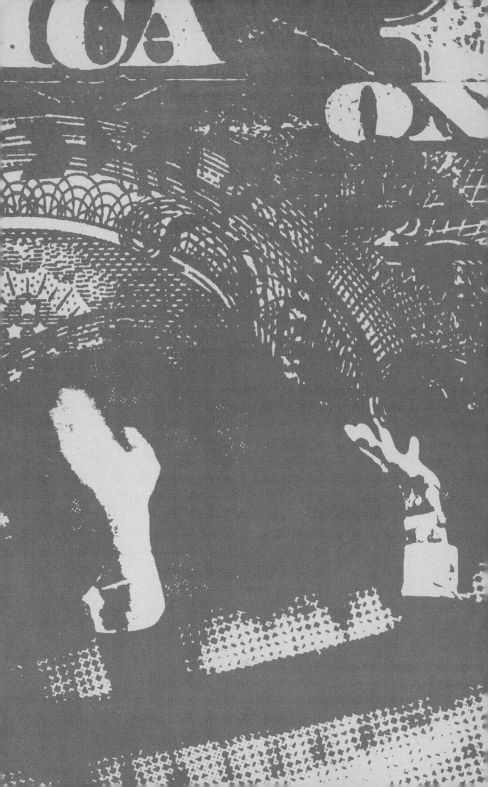

CORRUPTION IN THE AMERICAN POLITICAL SYSTEM

Larry L. Berg

Harlan Hahn

John R. Schmidhauser

University of Southern California

GENERAL LEARNING PRESS
250 James Street
Morristown, New Jersey 07960

To Mary, Andrea, Michelle, Thelma, Susan, Sarah, Martha, Steven, Paul, Thomas, and John C.

Manufactured in the United States of America

Published simultaneously in Canada

Library of Congress Catalog Card Number 76-9578

ISBN 0-382-18110-7

Preface

This book grew out of our strong conviction that political corruption in the United States is part of the political system rather than the result of the rise of an occasional "evil man." Our argument in no manner supports the crude suggestion that somehow because "they all do it, it's really not so bad." Instead, we have attempted to establish the argument and to support it with a variety of illustrative examples, both historical and contemporary. We hope that we also have been able to stimulate intelligent reappraisal, further inquiry and, ultimately, the difficult but necessary process of restructuring political institutions. Thus the task that we undertook is a dual one—and is addressed to interested participants and citizen-observers of the present political system as well as to students and practitioners in the field of political science.

Our intellectual obligations are numerous. Harlan Hahn acknowledges his appreciation for the stimulation and influence of the late V. O. Key, Jr. Larry Berg similarly acknowledges the impact of Llewelyn Werner, and John Schmidhauser recalls, with gratitude and high intellectual respect, both the teaching skill and rigor and the exemplary models of citizen participation of George W. Spicer and the late James Hart of the University of Virginia. A special thanks goes to former Assemblyman Winfield A. Shoemaker for his draft of material for the chapter on the California legislature and his valuable suggestions. We also want to express deep appreciation to our good friends Ed and Joyce Koupal, the founders and heart of the People's Lobby.

The long hours of discussion, writing, and revision were made much more livable because of the assistance and understanding of Mary Berg, Thelma Schmidhauser, and the vigorous youngsters who kept things lively in our households.

The secretaries at the University of Southern California, Debbie Kahn, Fritzi Fox, Cleatus Pomazal, and Marie Watson, have our deep appreciation for their excellent handling of the manuscript.

Larry Berg

Harlan Hahn

John R. Schmidhauser

Contents

1

Watergate in Historical Perspective: The Roots of Corruption in American Political Institutions

DURING THE SECOND TERM OF THE NIXON ADMINISTRA-
tion, the American people were subjected to a series of events that were
unprecedented. The discovery of an attempted burglary at the offices of
the Democratic National Committee in the Watergate building in
Washington, D.C., led to the revelation of a plethora of scandals that
threatened to undermine the foundations of the political system. The
indictment and conviction of many top government officials, as well as
the resignation and subsequent pardoning of a president, produced a
constitutional crisis that should compel all Americans to renewed consideration of the endemic problem of political corruption and to a
reexamination of the institutions of government. The purpose of this
book is to assist citizens and students of American politics in this reappraisal.

Perhaps the easiest way to explain the scandals that have plagued
American government both recently and in the past is to blame specific
individuals. This approach is exemplified in the judgment made by
Frank Mankiewicz,[1] who was Senator George McGovern's campaign
director in the 1972 presidential election. Mankiewicz concluded that
the Watergate crisis was the inevitable outcome of Richard Nixon's
"limitless appetite for victory and electoral triumph." In arguing that
"no one can point to a Nixon ideology, beyond winning the next election, or to personal boundaries of conscience as to how that might be
accomplished," Mankiewicz seemed to ascribe the scandal simply to

human foibles. A fundamental flaw in this position is that it tends to divert attention from institutional defects and weaknesses that may be responsible for corruption in the political process. It is remarkably similar to the notion that by ridding it of Boss Tweed, New York became "clean." It is the judgment of the authors of this book that the fault for the misconduct that was exposed in the Watergate episode cannot be attributed exclusively to a specific individual, to a group of people, or to one political party. Instead, the sources of corruption in the structure of American politics must be explored.

Another common interpretation of political corruption and of the Watergate crisis is reflected in Arthur Schlesinger, Jr.'s *The Imperial Presidency*.[2] Schlesinger asserted, "The unwarranted and unprecedented expansion of presidential power, because it ran through the whole Nixon system, was bound, if repressed at one point, to break out in another. This, not Watergate, was the central issue." Although few would deny that the power of the executive branch has grown at the expense of other governmental institutions, an exclusive preoccupation with the presidency ignores the manifestations of corruption in political parties, Congress, the courts, and at the state and municipal levels of government. In fact, it is the central thesis of this book that the explanation of corruption can be found in developments that have affected *all* public institutions. The events of Watergate and the Nixon administration are not the only scandals that have tainted American political life. Hence, the search for an understanding of the origins of political corruption must encompass an extensive examination of the foundations of the government process.

Consequently, the definition of corruption which is basic to this study embodies a systemic concept. Political corruption violates and undermines the norms of the system of public order which is deemed indispensable for the maintenance of political democracy.

Although some American scholars have investigated corruption in the political systems of so-called underdeveloped nations, most students of American politics have eschewed a serious treatment of such phenomena in the United States. Perhaps one reason has been the tendency to deemphasize or to understate corruption in this country. This position was espoused by Bayless Manning, former Dean of the Stanford Law School, who argued that the stress on problems such as conflicts of interest among public officials had become "a modern obsession . . . because American politics is highly susceptible to morality escalation." Therefore, he concluded, "we can afford the luxury of worrying about public harms before they happen.''[3] This remarkably complacent observation was published in 1964, before the tale of the Watergate episode had unfolded. But his article appeared at a time when many of the harbingers of the momentous moral and constitutional crises of the 1970s were visible, events which Manning blithely over-looked in extolling the virtues of the American system. His opinion thus can be distinguished from the posture of the many scholars who have conveniently ignored the existence of corruption. Ironically, he even asserted, "Though some may find it surprising, the fact is that in this country we are currently living in an era of unexampled honesty in public administration." According to Manning, this paradise of public propriety was created by the " . . . evolution of modern administrative techniques for fiscal control, development of a professional sense in the civil service, virtual elimination of the spoils system, spread of competi-tive bidding, increase in public education, enrichment of the economy, and other [unnamed!] basic shifts in the national organism . . . ."[4] By concentrating on the strengths of the political system to the exclusion of its defects, this analysis ultimately revealed the dangers of biased com-mentary and made for poor prophecy.

Another more conventional treatment of the issue was exem-plified by James Q. Wilson's "Corruption: The Shame of the States." In this essay, Wilson did acknowledge the existence of corruption, but he inexplicably preferred to devote much of his analysis to the empiri-cally unsubstantiated assertion that the states were (or had become) more corrupt than the cities. Wilson, however, did discuss three theories of political corruption. According to the first theory certain ethnic or minority groups were relatively uninterested in and un-influenced by ethical norms stressing probity and impersonal efficiency, but they were receptive to familial or group favoritism, personal (as distinguished from public) loyalty, and private gain. The second theory, allegedly derived from the works of Lincoln Steffens, journalist and reformer, was described as "a theory that corruption is the result of ordinary men facing extraordinary temptations." The third theory, which was based upon assumptions in the writings of Henry Jones Ford, turn of the century political scientist, posited a structural solution; name-ly, the unification of powers that were presumably divided by a con-stitutional system of checks and balances.[5]

Wilson's treatment of the remedies implied by each of these three theories of corruption also reveals some interesting deficiencies both in his own analysis and in the general literature that is available on this topic. First, it is instructive that all of the theories reviewed by Wilson were developed in the late nineteenth or early twentieth century. No American thinker, either before or since that time, apparently has presented ideas on the subject of corruption that were considered worthy of further examination. Second, Wilson's propensity to stereotype a preference for favoritism, personal loyalty, and private gain as an attribute of ethnic or minority groups rather than as a personality trait must be severely criticized. It constitutes not only an unwarranted and unconscionable aspersion upon the character of members of those groups, but it might be used by many other citizens as a rationalization to prevent representatives of those groups from attaining positions of political power. Third, Wilson commits a common fallacy by neglecting the broader ramifications either of corruption or of the possibilities of political change. Although both Steffens and Ford did consider the relationship between political and economic influence, and although both proposed alterations in existing political institutions, Wilson summarizes their recommendations for reform in relatively narrow terms. Of the type of corruption uncovered by Steffens, Wilson asserts that "the solution . . . is, obviously, to inspect, audit, check, and double-check." Similarly, Ford's structural remedy for corruption is described as reforms which were "precisely what the National Civic League and other reform groups have attempted by their espousal of the council-manager plan for municipal government and what strong advocates of strong and responsible political parties have sought with respect to state and national government."[6] Wilson's characterization of the reforms implied by all three theories of corruption does not suggest that there is a need for any further innovations in the political system. Instead, his account seems to denote traces of ethnocentrism and adherence to the status quo. Broader notions of the influences that generate corruption throughout the governmental process, and of the alternative mechanisms by which those influences might be restrained, were conspicuously ignored or avoided in Wilson's analysis.

The effort to preclude any consideration of structural changes in the political process also has been reflected in the tendency to restrict the definition of corruption to the commission of acts that are contrary to existing law. In his comparative study of corruption in several nations, James Scott acknowledged the difficulties associated with a formal legalistic definition:

> In a more general sense, our conception of corruption does not cover political systems that are, in Aristotelian terms, 'corrupt' in that they systematically serve the interests of special groups or sectors. A given regime may be biased and repressive: it may consistently favor the in-

terests, say, of the aristocracy, big business, a single ethnic group, or a single region while it represses other demands, but it is not *ipso facto* corrupt unless these ends are accomplished by breaching the formal norms of office . . . .[7]

There are several problems, however, in any attempt to distinguish between behavior that is corrupt or not corrupt only according to the yardstick provided by the law. Perhaps most important, it must be recognized that those who hold political power in any society are able to determine legality. Consequently, an exclusive reliance upon legal norms to identify corrupt activities could result in the danger that was presaged by the dialogues of the Greek philosophers, namely, the imposition of the axiom of Thrasymachus rather than the rule of Socrates, or the recognition of the authority of the powerful rather than of the just. (In Plato's *Republic* both engaged in a discussion of the bases of political authority; Socrates asserted the necessity for establishing an ethical basis, but Thrasymachus presented the argument that might makes right.) By limiting the delineation of corrupt or scandalous conduct to the criteria prescribed by existing statutes, there is the additional risk that citizens might be less likely to express their moral indignation about the unprincipled acts of public officials and to demand structural changes in the political system. Legal stipulations can often be stretched or amended to suit the purposes of politicians, and the public has a right not only to insist that their leaders observe more stringent standards of ethical behavior but also to force the construction of institutional arrangements that would prevent government officeholders from engaging in immoral or corrupt activities under the guise of the law. Corruption cannot be equated solely with illegal conduct; in fact, far more commonly, it involves extralegal or even technically legal activities. As a result, there is a need to replace those definitions of corruption that are based upon purely legal norms with a concept that can be used to identify and to distinguish activities and practices that undermine a constitutional system of law and justice.

Madison, de Tocqueville, and an Unknown Citizen

The unwillingness of most modern American political scientists to examine the roots of corruption effectively stands in sharp contrast to the works of James Madison and to the analyses of Alexis de Tocqueville and his contemporaries. Their discussions of issues concerned with public and private roles in society, as well as the relationship between economic and political power, were sufficiently broad and universal to provide a means of relating questionable or improper conduct to the constitutional system. Few subsequent commentators have approached those issues from this perspective. Their emphasis has, more often than not, been focused upon direct bribes and personal greed rather than upon fundamental or systemic corrupting influences within existing institutions. Exceptions are found in the studies of corruption by Arnold Heidenheimer and by Arnold Rogow and Harold Lasswell. As Rogow and Lasswell note, ''A *corrupt act* violates responsibility toward at least one system of public or civic order and is in fact incompatible with (destructive of) any such system.''[8] Indeed, their comment, which is the approach to corruption adopted in this book, constitutes a rare modern restatement of de Tocqueville's orientation. The perspective on the study of corruption offered by these men provides a useful basis for evaluating morality or immorality in the conduct of public officials by focusing on actions that comprise a threat to the constitutional order and to the values of a democratic society.

Basically, de Tocqueville's observations on America reflected his efforts to understand the components of democracy and to assess those forces that might enhance or diminish its future prospects. Consequently, his discussion of political corruption in the United States was a concomitant of his general treatment of the characteristics that made democracy possible in the social and economic environment of the new nation. De Tocqueville stressed that the relative equality of conditions ''naturally urges men to embark in commercial and industrial pursuits, and that it tends to increase and to distribute real property.''[9] Ironically, de Tocqueville also viewed these tendencies as containing the potential conditions that ultimately might undermine and corrupt democratic institutions in the United States.

Although little attention has been paid to this aspect of de Tocqueville's work by twentieth-century theorists, his comments on the dangers inherent in the concentration of social, economic, and political power were widely discussed and debated by contemporary American critics of his then new work. One of the most eloquent statements in this controversy was contained in a review of de Tocqueville's *Democracy in America* that was published in *The United States Magazine and Democratic Review* in July 1838.[10] The anonymous reviewer examined de Tocqueville's comments on the rise of an aristocracy in detail and also proposed an alternative proposition that was directly related to the issue of the corruption of democracy by persons of great wealth. He began his critique with a lengthy quotation from *Democracy in America* concerning the "influence of the legal profession," which de Tocqueville had described as "the real and only principle of aristocracy" in this country.

> "If I were requested," says our author [de Tocqueville], "to point out the seat of the aristocratic principle in the United States, I should answer, without hesitation, that it is not to be found among the wealthy, who are not combined together by any common bond of interest. The seat of the American aristocracy is with the judges on the bench and the lawyers at the bar.
>
> "The more I reflect upon what I have witnessed in the United States, the more fully am I satisfied that the lawyers are the most powerful class in the community, and the only real counterpoise to the influence of the democracy. In the United States we perceive at once how well the spirit that pervades the bar is fitted by its virtues, and even its defects, to neutralize the vices inherent in a popular government. . . .
>
> "The lawyers form, in the United States, a power, which is very little feared, and is even not much noticed; which carries no flag of its own; which yields flexibly to every passing exigency, and follows, without resistance, the movement of the body politic; but which, nevertheless, surrounds and embraces that body in all its members,—penetrates into all the classes that compose it,—works upon it secretly, and finally gives it any shape which suits its own pleasure."[11]

The anonymous reviewer found de Tocqueville's comments on the countervailing influence of lawyers and on the extent to which they permeated political movements somewhat "eccentric" and untenable, but he did not dismiss their accuracy. In fact, he concluded, "This theory is rather more plausible than the one just alluded to, of the 'omnipotence of majorities,' and agrees a good deal better, with a merely superficial view of the mode in which the public affairs are conducted in this country." The unnamed critic continued by describing the influence of attorneys in terms as applicable to modern America as they were to the era in which they were written.

> It is no doubt true that the legal profession furnishes a large proportion of the persons employed in the administration of the Government in all its departments, Executive, Legislative, and Judicial. It is also true that a very large proportion of the lawyers so employed habitually act with the political party which represents for the time, under whatever name, the "aristocratic" principle, and supply that party with its acknowledged and

ostensible leaders. From these apparent facts it is not very unnatural for a hasty observer to conclude with M. de Tocqueville that the legal profession forms, in fact, the real and substantial basis of the aristocracy . . . .

Yet, the anonymous reviewer was not content to allow the argument to rest at that point. He asserted that "though a superficial view of the facts . . . might lead to the conclusion that the legal profession forms . . . the basis of the . . . 'aristocratic tendencies,' which are developed . . . in this country, a more thorough examination of the subject shows very plainly that this is not the real state of the case."

Initially, the critic observed that de Tocqueville was incorrect in assuming that the public had failed to recognize or to be appalled by the influence of attorneys. He stated, "The opinion of M. de Tocqueville is not uncommon among ourselves . . . ." But, rather than forming a basis for their invisibility or respect, the reviewer noted that this attitude

> has contributed largely, in connection with other causes, to generate the unpopularity of lawyers as a class. For it is far from being true, as he [de Tocqueville] supposes, that they are less distrusted by the people than other educated men. It is notorious, on the contrary, that as a class, and with the rare exception of those who openly espouse the democratic cause, they are decidedly unpopular . . . .

Even more important, this contemporary commentator on de Tocqueville proceeded not only to identify what he considered the actual location of aristocratic tendencies in America, but also to explain its relationship to the legal profession in a manner that suggested a crucial source of corrupting political influences. His theory was stated in the following words.

> The members of the legal profession in this country are not the aristocracy but the agents, organs, or, to use a more appropriate term the "attorneys," of the aristocracy. The aristocracy is constituted by the owners of "accumulated wealth," and chiefly by the moneyed men of the great commercial cities. These are generally persons educated in the habits of practical life, and not very capable of pleading their own cause before the public. The lawyers undertake to do this for them; they occupy the foreground; they fill the legislative halls and the various departments of the Government; they talk and write upon all occasions, in season and out of season; in short, they take the responsibility, and bear the unpopularity, of keeping up a perpetual warfare upon the democratic tendencies that are constantly in action, and in the end generally carry all before them. The conspicuous position which the lawyers hold in the forefront

of the battle, gives them an imposing and formidable aspect. In reality, however, they are merely present in a representative character, and would declaim as loudly and as long for democracy as they now do against it, if they could be as well paid for their trouble . . . .

Thus, in the judgment of the reviewer, lawyers did not comprise the true aristocracy in America; instead, they were simply the agents of an aristocracy consisting of moneyed interests. As a result, members of the legal profession were the vehicle for transmitting the power of accumulated wealth and for injecting the influence of money into the political process. The services of attorneys were, of course, available to anyone who could afford them. But since the moneyed aristocracy has controlled the largest share of the resources expended for their talents, the words and behavior of practitioners of the law always have been dominated by the desires of persons with great fortunes.

De Tocqueville himself noted the growing concentration of political power among those who controlled the economic life of the new nation.

As the conditions of men constituting the nation became more and more equal, the demand for manufactured commodities becomes more general and more extensive; and the cheapness which places these objects within the reach of slender fortunes becomes a great element of success. Hence there are every day more men of great opulence and education who devote their wealth and knowledge to manufactures; and who seek, by opening large establishments, and by a strict division of labor, to meet the fresh demands which are made on all sides. Thus, in proportion as the mass of the nation turns to democracy, that particular class which is engaged in manufactures becomes more aristocratic . . . .[12]

In fact, he even implicitly acknowledged the ability of the wealthy to protect themselves from scandal by disavowing or disassociating from the activities of their agents. As de Tocqueville said:

The territorial aristocracy of former ages was either bound by law, or . . . bound by usage, to come to the relief of its serving-men, and to succour their distresses. But the manufacturing aristocracy of our age first impoverishes and debases the men who serve it and then abandons them to be supported by the charity of the public . . . .

Yet, even de Tocqueville did not seem to appreciate fully the political crises that might be precipitated by economic giants in American society. Although he recognized the potential threat posed by growing industrialization, de Tocqueville apparently did not believe that this trend would place the political system in serious jeopardy. Thus, he concluded:

> I am of opinion, upon the whole, that the manufacturing aristocracy which is growing up under our eyes, is one of the harshest which ever existed in the world; but at the same time it is one of the most confined and least dangerous. Nevertheless the friends of democracy should keep their eyes anxiously fixed in this direction; for if ever a permanent inequality of conditions and aristocracy again penetrate into the world, it may be predicted that this is the channel by which they will enter.

De Tocqueville's assertion that the manufacturing aristocracy comprised "one of the most confined and least dangerous" elites was seriously challenged by the reviewer for *The United States Magazine and Democratic Review,* who contended:

> The possession of accumulated wealth is the only thing which can give an individual substantial political power; that is, the power of commanding the services of others. Superiority in intellectual and physical qualities, natural or acquired,—strength, talent, learning, skill, dexterity, in the arts,—are only so many means of "rendering service" to others with greater facility or effect. But to render services is a very different thing from commanding them. The exercise of these valuable qualities may produce wealth, and bring with it political power; but their possessors, as such, are the "servants," and not the "masters" or "rulers," of those who employ them. This is the position of the lawyers as a class in relation to the moneyed men. The only lucrative part of a lawyer's business is that which is connected with the management of property, and especially property accumulated in large masses, and employed in an active way. The lawyers, as a class, depend for success in life upon being employed by the owners of property, and particularly of accumulated property. They are, therefore, virtually, with all their superiority of education, and, as a body, of intellectual power, the mere agents, factors, or, in one word, servants of the moneyed men. Their political career, if they go at all into politics,—which the most prudent carefully avoid,—is entirely subordinate to the professional, which furnishes their means of subsistence; and they fall, accordingly, without effort, into any political course which the interest of their employers may happen to dictate.

By stressing the economic connection between the legal profession and the manufacturing aristocracy, therefore, this unnamed critic of the early nineteenth century developed a critical point that de Tocqueville had apparently ignored or overlooked. It is that the corrupting influence of concentrated wealth often is not exerted directly in the political process, but the law and public policies enacted by government frequently interface with this influence through the actions of lawyers, politicians, and others who serve as the agents of the moneyed aristocracy.

Perhaps even more important, the observations on contemporary affairs recorded by de Tocqueville's reviewer comprised an important contribution to an understanding of the then prevalent views of political morality. The conditions that the perceptive French visitor predicted would become a future threat to the integrity of democratic institutions *already* were perceived as tangible and current in the 1830s. By that time, America had experienced a series of scandals that usually involved the interplay between social and economic power, political subservience to this influence, and the attempt to make aspects of unethical conduct either legally or morally acceptable.

In many respects, the emergence of immorality in American politics reflected the failure of the framers of the Constitution to construct governmental institutions that would eliminate or minimize corruption. In *The Federalist* and other writings, the principal architects of the American political system explicitly stated that this system was designed to protect the public from avarice and scandals. In *Federalist* Number 10, for example, James Madison made the crucial observation that institutions rather than men provide the only certain defense against immoral behavior. Madison felt that the principal threat to democratic governments arose from "the mischiefs of faction," or the tendency of men to join together in the pursuit of political benefits. Madison did not believe that politicians could be entrusted to regulate the conflict that inevitably results from these activities. He wrote, "It is in vain to say that enlightened statesmen will be able to adjust these clashing interests, and render them all subservient to the public good. Enlightened statesmen will not always be at the helm."[13] Madison correctly identified the inherent dangers of the situation. His statement not only contains a prophetic identification of the issues that might prompt men to engage in corrupt practices, but it also reflects a profound understanding of the effects that those influences could have upon both legislators and the general public.

> No man is allowed to be a judge in his own cause, because his interest would certainly bias his judgment, and, not improbably, corrupt his integrity. With equal, nay with greater reason, a body of men are unfit to be both judges and parties at the same time; yet what are many of the most important acts of legislation, but so many judicial determinations,

not indeed concerning the rights of single persons, but concerning the rights of large bodies of citizens? And what are the different classes of legislators but advocates and parties to the causes which they determine? Is a law proposed concerning private debts? It is a question to which the creditors are parties on one side and the debtors on the other. Justice ought to hold the balance between them. Yet the parties are, and must be, themselves the judges; and the most numerous party, or, in other words, the most powerful faction must be expected to prevail. Shall domestic manufactures be encouraged, and in what degree, by restrictions on foreign manufactures? are questions which would be differently decided by the landed and the manufacturing classes, and probably by neither with a sole regard to justice and the public good. The apportionment of taxes on the various descriptions of property is an act which seems to require the most exact impartiality; yet there is, perhaps, no legislative act in which greater opportunity and temptation are given to a predominant party to trample on the rules of justice. Every shilling with which they overburden the inferior number, is a shilling saved to their own pockets.[14]

First, Madison recognized the inherent problem of conflicts of interest, which arise whenever elected officials with a salary or financial investments confront the dilemma implicit in casting a vote or in making a decision relevant to their holdings. In this circumstance, officeholders must consult their own self-interest among the many other interests that might be served by their action. While some people may find it possible to act contrary to their self-interests, the mere existence of economic considerations is almost certain to be a source either of serious temptation or of severe strain. Second, Madison was aware that human beings are not angels. Thus, since legislators and other officials are required to make an extended series of decisions that impinge upon powerful economic interests, there is a strong likelihood that elected representatives may use some of those decisions either to advance their personal fortunes or to repay their obligations to others who have sponsored and subsidized their political careers. Finally, he admitted that the ultimate victim of any political system that is sustained by private contributions is the average taxpayer. Through subtle and covert process, as well as from direct bribery and favoritism, powerful economic interests in America have reaped political subsidies and rewards that shift the burden of the cost of government to the rank-and-file citizen who must pay for these through taxes. Coupled with the statement that "the most common and durable source of factions has been the various and unequal distribution of property,"[15] Madison's analysis comprises a useful theoretical perspective for the study of corruption among all public decision makers who must choose between competing alternatives.

The Background of Corruption in America

Madison had hoped that such devices as federalism, the separation of powers, and checks and balances would prevent corruption ·in the American political system, but defects became apparent soon after the Constitution was ratified. Significantly, the first major scandal in American history, the so-called Yazoo land fraud, involved the interplay between money and political decision-making. Despite the efforts of the Founding Fathers to design political institutions that would serve as a barrier to the commission of corrupt acts, the temptations offered by land speculation in the new republic apparently were too strong for many politicians to resist.

In 1795, the state of Georgia asserted its right to determine the disposition of a vast tract of land (named the Yazoo tract after its major river) comprising much of the land area of the present-day states of Alabama and Mississippi. This land also was claimed by three competing powers: the government of Spain, the federal government of the United States, and a confederation of Indian tribes. It was occupied by the Cherokee, Creek, Choctaw, and Chickasaw tribes, but the state had made no legal agreement with those tribes for transferring possession of the land. In the face of these claims, at the importuning of four politically influential land-development corporations, the Georgia legislature was persuaded to sell a huge segment, thirty-five million acres of the western territory, at only one and one-half cents per acre.

The cast of characters in this transaction included some of the leading politicians of that era. The members of the New England Mississippi Land Company, which purchased approximately one fourth of the original Yazoo tract, included such prominent New Englanders as Samuel Dexter, Gideon Granger, Perez Morton, Samuel Sewall, and James Sullivan, who were prominent in the economic and political affairs of the states of Connecticut and Massachusetts. Among the leading promoters of the sale were two United States Senators, James Gunn of Georgia and Robert Morris of Pennsylvania; two Congressmen, Thomas P. Carnes of Georgia and Robert Goodloe Harper of South Carolina; and three prominent jurists, Associate Justice James Wilson of the United States Supreme Court, federal district Judge Nathaniel Pendleton, and William Stith, justice of the superior court of Georgia. The economic and political position of these men is illustrated by the status occupied by Robert Morris, described by historians as "the financier of the American Revolution," who combined politics with a major preoccupation with land speculation and high finance. The dual role played by these men in the development of the new nation demonstrated the institutional relationship between financial enterprise and governmental corruption that had already developed at that time.

The conflicts unleashed by the sale of the Yazoo lands had a profound impact upon American political institutions. Ultimately, the Jeffersonian Republican party split over the issue. But, in the wake of the disclosure, amid charges of the wholesale bribery of the Georgia legislature, opposition to the sale was led by Congressmen James Jackson and John Randolph. In terms strangely unlike the language used in the debates on the Watergate scandal almost 180 years later, Randolph described one opponent as "a man of splendid abilities, but utterly corrupt. He shines and stinks like a rotten mackerel by moonlight."[16]

Ultimately, however, the principal participants in the graft scheme suffered less than might have been expected. One of the original organizers of the land deal, Robert Goodloe Harper, joined another prominent attorney hired by the speculative land companies, Alexander Hamilton to prepare a legal brief that outlined a novel and broad interpretation of the constitutional commerce clause that was accepted by Chief Justice John Marshall of the U.S. Supreme Court. The land speculators won a great victory in the historic case of *Fletcher* v. *Peck* (1810), which was the first Supreme Court decision to invalidate a state law on the grounds that it violated the national Constitution. The speculators were declared "innocent purchasers," although many of them participated in corrupting the Georgia legislature, and they were reimbursed by Congress for their losses.[17] Subsequently, the alleged innocent purchasers received over four million dollars in compensation. The New England Mississippi Land Company received $1,077,561.73 and the Union Bank of Boston acquired $82,354.21. The prominent political and economic leaders from Connecticut and Massachusetts also fared well. Samuel Dexter received $67,104.22, William Sullivan was granted $14,880.94, and the estate of Samuel Sewall was awarded $13,771.45. Many of the original speculators and the prominent New England purchasers continued to be accepted in the most distinguished social and political circles. In many respects, they did not fare as badly as the critics of the transaction who were accused of gaining political advantage by their opposition.

This development might have caused some pain to James Jackson who had written to a close friend one year before the sale, "I have really a good mind . . . to leave Congress and Congress things, turn speculator and go snacks at home with the best of them. There is a damn sight more to be got by it, depend on it, and I have not got one sixpence ahead, since I undertook [being a Congressman]."[18] Jackson, who was the principal Georgia opponent of the sale, later was elected to the U.S. Senate, but he died in 1806 before the parties to the transaction won their ultimate legislative and judicial victories. Moreover, John Randolph, the Speaker of the U.S. House of Representatives who led early successful fights against the Yazoo speculators, was eventually deposed. The final outcome of the first major political scandal in American history, therefore, yielded an ironic but instructive conclusion: the major participants in those corrupt practices ultimately enjoyed greater economic and political success than the opponents who condemned their actions. In this incident, those who sought to subvert the political system for their personal purposes triumphed over the victims and the critics of immoral conduct.

In many respects, however, the institutional response to this scandal may have been even more significant than the dramatic actions of some of the prominent individuals in the controversy. The reaction of the entire political system to the issues raised by the Yazoo affair served as cues and incentives to contemporary political leaders and their successors. The eventual resolution of the conflict reflected some insights on prevailing American concepts of corruption and on the rewards and punishments imposed upon persons involved in corrupt practices that did little to encourage citizens who expected higher standards of ethical conduct from their public servants. Although the Yazoo incident raised several important constitutional issues, it did not produce any major structural changes that might inhibit or prevent similar episodes from occurring in the future.

The growing monetary and political power of speculative entrepreneurs was often contrasted with the stability and contentment of a society dominated by groups of artisans and small farmers that were socially and economically equal in many regions of America during the late eighteenth and early nineteenth centuries. For example, Justice William Johnson, who was appointed to the Supreme Court by Thomas

Jefferson, wrote nostalgically of colonial Charleston, South Carolina, in the period of his childhood:

> The luxuries of the day were within the reach of a moderate fortune, and few could be said to be elevated above one common level. Hence social happiness was not disturbed by the workings of envy, or the haughty demeanor of upstart pride. The party in power felt and acknowledged that they had been called to the government by the voice of the people; and the people blended with a respectful deportment . . . .[19]

Johnson ascribed the social health and contentment of the city during that period to an equality of possessions and privileges. By the time of Jefferson's death in 1826, however, Johnson had abandoned his earlier optimism. In his *Eulogy on Jefferson*, Johnson described Jefferson's views in the following words:

> He knew that avarice was the besetting sin of a republican government. That the very security with which property was possessed, not less than the influence which it confers . . . fostered a devotion to its acquisition, which he would have directed to more exalted objects. He dreaded the noxious and baneful influence of a passion for gain—in its progress degrading to national character; dangerous to the tranquility of the world; fatal to every ennobling sentiment; destructive to every social feeling; and when become the ruling principle of a government, converting man into a ferocious animal.
>
> He dreaded the possible growth of that most degrading of all aristocracies, which, having its basis in the distribution of pecuniary favors, like the wand of Circe, converts men into swine: that power, before which the stately port of the freeman shrinks into the cringe and smile of the knave, or more degraded sycophant.[20]

The rise of corrupting influences, which Madison had feared and which de Tocqueville and his critic were to observe in the next decade, seems to have emerged early in American history.

The widespread ideas on public morality, which disturbed these men, as well as such contemporary political leaders as Johnson and Jefferson, seemed to reach a low point in the nineteenth century. Among the politicians whose careers can be offered as testimony for that statement was the renowned Daniel Webster. In 1833, for example, when the renewal of the charter of the Second United States Bank came before Congress, Senator Webster wrote a letter to the bank's president, Nicholas Biddle, containing a direct request for money: ''I believe that my retainer has not been renewed or *refreshed* as usual. If it be wished that my relation to the Bank should be continued, it may be well to send me the usual retainer.''[21] Subsequently, it was revealed that Webster's personal coffers were not the only sources that had been "refreshed" by money from the U.S. Bank. According to a memorandum written by Biddle in 1837, personal "loans" were made at least to fifty-four other members of Congress, as well as newspaper editors and high government officials. In addition to Webster, who received loans of $17,782.86, the list included the names of Henry Clay and John C. Calhoun, "as well as numerous former cabinet members, three vice-presidents of the United States, and several of the leading editors of the country.''[22]

The hope that corruption might be avoided by a predominantly agrarian society in which political power was divided among numerous jurisdictions and agencies of government soon collapsed amid the growth of industrialization and financial interests. Perhaps nowhere was this trend more clearly illustrated than in the seemingly tranquil agricultural state of Iowa. Immediately after the election of Abraham Lincoln in 1860, a group of Iowa politicians and their counterparts from other states descended upon Washington, D.C., to secure railroad legislation, contracts for trade with the Indians, and other prizes from the new administration.[23] The leader of this group was General Grenville M. Dodge, a railroad promoter who subsequently used business favors, easy loans, free railroad passes, and the control of newspapers and patronage to establish a dynasty that virtually controlled politics in Iowa as well as other states for the remainder of the century.[24] Dodge and his hand-picked agent, Senator William B. Allison of Iowa, played a prominent role in the scandal arising from the efforts of the directors of the Union Pacific Railroad to create a phantom construction company called Crédit Mobilier. As agents for the railroad, the directors of the "construction" company charged exorbitant prices for the completion of the 667 remaining miles of the Union Pacific. To forestall an investigation of this transaction, which may have earned Crédit Mobilier as much as $23,000,000 but which ate up congressional grants to the railroad, the directors distributed stock to influential congressmen.

In 1870, Dodge also secured the leadership of a commission to supervise the construction of a new state capitol in Iowa. Within three years, it was discovered that the foundation stones were crumbling and had to be replaced at a cost of $52,000.

Although the predominant influence of the railroads was challenged by periodic agrarian and third-party movements, none of those efforts was notably successful in curbing their power.[25] In 1886, for example, sixty-one antirailroad bills were defeated in the Iowa legislature, and "the few that did pass were all modified and weakened in later years."[26] While mining, manufacturing, and other interests were acquiring predominant influence in different regions of the country, in Iowa and many other states the railroads achieved the merger of economic and political power that had been the major concern of de Tocqueville and his anonymous critic.

The moral standards of American political life probably reached their nadir in the second half of the nineteenth century. The effort of political leaders to secure special favors from the infant Republican party during the Civil War was followed by the scandal-ridden administration of President Ulysses S. Grant, by the graft and abuses of authority which occurred during the Reconstruction era in the South, and by the infamous Hayes-Tilden electoral college compromise of 1876, in which the outcome of a presidential election was virtually exchanged for policy concessions including the removal of federal troops from the South. Perhaps even more important, however, giant economic interests were using money flagrantly and extravagantly to secure a privileged and protected position in American society. The level of political ethics was so low that railroad president Collis P. Huntington openly justified his bribery of public officials by saying, "If you have to pay money to have the right thing done, it is only just and fair to do it."[27] By the end of the century, the United States Senate had become known as a "millionaire's club," in which membership was obtained either by men who possessed great wealth or by their agents, whose candidacies for political office had been sponsored and subsidized by dominant economic interests.

The influence of money was not confined to the legislative and executive branches of government. Comparable forces also were working on the judiciary. In this sphere of the political process, judges were constantly beset by the dilemma of remaining on the court or of pursuing a more lucrative career in private practice. Perhaps nowhere was this quandary better expressed than in the confidential letter of Justice Benjamin P. Curtis concerning his resignation from the United States Supreme Court. His words not only revealed a candid appraisal of public life in mid-nineteenth-century America, but they also reflected the thoughts of a lawyer who could command a greater salary in the private sector of the economy than on the highest judicial tribunal in the country.

> Before [September] I shall have to come to a decision upon a matter of great moment to myself,—whether to continue to hold my present office. The expenses of living have so largely increased, that I do not find it practicable to live on my salary, even now; and, as my younger children will soon call for much increased expenses of education, I shall soon find it difficult to meet expenses by my entire income . . . . Added to this, I cannot have a house in Washington, and I must either live apart from my family for four to six months every year while I go there, or subject them to a kind of migrant life in boarding-houses, neither congenial or useful . . . . But I do not myself think of great public importance that I should remain where I believe I can exercise little beneficial influence and I think all might abstain from blaming me when they remember that I have devoted six of the best years of my life to the public service, at great pecuniary loss, which the interest of my family will not permit me longer to incur. I have no right to blame the public for not being willing to pay a larger salary; but they have no right to blame me for declining it on account of its inadequacy.[28]

Similar pressure was felt by Justice Samuel Freeman Miller, who served from 1862 to 1890. His biographer Charles Fairman described private corporate expansion at the expense of public prestige in the following terms:

> In a day when public virtue was not commonplace, Miller remained poor, honest, unwarped in sympathy or intellect. He lived well as befitted his office, but his personal tastes were of the simplest. Congress, he felt, was generous in compensating the justices at $6,000, presently $10,000 per annum. In this he was speaking for himself. For when he had lost Judge Dillon as a colleague on the circuit, and then Judge McCrary, both of whom became counsel to railroad companies, he expressed his regret that by a niggardly policy and insufficient salaries, the best offices of the country, especially its judicial offices, are abandoned for the pursuits of private life. One Sunday morning Roscoe Conkling called by appointment on Judge Miller. At lunch the latter remarked that Conkling had brought him offers of four retainers at $25,000 each, to act as consulting attorney for certain New York firms, the employment leaving him free to represent any other interest not competing with his clients. The question instantly was, ''Well, what did you say?'' Mrs. Miller would have been well content to have so much larger an income. Miller's reply was that he had told Conkling that he supposed he must still be worth $10,000 to the government. He would not consent to Mrs. Miller's investing in property

along Sixteenth Street lest it appreciate greatly and he be accused of speculation. Whatever he had in his purse was available to all who had claims upon him.[29]

Undoubtedly there were many judges, such as Justice Miller, who remained impervious to the economic rewards available to them. Perhaps there were others who succumbed to the temptation. James Willard Hurst has argued as follows:

> Definite standards of ethical behavior for the bench crystallized in the nineteenth century, whatever the varying practical effect in different levels of courts. As late as mid-twentieth century, no comparably definite ideal had become set for the legislature.[30]

Perhaps even more significant than the corruption of lawyers and judges by personal greed, however, was the aggregate effect of economic resources upon the legal profession. As reformer Louis D. Brandeis noted, "Instead of holding a position of independence, between the wealthy and the people, prepared to curb the excesses of either, able lawyers have, to a greater extent, allowed themselves to become adjuncts of great corporations and have neglected the obligation to use their powers for the protection of the people."[31]

Lawyers not only form a crucial link between wealthy clients and the average citizen but also between powerful economic interests and the political process. During the nineteenth and twentieth centuries, those interests have scored a seemingly endless succession of legal victories. Most of the battles have been won initially in legislative assemblies and in executive agencies. But the laws and regulations enacted by those agencies ultimately are applied and enforced by the courts, and decisions of the judiciary frequently have upheld those rules at the expense of the people. Moreover, political decisions, once they have gained the sanctified imprint of the law, have an awesome effect in shaping subsequent definitions of corruption and unethical conduct. As a result, judicial as well as legislative and executive branches of government have played a significant role in perpetuating the special privileges and advantages gained by major economic interests.

The Drive for Institutional Change

Major attention during the late nineteenth and early twentieth centuries, however, was focused on the corruption that had emerged at the local level in America. In part to overcome the dispersion of authority and the absence of needed services in municipal government, many cities developed a so-called "machine" within the framework of the dominant political party that was headed by a single leader or "boss." But unlike the legal profession or government at the state and national level, which was controlled by WASP residents, these urban organizations were dominated by European ethnic groups, who had arrived in the waves of immigration during the nineteenth century. Although the "machines" were anathema to the reformers who sought to destroy them, they fulfilled many important "latent" functions by providing welfare services to needy immigrants, by humanizing government, and by bridging the gap between the urban dweller and political authority.[32] In fact, perhaps the clearest justification of the existence of a political "machine" was provided by Martin Lomansey, the political boss of Boston, who told muckraker Lincoln Steffens in 1915, "I think that there's got to be in every ward somebody that any bloke can come to—no matter what he's done—and get help. Help, you understand; none of your law and justice, but help."[33]

Despite these admirable motives, however, a primary purpose of the "machine" was to maintain the dominance of politicians who held top leadership positions in the organization. To achieve this objective and to serve the needs of their supporters, vast numbers of patronage or public jobs were distributed on the basis of political loyalty rather than of personal merit. A similar goal was pursued by stuffing ballot boxes and by bribing voters. In addition, many "machine" leaders recognized the benefits to be derived from public life by capitalizing on the opportunities provided by advance knowledge and political connections. If politicians learned of the planned location of a city park, for example, many saw no ethical problems in purchasing adjacent land that would double or treble in value after the park was opened. In the forthright language of George Washington Plunkitt of New York's Tammany Hall, this practice, essentially similar to the activities of national and state officeholders, was termed "honest graft."[34] Perhaps most important, the rise of the urban political "machine" coincided with a period in which cities were confronted with the need to grant numerous franchises for transportation, utilities, sewer systems, and other municipal enterprises. The award of those contracts frequently was accompanied by bribery, kickbacks, and payoffs to leaders of the "machine." As Steffens pointed out, those scandals could not have occurred without the willful cooperation and collusion of large business interests.[35] In city as in state and national politics, the conjunction of economic and political power seemed to form a major source of corruption.

To curb these abuses, municipal reformers were not content simply to elect "better men" to public office. Instead, they sought to achieve institutional changes in the framework of city government that allegedly would prevent corruption from occurring again. While a portion of their energies was devoted to the election of wealthy reform mayors such as Hazen S. Pingree of Detroit, James D. Phelan of San Francisco, Seth Low of New York, Thomas L. Johnson of Cleveland, and Samuel M. ("Golden Rule") Jones of Toledo, Ohio, perhaps the most lasting contributions of the reform movement were reflected in the demands for structural changes at the local level. Promoted as a single plan by organizations such as the National Municipal League, the program advocated the election of city councilmen by a nonpartisan ballot on an at-large basis rather than by wards, the enactment of civil service requirements, and the appointment of a city manager who (it was hoped) would manage the affairs of the city according to administrative rather than political criteria. Although several early reform proposals included a call for voting by various methods of proportional representation to increase the political voice of minority segments of the community, this provision was abandoned by most cities. In general, the institutional alterations advanced by the reformers were designed to eliminate corruption by implementing the values of economy, efficiency, and professionalism in city government.

A similar effort to restrict the influence of railroad, mining, and manufacturing interests emerged at the state level. Although the so-called "progressive movement" was led by many charismatic personalities including Senators Robert M. La Follette of Wisconsin, George W. Norris of Nebraska, Albert B. Cummins of Iowa, and Hiram Johnson of California, a major thrust of this movement was devoted to the creation of changes in political institutions rather than in government personnel. In addition to the adoption of civil service reforms and the establishment of regulatory commissions, which were also proposed at the state and the national level, their platforms called for several structural alterations that were intended to enhance rather than diminish the power of the general public. Perhaps the most important innovations were the direct primary, the initiative, the referendum, and the recall.[36] Basically, each of these reforms was designed to allow the people to govern themselves directly rather than acting through intermediaries in the selection of candidates who might be rejected by established party organizations, the proposal of issues or policies that might be buried by recalcitrant officials, the passage of measures that might be blocked by legislative assemblies, and the removal of officials who might otherwise serve out their terms unmindful of public disapproval. Unlike most reforms proposed for cities, therefore, these structural changes were planned to decentralize rather than centralize political authority and to increase popular rather than elite control of governmental institutions.

Although fewer reforms were adopted by the federal government during the progressive era of the early twentieth century, many institutional changes were advocated to control the corrupting influence of economic interests. Moreover, the modifications that were made in the structure of the national government at this time were not notably successful. Several regulatory commissions were established, for example; but most of those agencies eventually were captured by the very industries they were supposed to regulate. Perhaps most important, however, Congress apparently felt that it could control the pernicious influence of money in politics by imposing limitations on campaign contributions and by requiring disclosure of those donations. As the result of agitation led by Perry Belmont, Democratic campaign treasurer of 1904, Congress finally passed a bill in 1910 that required candidates for Congress and political committees to report campaign receipts and expenditures. Following the exposé of efforts by Ohio's Senator Mark Hanna to obtain financial contributions from businessmen for Republican candidates and similar events, a law was enacted in 1907 that prohibited banks and corporations from contributing to presidential or congressional campaigns. This prohibition was extended to utilities by the Public Utility Holding Company Act of 1935 and to labor unions by the Smith-Connally Act of 1943 and the Taft-Hartley Act of 1947. Similarly, the Corrupt Practices Act, and the Hatch Act of 1940, attempted to impose absolute ceilings upon the amounts spent by campaign committees and upon the amounts donated by private individuals. Through a variety of devices, ranging from the creation of "paper" organizations to the suppression of information, however, both candidates and contributors have managed to circumvent those regulations. Neither the laws passed by Congress during the progressive era nor by their successors in subsequent decades were successful in fulfilling the objectives of reformers. Efforts to require financial disclosure and to impose limitations on campaign expenditures and contributions have not been an effective weapon against the effects of money in the electoral process.

But even more important than the reforms adopted by Congress were several other proposals that were advanced during the progressive era. In a message to Congress on December 3, 1907, President Theodore Roosevelt diagnosed the weaknesses of conventional approaches to the problem of corruption and offered an important new proposal.

It is well to provide that corporations shall not contribute to presidential or national campaigns and furthermore to provide for the publication of both contributions and expenditures. There is, however, always danger in laws of this kind, which from their very nature are difficult of enforcement, the danger being lest they are obeyed by the honest, and disobeyed by the unscrupulous, so as to act only as a penalty upon honest men . . . . There is a very radical measure which would, I believe, work a substantial improvement in our system of conducting a campaign, although I am well aware it will take sometime for people so to familiarize themselves with such a proposal as to be willing to consider its adoption. The need for collecting large campaign funds would vanish if Congress provided an appropriation for the proper and legitimate expenses of each of the great national parties, an appropriation ample enough to meet the necessity for thorough organization and machinery, which requires a large sum of money. Then the stipulation should be made that no party receiving campaign funds from the Treasury should accept more than a fixed amount from any individual subscriber or donor, and the necessary publicity for receipts and expenditures could without difficulty be provided.[37]

Roosevelt was essentially accurate in noting that attempts to control the influence of money by limitations or publicity not only are difficult to enforce, but they also penalize the honest man. In fact, his suggestion that contributions above a fixed amount should be limited and publicized rather than forbidden seemed inconsistent with his preceding comments. But he was probably correct in assuming that the proposal for public funding of campaigns would encounter serious resistance and criticism.

Some indication of this resistance was provided by the only state attempt to implement a law that required public financing. Colorado passed a law in 1909, providing that the expenses of campaigns should be paid only by the state and by the candidates themselves. Interestingly enough, candidates were not permitted to spend more than 40 percent of the first year's salary of the office to which they were aspiring, and it was a felony for any other person to give or to receive campaign donations. Under the stipulations of this act, the Colorado treasurer was required to pay the state chairman of each political party twenty-five cents for each vote cast for that party's gubernatorial nominee in the last election, with one-half of the total sum allocated for campaign purposes and one-half to be distributed among the county chairmen of the party. But when the Republican and Democratic state chairmen sought the funds to which the law entitled them, they were refused, and their petitions to the state supreme court for an order compelling payment were met by a demurrer from the attorney general. The demurrer was sustained by the courts on the ground that the act was unconstitutional, but the court did not file a written opinion or provide an explanation for its decision.[38] Thus, the first state experiment with public financing of political campaigns ended in frustration and confusion.

Politicians, however, were not the only observers who proposed structural changes to stem the growth of corruption in American politics. Besides such muckraking journalists as Upton Sinclair, Gustavus Myers, and Lincoln Steffens, a number of early political scientists including Woodrow Wilson, A. Lawrence Lowell, Henry Jones Ford, and Frank J. Goodnow endorsed specific ideas for institutional alterations in the political system. Much of their work reflected an admiration for parliamentary forms of government, and many of their proposals were focused on programs to restructure political parties.[39] But, in presenting comprehensive plans for improving the moral quality of American politics, the first practitioners of political science in this country performed an invaluable service to the political system.

This approach stands in sharp contrast to the orientation of many political scientists. Illustrative of this attitude was a study by Nelson Polsby in which he sought to trace the institutional maturation of the U.S. House of Representatives. Although this research did not attempt to assess the amount of corruption in the House directly, it did examine the evolution of ethical norms by which, as Polsby noted, "Precedents and rules are followed; merit systems replace favoritism and nepotism; and impersonal codes supplant personal preferences as prescriptions for behavior."[40] Overlooked in Polsby's analysis were both the important value of legislative assemblies described by Allan Kornberg as the tendency "to defend members against external criticism"[41] and the emphasis on ethical standards of legislative conduct that characterized the work of H. Hubert Wilson.[42] By underplaying the investigation of the institutional sources of corruption in American politics, specialists in executive as well as legislative politics have been guilty of a serious omission that undermined their ability to provide expert commentary on the Watergate scandal. Furthermore, contemporary political scientists have devoted relatively little attention to the examination of political parties and political participation, which might serve as vehicles for the reform of the political system.

In short, the evidence does not suggest that there has been a major improvement in the ethical standards of American politics since the progressive era. In the House of Representatives, for example, conviction of a crime (or the strong probability of such conviction) apparently has not been considered a "disqualification for the high office of serving in Congress."[43] Despite the ouster of Adam Clayton Powell, Jr., during the 1940s and 1950s several Congressmen including J. Parnell Thomas of New Jersey, Walter E. Brehm of Ohio, James M. Curley of Massachusetts, and Andrew J. May of Kentucky were either fined or imprisoned without being subjected to disciplinary action by the House.

Similarly, scandals have not ceased to afflict the executive branch of government. During the Harding administration, Secretary of the Interior Albert B. Fall was accused of receiving more than $385,000 from two corporations that had leased the Elk Hills oil reserves in California and the Teapot Dome reserves in Wyoming. Although Fall was eventually fined $100,000 and sentenced to one year in jail for accepting a bribe, the representatives of both companies escaped conviction on this charge.[44] Furthermore, the tenure of almost every succeeding president has been tainted by charges of corruption ranging from the "five-percenters" in the Roosevelt era, to the gift of deep freezers during the Truman administration, and to the acceptance of vicuña coats by Sherman Adams during the incumbency of President Eisenhower. Corruption has seemed to be an endemic rather than a transitory or ephemeral feature of the American political system.

But the principal area in which political scientists have failed to contribute to the analysis of corruption has been the study of elections and campaigns. As Jean Blondel observed, "It is a sad comment on the somewhat academic character of political parties studies, that so many have neglected, or treated as secondary, the question of party finance. We all know that the style of life of individuals is markedly shaped by levels of private incomes and by patterns of consumption; yet political parties are rarely considered in the same way."[45] But it must be remembered that the origins of the scandal that resulted in the first resignation of a president in American history can be traced to an illegal raid on the headquarters of the opposition party and to the receipt and expenditure of vast sums of money in the 1972 presidential campaign. While most writers have tended to treat the subject as a peripheral issue, partisan finance is perhaps the "centrally important" factor in determining the distribution of influence in a political system.[46] In fact, it is the central thesis of this book that a major source of systemic corruption in America can be found in the interface between economic resources and political power that occurs primarily in election campaigns and to the inequities that it produces.

NOTES

1. Frank Mankiewicz, *Perfectly Clear: Nixon from Whittier to Watergate* (New York: Quadrangle—New York Times Books, 1973).
2. Arthur Schlesinger, Jr., *The Imperial Presidency* (New York: Houghton Mifflin, 1973).
3. Bayless Manning, "The Purity Potlatch: An Essay on Conflict of Interests, American Government, and Moral Escalation," *Federal Bar Journal* 24 (Summer 1964):248.
4. Ibid., p. 246.
5. James Q. Wilson, "Corruption: The Shame of the States," *The Public Interest* 2 (1966):30.
6. Ibid.
7. James C. Scott, *Comparative Political Corruption* (Englewood Cliffs, N.J.: Prentice-Hall, 1972), p. 5.
8. Arnold A. Rogow and Harold Lasswell, *Power, Corruption, and Rectitude* (Englewood Cliffs, N.J.: Prentice-Hall, 1963), pp. 132–133. Also see Arnold J. Heidenheimer, *Political Corruption: Readings in Comparative Analysis* (New York: Holt, Rinehart and Winston, 1970).
9. Alexis de Tocqueville, *Democracy in America,* Vol. 2 (New York: Schocken Books, 1967) p. 304.
10. Anonymous [Critique of Alexis de Tocqueville's *Democracy in America*], *The United States Magazine and Democratic Review* (July 1838), pp. 341–349.
11. Ibid.
12. De Tocqueville, *Democracy in America*, 2: 192–194.
13. Alexander Hamilton, James Madison, and John Jay, *The Federalist,* Vol. I (Washington, D.C.: M. Walter Dunne, Publisher, 1901), pp. 65–66.
14. Ibid., p. 65.
15. Ibid., p. 64.
16. C. Peter Magrath, *Yazoo: Law and Politics in the New Republic* (Providence, R.I.: Brown University Press, 1966), p. 40.
17. Ibid., pp. 1–117.
18. Ibid., p. 11.
19. Justice William Johnson, *Life of Greene,* Vol. 1, reproduced in part in Donald S. Morgan, *Justice William Johnson, the First Dissenter* (Columbia: University of South Carolina Press, 1954), pp. 219–220.
20. Ibid.

21. Quoted in James Willard Hurst, *The Growth of American Law* (Boston: Little, Brown, 1950), p. 367.

22. Paul H. Douglas, *Ethics in Government* (Cambridge, Mass.: Harvard University Press, 1952), pp. 15, 108.

23. Leland L. Sage, *William Boyd Allison* (Iowa City: The State Historical Society of Iowa, 1956), p. 43.

24. C. Vann Woodward, *Reunion and Reaction* (Garden City, N.Y.: Doubleday, 1956), pp. 78–104.

25. Harlan Hahn, *Urban-Rural Conflict: The Politics of Change* (Beverly Hills, Calif.: Sage Publications, 1971), pp. 42–54.

26. Russel B. Nye, *Midwestern Progressive Politics* (New York: Harper & Row, 1965), p. 66.

27. Quoted in Richard Hofstadter, *The American Political Tradition* (New York: Vintage Books, 1958), p. 165.

28. Benjamin R. Curtis, *The Life and Writings of Benjamin Robbins Curtis* (Boston: Little, Brown, 1879), pp. 247–248.

29. Charles Fairman, *Mr. Justice Miller and the Supreme Court 1862–1890* (Cambridge, Mass.: Harvard University Press, 1939), pp. 426–427.

30. Hurst, *Growth of American Law*, p. 63.

31. Quoted in Richard Hofstadter, *The Age of Reform* (New York: Vintage Books, 1960), p. 161.

32. Robert Merton, *Social Theory and Social Structure* (New York: The Free Press, 1957), pp. 71–81.

33. *The Autobiography of Lincoln Steffens* (New York: Harcourt Brace Jovanovich, 1931), p. 618.

34. William Riordan, *Plunkitt of Tammany Hall* (New York: E. P. Dutton, 1963).

35. For a discussion of the distinction implied by this comment, see Hofstadter, *Age of Reform*, pp. 262–265. Also worthy of note is Nebraska's adoption of a unicameral legislature, which seemingly was designed to promote the centralization rather than the dispersion of authority.

36. Even though each of these proposals also was adopted at the local level, they seemed to have their major impact upon state politics. Significantly, none of these reforms have been implemented at the national level.

37. Quoted in Earl R. Sikes, *State and Federal Corrupt-Practices Legislation* (Durham, N.C.: Duke University Press, 1928), pp. 249–250.

38. Ibid., pp. 144–145.

39. For an analysis of their ideas, see Austin Ranney, *The Doctrine of Respon-*

sible Party Government (Urbana: University of Illinois Press, 1962), pp. 25–110.

40. Nelson W. Polsby, "The Institutionalization of the U.S. House of Representatives," *American Political Science Review* 62 (March 1968): 145.

41. Allan Kornberg, "The Rules of the Game in the Canadian House of Commons," *Journal of Politics* 26 (May 1964):359.

42. H. Hubert Wilson, *Congress: Corruption and Compromise* (New York: Rinehart, 1951).

43. George A. Graham, *Morality in American Politics* (New York: Random House, 1952), p. 89.

44. John D. Hicks, *Republican Ascendancy, 1921–1933* (New York: Harper & Row, 1960), pp. 75–76.

45. Jean Blondel, "Preface." In Arnold J. Heidenheimer, ed., *Comparative Political Finance: The Financing of Party Organizations and Election Campaigns* (Lexington, Mass.: D.C. Heath, 1970), p.f.

46. Ibid., p. 3.

2

Corruption
and
the
Responsible
Citizen

ACCORDING TO THE CLASSIC TEXTS ON DEMOCRATIC politics, "responsible citizens" include persons who exceed the minimal requirements of voting on election day. "Responsible citizens" also seek to augment their influence at the ballot box by engaging in a variety of activities such as working within political party organizations, writing to elected representatives, participating in the election of party nominees, persuading others to vote for particular candidates, and contributing financially to the support of political campaigns. In fact, from the time they enter their first high school civics class through their college courses in political science, students are taught that the only way they "can really accomplish something in politics" is by supplementing their votes with time, effort, and money. Americans are told that achieving important political objectives is "hard work," and they are frequently enjoined to demonstrate their convictions by making monetary donations. In fact, the polemical appeal to "become active in politics" and to "support the candidate of your choice" with financial contributions long has been an important part of the conventional wisdom of political science.

The problem with this pitch, of course, is that it is seldom heeded. Actually, only a small proportion of private citizens attempt to enhance the impact of their votes with financial contributions to favorite candidates. An even smaller number of citizens seems willing to expand their influence by engaging in the everyday jobs of politics such as licking postage stamps at campaign headquarters, distributing political literature at public gatherings, or canvassing neighborhoods in behalf of their candidates. One summary of the available information about these activities concluded:

> Only about 4 or 5 percent are active in a party, campaign, and attend meetings. About 10 percent make monetary contributions, about 13 percent contact public officials, and about 15 percent display a button or sticker. Around 25 to 30 percent try to proselyte others to vote a certain way, and from 40 to 70 percent perceive political messages and vote in any given election.[1]

Those statistics are comparable to the results of other studies.[2] The idea of augmenting the influence of one's vote by intense political activity may be a good one, and it might even occasionally elicit a popular response in the classroom,[3] but it is seldom practiced in daily life.

The overwhelming evidence, which indicates that citizens do not adhere to the model prescribed for them by the textbooks, often evokes a despairing shrug among professors of political science, and is viewed as a source of dismay by some political reformers. But the reasons for the public's apparent indifference to political activity and for the reluctance to donate small amounts to political collection plates are seldom examined intensively. When explanations are offered, they are usually confined to relatively superficial references to "public apathy." Both politicians and political scientists have been inclined to fault rank-and-file citizens for their failure to offset the influence of large campaign contributions and to eradicate the evils of political corruption.

It is the unorthodox thesis of this chapter that the public might not bear the exclusive blame for this apparent departure from the standards of "responsible citizenship." Rather, the fault may lie with the expectations that have developed concerning political behavior and with the institutions that have been created for political activity. There may be important reasons why most people are reluctant to shell out their dollars to campaign coffers and why politics just do not matter to them. The explanation for the failure of citizens to supplement their ballots through political activism and campaign contributions requires more careful analysis and more extensive research than has been conducted thus far. This chapter suggests some propositions that might guide such an inquiry.

Voting Behavior and the "Responsible Citizen"

The literature on voting behavior illustrates both the difficulties of this enterprise, as well as the gap that often separates theory and practice. According to classic postulates, the responsible voter in a democracy was a citizen who carefully examined the qualifications of the rival candidates, dispassionately evaluated their positions on the major issues of the day, and expressed an enlightened and objective judgment at the ballot box.

Yet, early surveys of voting behavior revealed an abysmal lack of political knowledge and information. Most voters displayed a wretched grasp of controversial issues, and few even knew the names of their representatives in Congress. Furthermore, subsequent research indicated that electoral decisions seem to be shaped not only by social class but also by identification with a political party and that these partisan loyalties often are transmitted—almost genetically—from generation to generation.[4]

The findings of this research appears to raise some troublesome questions for democratic politics. How can citizens exercise their "enlightened judgment" if they do not even know the names of candidates or basic facts about major issues? How can the results of an election mean anything if voters are merely registering longstanding partisan allegiances inherited from their forebears? How *does* democracy operate, and how *can* it survive?

An increasing amount of research suggests a need both to reduce our expectations of democratic voters and to revise our notion of electoral rationality and responsibility. Some evidence, for example, indicates that those voters who change their political preferences between elections, and who thus frequently determine the outcome tend to endorse candidates with similar positions on issues that are salient to them. As V. O. Key, Jr., concluded, "Voters are not fools. To be sure, many individual voters act in odd ways indeed; yet in the large the electorate behaves as rationally and responsibly as we should expect, given the clarity of the alternatives presented to it and the character of the information available to it."[5] Efforts to disentangle the interrelated effects of candidates, issues, and party orientations indicate that issues may play a more important role in molding voters' preferences than has been commonly supposed.

The apparent discrepancy between the classic model of the responsible citizen and empirical studies of electoral behavior may have arisen from a misunderstanding of the requirements of rational voting. In many respects, the major tenets of classic democratic theory seemed to bear a striking resemblance to the political ethos that Richard Hofstadter believed was "founded upon the indigenous Yankee-Protestant political traditions, and upon middle-class life."[6] According to Hofstadter, this system of political ethics

assumed and demanded the constant, disinterested acti[v]
in public affairs, argued that political life ought to be
degree than it was, in accordance with general princ[i]
laws apart from [and] . . . superior to personal needs,
common feeling that government should be in good part an effort to
moralize the lives of individuals, while economic life should be inti-
mately related to the stimulation and development of individual character.[7]

Although his characterization has been used for various purposes, including the formulation of a peculiar notion that some citizens display a
stronger sense of "public-regardingness" than others,[8] it has been
employed almost exclusively in the study of voters rather than of public
officials. In short, this image of democratic men seems to presuppose
that correct political decisions can be made only when voters act altruistically rather than on the basis of self-interest.

The failure of many citizens to become actively involved in political campaigns or to donate small amounts of money to the candidates of
their choice does not necessarily imply a basic flaw in the public's sense
of responsibility. When politicians and professors exhort their listeners
to "augment their electoral influence," they frequently base their arguments upon altruistic principles or upon the claim that individuals
should take such action simply because their own personal standards of
responsible citizenship demand it. In making this appeal, they seem to
commit the same errors that have afflicted students of voting behavior.
People seldom are motivated solely by altruistic concerns, and actions
rationalized by altruistic principles often reflect paternalism and dis-
guised self-interest. It is only rarely that citizens feel impelled to engage
in political activity or to make contributions simply because they are
regarded as the proper or the prescribed things to do.

Yet, there is no intrinsic reason why voters who seek to further
their own interests at the ballot box are acting less responsibly or less
rationally than those who are motivated by altruism. In fact, a convincing case could be made that "the public interest" is apt to be achieved
by the cumulative actions of persons expressing their self-interest rather
than by altruistically motivated individuals who base decisions upon
their own perceptions of the welfare of others. Fundamentally, in an
election, voters are called upon to make a choice between competing
values. Such value judgments frequently do not require detailed knowledge of the facts of political controversies, and they may often reflect a
long-standing attachment to traditional beliefs and loyalties. A choice
between competing values does not necessarily demand a total absence

of emotions or the formation of neutral, dispassionate opinions. Paradoxically, evidence that seems to suggest what others have characterized as the irresponsibility of voters may not be inherently incompatible with the standards of citizenship in a democracy.

Furthermore, the reluctance of many citizens to become actively involved in politics might be related to fundamental defects in the political system. As many commentators have observed, the rhetoric of party platforms and campaign oratory hardly is conducive to the exercise of enlightened judgment; and the mass media occasionally fail to fulfill their awesome responsibilities of providing voters with the information necessary to make a logical decision. In fact, candidates frequently have been urged to moderate their positions on policy issues and to withhold detailed or technical material from the public as the most feasible method of gaining elective office in America.

As Murray Levin has noted:

> A citizen may judge the candidates in terms of so-called "rational," "realistic," or factual standards—his past performance as a legislator contrasted with his campaign promises, for example, or his involvement (or lack of involvement) with so-called corrupt practices . . . . This "rational" estimate, of course, can be made only if the "facts" are available, but the "facts" are either not readily available, or difficult to evaluate . . . . Consequently, the "honesty" of the candidate is often the variable about which most information is demanded by voters who wish to make a "meaningful" decision. However, information concerning the honesty of the candidate is difficult to secure because corrupt and dishonest activities are carefully hidden from the public.[9]

Modern campaigns do not resemble the titanic battles of an earlier era that involved candidates who were clearly identified with the interests of their economic supporters such as railroads, mining companies, or reform movements. Since politicans seldom make a vigorous effort to publicize the sources of their campaign donations or the nature of their obligations to financial backers, voters often are required to choose between competing candidates in the same way that they select their friends. For example, if honesty is considered a virtue of overriding importance, characteristics such as the warmth of a candidate's smile, the strength of a handshake, and apparent sincerity may loom large in the perception of others.

In a subsequent study, Levin elaborated on the damaging effects that the absence of information about the candidates can have upon the general public:

Classical democratic theory also leads democratic man to expect rational and honest behavior on the part of public officials. In a political system in which many individuals believe that corruption is widespread and political power is concentrated and abused, these expectations of the citizen are not met. Citizens come to believe that they are foreigners (aliens) in their own political world. For them the political structure, as a system of prescribed performances, has ceased to exist.[10]

Consequently, many voters have developed a sense of alienation or estrangement from the political process. As one of the authors noted previously:

> Although alienation initially was characterized by some researchers as an essentially psychological trait that emanated from the individual and that could be alleviated most effectively by dealing with persons on an individual basis, others began to realize that alienation also might have external environmental sources. Instead of regarding alienation as a deviant or abnormal state of mind, an increasing number of scholars gradually were persuaded to recognize the possibility that people who experienced a sense of alienation might have a plausible basis for their feelings. Actually, the organizations and institutions provided by an urbanized society may be more conducive to the growth of estrangement and disaffection than to the development of rapport and security. Thus, attention naturally was shifted from individual cures to the goal of restructuring institutions so as to minimize alienation. While this trend has led to an emphasis in sociology on the creation of social structures that might diminish the gap among all members of society, it has also resulted in a concentration in the political sphere on efforts to reduce the distance between the public and government decision-makers.[11]

This is a form of alienation or inefficacy that stems from perceived flaws in the political system rather than from individual pathology.[12] Moreover, there seems to be a close relationship between systemic corruption and this type of "systemic inefficacy." The growth of widespread feelings of alienation, fueled by the issues of political corruption, poses a serious danger to American political institutions.

Actually, the public belief that politics is a corrupt and dirty business is longstanding in American politics. This logic is often reflected in the unspoken assumption that political activities or small campaign contributions are futile in the face of slick and powerful adversaries. The same belief is more frequently voiced in the observation that the "big boys" run politics and that the "little man" is overpowered in the game. In 1943, a national survey revealed that 48 percent of the American public agreed that "it is almost impossible for a man to stay honest if he goes into politics." Only 42 percent disagreed, and 10 percent were undecided.[13] In addition, there is evidence that this sentiment has grown. In 1970, 35 percent of the American people believed that political corruption had increased in the past ten years.

This attitude apparently has been inspired in large measure by the massive expenditure of money in election campaigns. As Levin noted in quoting several rank-and-file voters,

> Campaign contributors are stereotyped as buyers purchasing future political favors. The extravagance of the campaign is interpreted by many as a measure of the degree to which the candidate is under obligation to pay back a profitable return. "He spent too much money campaigning. I thought of where all those funds came from . . . . I felt he made deals with backers of the campaign . . . . Everyone was supporting him, it seems as though there was a fear of him."[14]

A series of obvious facts give credence to these somewhat diffuse concerns and require careful analysis. The next several sections of this chapter are devoted to a consideration of some of the sources of systemic corruption in the American electoral process.[15]

Money: The Only Continuing Investment in Politics

One of the most distinctive characteristics of political activity is that it occurs on a sporadic basis. Citizens are given the opportunity to vote, for example, only at specified intervals. Even such alternate forms of political activity as working within a political party, writing to legislators, and participating in a campaign usually are appropriate only at prescribed times. The sporadic, episodic, and intermittent nature of political activism has several significant implications. It does not provide voters with an adequate foundation for a continuing involvement in political life. Unlike the employee whose constant presence at work could form the basis for loyalty to a corporation, citizens seldom experience the impact of government as a persistent everyday event. Attention to politics is at best a peripheral and part-time job, entailing only a few hours or minutes a week. Moreover, it is hardly the type of work that is likely to produce immediate benefits. Even the most vocal exponents of the classic model of "responsible citizenship" would be hard-pressed to show why consistent attention to political matters is necessary for the momentary decision that one makes in a polling booth. The institutions that have been created to facilitate public influence on government policy simply do not provide the basis for continuing participation in politics; and rank-and-file citizens may not be able to justify the amount of time and energy that some observers feel should be spent on political activity.

It may be that the only person who has a continuing investment in political campaign affairs is the contributor, especially the large contributor. While other members of society may become involved in politics only as part-time workers of minor consequence, contributors can legitimately cast themselves in the role of the stockholders and, in this capacity, can receive the benefits to be derived from exercising influence at critical moments, as well as the pleasure of watching the value of the stock rise and fall as the supported candidates achieve greater or lesser degrees of political influence. In many cases, the principal benefit to be obtained from a contribution is the investment itself and the knowledge that it provides the stockholder or investor with a stake in the career of the candidate. Thus, the role of the contributor is somewhat analogous to the position of the backer of a Broadway show, the "angel" who foots the bill for theater productions. In fact, evidence suggests that many contributors view their donations to political campaigns as a kind of "insurance policy," which is purchased as a "safety precaution" instead of as a promise of guaranteed returns. Even if contributors find that they need not use the political leverage to which the donation has entitled them, the investment still provides them with a continuing sense of enjoyment and psychic satisfaction that noncontributors do not experience.

In many cases, of course, the relationship between campaign contributions and government rewards continues to operate on a direct quid-pro-quo basis. Although politicians normally are reluctant to discuss such arrangements, some insight into this type of investment was provided by John F. Kennedy, a former night watchman at a safety razor company, who capitalized on his name to become the state treasurer of Massachusetts without the benefit of massive financial backing.

> The winning candidate is in a position to dispense largesse. The return on a successful political investment may be higher than that on a blue-chip stock. However, return on capital depends upon the size of the investment. Kennedy remarked, "They'll have their agents call up people and say, 'If you give a hundred dollars you are put on the preferred list. If you give a thousand dollars, you're a bond holder.' "[16]

In addition, the contributor, or the political "angel," can rest comfortably with the knowledge of having a major advantage over persons who must rely on other means of attempting to exert influence. Opportunities for political activism usually emerge at specific periods before an election or at the height of a controversy; and citizens who seek to exercise power in this manner often encounter major constraints on their time as well as serious difficulties in mobilizing during those moments. By contrast, "angels" with a continuing investment can employ leverage when and where they choose. For some persons, money may be a more elastic resource than time, and contributors often occupy a superior position vis-à-vis those who are compelled to pursue other methods of political persuasion.

Ironically, the citizen whose principal form of political involvement consists of investing in the careers of candidates also seems to occupy a position of status and respect in American society. "Angels" who contribute money to politics, but who do not engage in other types of activity, seldom are castigated or criticized for their failure to participate fully in the governmental process. On the contrary, they are extolled for their philanthropy; they are depicted as models of "civic-minded" individuals. Cash contributions, of course, comprise only one means of augmenting the influence of a person's vote; but, even for the most enthusiastic advocates of "responsible citizenship," this method seems to be sufficient. Little more is expected or required.

In many respects, this perspective appears peculiar because of the strong emphasis that is placed upon personal responsibility both by the proponents of this doctrine and by American society in general. Although the practice of avoiding the military draft by hiring a substitute to serve in one's stead was abandoned in the United States after the Civil War era, it has persisted—in a somewhat modified form—in political life. By making a substantial financial contribution, citizens are excused from the obligations of other types of political activity. "Angels" are permitted to "buy their way out" of the toil and drudgery of political activism without suffering any loss of honor or respect.

Yet, there is always a basis for potential conflict between the large campaign contributors and the "consumers" of politics who simply vote without donating funds to a candidate. As V. O. Key, Jr. observed:

> It is probably fair enough to conclude that men of wealth on the whole use money in politics to protect what they regard as their interests. Their votes are few in a regime of popular government and they build their political defense by the use of money. Others have votes; they have

money. The two are, if not in perpetual conflict, always potentially at loggerheads.[17]

Nevertheless, for a variety of reasons to be explained, it appears that the "angels" are in a position to exercise greater influence than are those who simply vote or work in a political party.

Perhaps the principal evidence for this conclusion can be traced to the pressing need that has developed in politics for vast sums of money. In part, this trend has been promoted by the increasing costs of the mass media. Between 1956 and 1968, for example, expenditures for television time in presidential elections increased from $6.6 million to $27.1 million; the cost of radio publicity jumped from $3.2 million to $13.3 million; and the price of newspaper advertisements grew from $4.3 million to $11.6 million.[18] Moreover, only a small proportion of the American public appears willing to pay the bills. Politics, as a corporation, probably is suffering from what might be termed underinvestment. As a result, the "angels" may be treated with exaggerated deference and courtesy, regardless of the actual opinions that may be formed of them both by professional politicians and by the propagandists of "responsible citizenship." Money talks, and those who desperately need money are prepared to listen.

Public and Private Methods of Voting

There is a simple but crucial difference between votes and campaign contributions as methods of exerting political influence. On election day, at least theoretically, all voters are equal; and one person's vote is supposedly no more valuable than another's. On the other hand, the resources available for political activism and contributions are fundamentally unequal—some people clearly have more free time to devote to political activity than others. What is even more obvious, certain individuals enjoy a substantial advantage in their ability to allocate money and economic power for political purposes.

The simplest method of illustrating the effect of this disparity is to examine the differences between the private market and public elections. In many respects, the free market can be compared to an election in which consumers, who act as voters, are presented with a series of choices between different brands of the same product. In this "election," the brand that is purchased most frequently by the most consumers commands the largest share of the market. The major distinction between the private market and an election is that, in an election, each voter is granted only one ballot; but, in the free market, each consumer possesses a "voting strength" or a purchasing power that is proportionate to the amount of money allocated to a particular brand of a product. Thus, if Consumer A purchases 500 items of Brand X at one dollar each, while Consumer B buys 5 items of Brand Y at the same price, Brand X has, in effect, received 495 more "votes" than Brand Y. Hence, Consumer A has 100 times more "voting strength" or purchasing power than Consumer B. The difference, of course, can be attributed to the fact that Consumer A has more dollars or resources to spend on this product than Consumer B. This practice contrasts sharply with the principle of equality that is presumed to govern the conduct of public elections. While voting in an election is founded upon the principle of equality, voting in the private market is based upon the amount of resources available to the consumer.

The process of selection that determines the operation of the free market system undoubtedly produces some inequities. A major flaw arises from the fact that it tends to favor the needs and preferences of the affluent. Since rich consumers have more resources to spend, manufacturers naturally tend to produce a greater number of goods that cater to their tastes and whims. Perhaps one of the few factors that operates to maintain an equilibrium in the free market system is the fact that poor people outnumber the rich. But in a society operating on truly egalitarian principles, citizens would be allocated one vote for each of the products they consume, and products might be designed by manufacturers to serve the needs of the greatest number rather than the preferences of those with the most resources.

Even more important than the inequity of the private market system is the tendency of similar inequalities to affect the results of public elections. Clearly, for example, a citizen who contributes one hundred dollars to a political campaign is in a position to exercise more influence on the choice of the "products" than another person who donates only one dollar to an opposing candidate. Similarly, "angels" who not only cast their ballots but contribute a substantial sum to the candidate of their choice are able to exert more influence upon the outcome of the election than persons who vote but do not contribute. The present system of obtaining private contributions to finance campaigns injects an element of inequality in American elections that is not unlike the principles of the private marketplace. "Angels" with sizable resources enjoy an advantage in determining the choice of candidates that is analogous to the role of the affluent in shaping the selection of consumer goods.

This analysis, of course, depends upon the assumption that money makes a difference in politics. It does; while money does not have an unfailingly causal relationship to political success, it is usually decisive. According to V. O. Key, Jr.,

> A census of all races for all offices—congressional, state, and local—would probably show that most, but by no means all, winners had had the larger campaign purses . . . . Winners have a habit of attracting money. Yet it seems equally clear that in the really big elections, the presidential sweepstakes, the size of the campaign chest does not in itself control the outcome—although big donors may not be neglected after the election.[19]

Occasionally, candidates win elections even though their opponents outspend them by sizable margins, and candidates with large campaign budgets do not necessarily emerge victorious solely because of their ability to spend more money.

If cash were the sole factor that shaped the results, there probably would be no need to hold elections. Aspirants to public office would simply issue an appeal for contributions, and the candidates who succeeded in amassing the largest war chest for the campaign would be declared the winner. The outcome of elections then would be dictated by the preferences of "angels" with the greatest amount of money to donate to political campaigns. As a result, nominees for elective office could concentrate their energies exclusively upon the affluent, ignoring those who were either unwilling or unable to aid their political careers.

It may be a source of consolation to some that money does not always decide the results of elections and that candidates still are compelled to devote some attention to voters (as well as to "angels") in their quest for political success. But the influence of money in politics seems equally and undeniably obvious. Several important questions, therefore, remain to be answered. How much of a difference does money make in politics? What is the difference in the amount of influence available to an "angel" in comparison with a citizen who does not donate to political campaigns? What effect does this difference have upon the general public?

The Principle of "Weighted Votes"

Although the precise measure of the phenomenon remains elusive, it seems clear that all citizens do not exert equal influence upon the outcome of elections. The idea of "augmenting one's electoral influence" by participating in political activity or contributing to campaign funds, which is so widely preached by politicians and political scientists, is predicated upon that fact. Time and money can produce a "multiplier effect" in politics. Thus, if one individual persuades another person to support a particular candidate, the strength of one vote, in effect, doubles. In a similar success with two persons, that individual's electoral influence triples; three converts quadruple electoral influence, and so on. In many respects, the process of gaining political power has not changed significantly since the days of George Washington Plunkitt who began his political career (which, it will be recalled, eventually earned him a prominent place in New York's Tammany machine) by gathering the support of his relatives, friends, and acquaintances, and by reporting to ward and district leaders that he "controlled a bloc of votes," which he could deliver on election day.[20]

But the potential wielder of political influence also must confront several new and seemingly unfamiliar problems. What is the most effective method of magnifying one's voting power? Can it be done simply by talking to people and by persuading them to cast their ballots on the same side? Or does it require the citizen to allocate personal resources to purchase advertising in the mass media?

There is no single definitive answer, but available evidence suggests that the much touted effects of expensive mass media advertising may not be totally exaggerated. In politics or in the private market, the initial requirement is brand identification or "getting the name known." The mass media can contribute significantly to the attainment of that objective. Moreover, research has demonstrated that the media often may play an important role in stimulating subsequent political discussion among friends and relatives.[21]

The problem then becomes one of measuring the amount of political influence that can be acquired by various methods of supplementing the strength of a person's vote. An "angel" who votes in an election and who contributes money to a favorite candidate obviously is in a position to have a greater effect upon the outcome than a person who merely votes but who makes no financial contribution. Similarly, a citizen who votes and who spends time attempting to persuade others to support a favorite candidate probably has more influence than someone else who confines political activity to the polling booth. Since the mass media offer such an effective and expensive method of political persuasion, the "angel" who contributes money to a political campaign is able to communicate a message to a larger number of voters and to affect a larger number of electoral decisions than the person who engages in face-to-face contacts. Clearly, a certain—and perhaps substantial—sum of money is required to offset the effects of a given quantity of time. Fifty hours of campaign work, for example, may have a greater impact in gathering additional votes than a one dollar contribution. But, in general, the advertising that only money can buy offers a more expedient method of reaching voters than do time and effort.

Although no precise formula has yet been devised, it does seem possible to develop a method of measuring the amount of electoral strength or influence produced by various types of political participation. Such an equation would have to include the effects of other forms of political influence, such as endorsements by prominent leaders or organizations, as well as campaign contributions and the conventional tasks of political activists. But, for the sake of simplicity, this analysis will be confined to voting and to financial contributions. As a starting point, it might be pointed out that a citizen who votes is at least able to exercise some influence upon the outcome of an election, while a person who fails to vote or to perform any other type of political activity probably exerts no power whatsoever. Let us assign the symbol X to the value of a person's vote. The supplemental influence to be gained by engaging in political activity could be represented by Y. And the additional power that could be exerted by contributing money to a political campaign can be designated as Z. The equation, of course, is not perfected sufficiently to tell us the value that can be attached to any of these acts. What we would like to know is the number of X's equal to various amounts of Y or Z, or the number of votes that will be produced by a given sum of financial contributions or by a specific number of hours of campaign work. Unfortunately, existing research on political campaigns does not provide an answer.

But the analysis does tell us something of potentially greater significance. It indicates that a person who engages in $X + Y + Z$ is capable of exerting much more political influence than someone who simply performs X. The effects of political influence are at least partially cumulative. The outcome of political campaigns probably is determined, to a much greater extent than many observers have been willing to admit, by a system of "weighted voting." In elections, as well as in the private marketplace, "angels" with the most resources are able to exert a greater influence upon the choices made by the American public than people who lack resources. The practice of "weighted voting" is totally consistent with the doctrine of augmenting strength; but, in a fundamental sense, it is also a clear ... principle of equality in voting, which lies at the heart of ... system of free elections.

...tion, there are several factors that compound and compli-... ...cts of "weighted voting." It is entirely possible that the impact of large contributions might tend to overshadow or to outweigh the value of political activity. Certainly, a voter who participates in X (voting) plus Y (activism) plus Z (financial contributions) is exerting more influence than a person who engages in $X + Y$ or $X + Z$. But it is not clear that a citizen who performs $X + Y$ has more power than an "angel" who performs $X + Z$ or even someone who performs Z alone. Cash may easily offset the effects of political activity. Although we do not know the exact amount of money that may be necessary to outstrip any given quantity of political activity or the dollars that might be required to garner a specified number of votes, it seems evident that the costly opportunities provided by the mass media have enhanced the value of money at the expense of other types of political activity. In the system of "weighted voting" that has evolved in America, money seems to be the principal weight.

Since the bulk of campaign expenses are paid by large gifts acquired from a limited group of "angels," it appears that those contributors have traditionally played a disproportionate role in shaping the political sentiments of American voters. In 1936, almost one half of the total receipts of both the Republican and Democratic national committees were furnished by 1,945 contributors of $1,000 or more; and, in 1952 approximately two-thirds of the expenses of major national campaign committees were provided by donors of $500 or more.[22] Big contributions probably have influenced more voters than any other single factor in political campaigns. Thus, the "angels," regardless of whether or not they vote themselves, may have cast more "weighted ballots" in elections than any other segment of the population.

"Opting Out" of Politics

The operation of "weighted voting," and the belief that there are widespread inequities in the electoral process, is a familiar concept to the general public. Many Americans have long felt that the power of their votes, or their meager efforts to affect the decisions of friends and neighbors, were no match for the enormous influence wielded by powerful interests. According to a Harris survey reported in July 1973, 69 percent of the American people believe that "large corporations have a great deal of influence in Washington." Only 7 percent feel that "the average citizen" has comparable power. In addition, 62 percent of the public expressed the conviction that they had "hardly any or almost no" influence in running the government. The mass of citizens have tended to shun the opportunity to donate to campaign coffers and to participate in other forms of political activity because they felt their limited resources would be outmatched by a small group of rich and influential "angels." As the preceding analysis indicates, there is more than a grain of truth in this hard-headed perspective. Perhaps the most devastating effect that private contributions have had on American political life is upon the political attitudes and beliefs of the public.

The conventional response to this skepticism, especially among exponents of the doctrine of augmenting electoral influence, has been to blame the public. In some cases, the people have been counseled to act as though the results of elections were still determined by the principle of equality, although abundant evidence indicates this is false. In other circumstances, politicians and political scientists have urged citizens to ignore the overwhelming odds that seem to militate against their success. William C. Mitchell's advice is typical:

> A voter becomes more realistic as he recognizes serious limitations on his capacity to influence the working of the system. But when he does he is in a better position to pursue whatever ends he chooses. This voter should also recognize that not everyone exercises the same amount of influence on policy in the United States. This revelation may be disheartening, but it can act as spur to more successful participation. Knowledge of where the power is and where it is not enables the interested citizen to concentrate his efforts in the most fruitful places.[23]

Faced with the clear prospect that the average voter, the part-time political activist, and the small contributor are likely to be outclassed in politics, the principal response of the advocates of "augmenting electoral influence" has been to seek to spur citizens to even greater—almost Herculean—efforts.

The reaction to this advice may be almost like the response that a jockey receives when whipping a horse that is trailing the pack in the home stretch. The horse may react—at least momentarily—with renewed effort. It is equally likely, however, that the horse, sensing that a stretch drive would be futile and perhaps self-defeating, may rebel at the whip and continue his losing pace. In the face of almost insurmountable handicaps, little may be gained by demanding intensified effort.

It is also untrue that citizens have been apathetic or indifferent to the inequities created by the expenditure of vast sums of money in American elections. Some commentators, including Dan Nimmo, have chastised the people for their failure to make earnest attempts to overcome the advantage of the rich and the powerful:

> If asked, many Americans may criticize the high cost of campaigning for public office; the simple fact, however, is that the American public is generally indifferent to the problem and will readily tolerate higher campaign spending in the future. Indeed, the evidence of the Goldwater and Nixon campaigns of recent years indicates that individual Americans are bothered not by the amount of campaign spending but by how to raise the money. The large number of small donations in recent campaigns suggests that many citizens intuitively see campaign costs as a way of keeping riffraff out of American elections . . . . On the basis of the recent history of campaign funding in the United States, it seems unlikely that effective controls will be established that will truly open the new technology of elections to rich and poor alike.[24]

This statement is directly contradicted by the findings of public opinion polls. In a survey conducted after the 1968 election, 66 percent of the American people favored a law limiting the total amount of campaign expenditures. A similar Gallup poll taken after the 1970 elections revealed that 78 percent of the people approved such regulation. By 1971, public support for rigid ceilings on campaign finances had risen to 80 percent. Even before the outbreak of the Watergate scandals, therefore, an overwhelming proportion of the American public endorsed strict laws to control the influence of private contributions in political campaigns. Nimmo's comment may reflect the views of "angels" on large contributors, who pay the largest share of campaign costs, but it certainly does not express the opinions of millions of rank-and-file American voters, or the "riffraff," who implicitly understand the inequities that effectively exclude them from meaningful participation in politics.

The tendency to blame the public both for its failure to correct the abuse of the existing method of campaign financing and for its reluctance to devote greater effort to political activity seems to reflect a fundamental misunderstanding of the nature of systemic corruption. The source of the evil cannot be fully ascribed to personal causes; instead, it can be traced to the institutional arrangement of the political system that permits the rise of corrupting influences, such as money, in American elections. Most people recognize the obstacles that restrict their probabilities of attaining important political objectives; they are aware of the crucial impact of large contributors and powerful interests upon the outcome of the vote; and they realize the severe limitations upon their own resources that reduce their ability to wield decisive influence. Their reactions to political events are conditioned by all of these considerations, and their logic is difficult to challenge. Given the inequities that permeate the electoral process and the influence exerted by private contributions that perpetuate a system of "weighted voting," the reluctance of many people to apportion their energy to political activity or to invest in campaigns seems understandable. Tilting at windmills might be a popular sport for whose who have the resources and the inclination to pursue this form of entertainment, but for a large number of people who must devote their time and money to more pressing concerns, it is not regarded as a profitable activity. Many citizens have not "copped out" of politics; they have "opted out." They simply have decided that the odds against securing their goals through political activity or contributions are too great to justify their involvement in the game.

Perhaps the most serious consequence of existing inequities in the electoral process has been the development of a deep and profound sense of alienation among the American public. According to a nationwide survey of American adults, 62 percent felt that "nothing I ever do seems to have any effect upon what happens in politics." Similarly, 54 percent believed that "most politicians are looking out for themselves above all else," and 65 percent agreed that "many politicians are bought off by some private interest." Perhaps most important, 61 percent thought that "the people who really 'run' the country do not even get known to the voters."[25] Moreover, this attitude seems to be growing. Other national polls have indicated that a general sense of alienation has spread from 24 percent of the people in 1966 to 35 percent in 1971 and to 42 percent in 1972. As one study of this subject concluded, "American politics has become the politics of alienation."[26]

There is evidence suggesting that alienation can be attributed to fundamental defects in the political system. As noted elsewhere,

> Although most researchers have tended to conceptualize alienation and efficacy almost exclusively in personal terms, or according to the individual's conception of his own ability to influence political events, feelings that denote a lack of efficacy or a sense of alienation also may stem from a belief that political leaders and government institutions are unre-

sponsive to the needs and desires of the people and that any attempt to exert influence upon them would be futile . . . . People may differ not only in the extent to which they possess confidence in their own ability to influence the course of political events but also in the extent to which they are willing to invest confidence in governmental institutions and leaders . . . . Finally, individuals may or may not feel that their political institutions and superordinates have the capacity to satisfy their needs. They may not find fault with those individuals working in government or with elected officials; but they simply believe either that the power to address their needs lies elsewhere or that the whole system is too cumbersome to act. It is a frequently heard complaint that bureaucracy has become too overgrown to meet today's problems. Likewise, there may be perceptions that local and state governments have little power to affect the major problems of our society. An individual may feel that he/she could influence the local mayor, yet still believe that would not be successful in securing his/her needs.[27]

The belief that the average voter has little impact upon government decisions and that powerful interests frequently determine the outcome of major controversies has prompted many people to refrain from political action. It has also inspired the emergence of a growing sense of estrangement or disaffection from public institutions and leaders. The latter development may be even more serious than the former. Citizens who are temporarily discouraged might be induced to return to the political fray, if at least a measure of equality can be restored to the process, and if it can be demonstrated that they have a chance of fulfilling their ambitions through political activity. But the deeply alienated may be so fundamentally "turned off" to politics that they may never be brought back to active political life, regardless of the changes or reforms that are made in existing methods of political decision-making.

Confronted by overwhelming odds, the citizen who believes that there are serious weaknesses in the political system has few available means of registering discontent. Perhaps the most common response is reflected by the failure to vote or to engage in other forms of political participation.[28] Although this reaction has been widely criticized, it does embody a rational component. The determination to abstain from political activity often may be a realistic response to restrictions that have been imposed upon the opportunity to exert meaningful influence rather than a desire to avoid the obligations of citizenship. Since few individuals are able to realize major rewards from political action, there is little incentive to become involved. "Similarly, the rhetoric of alienation—'They're all crooks,' 'It doesn't make any difference who wins'—is a remarkably effective time-saving device. By lumping all candidates together as equally bad, the alienated voter need not invest scarce resources evaluating relative 'evils.' "[29]

The rejection of the opportunity to vote or to contribute money to campaigns is a value judgment that has been reached by a large segment of the American public. Just as the decision to support one candidate rather than a rival reflects a choice between competing values, the refusal to participate also might signify deeply felt values about the process itself. Nonvoting is as much a political act as voting. And the same might be said about ignoring the political collection plate. The values expressed by those acts, however, seem to comprise a fundamental repudiation of the concept of "augmenting electoral influence." Many voters feel that the cards are stacked against them and that the conditions of the electoral process are unequal and unfair. For them, the value of equality may outrank the value of participation, and the only means they have of recording this value is by refraining from involvement in political activity or contributions.

Unfortunately, the values expressed by withdrawing from politics are almost completely negative. In fact, as the number of citizens who feel impotent in the face of the present system of elections and campaign financing grows, the likelihood of eliminating those inequities diminishes. The game of politics seems to operate according to an inflexible law: The greater the number of people who refuse to become involved in politics, the greater the influence exercised by those who remain.[30] Every discouraged activist and small donor who leaves politics automatically increases the influence of "angels" with the most resources to invest. There are always powerful interests prepared to fill the vacuum that is produced by the absence of the rank-and-file citizen in politics. By abandoning the field of battle, the average voter leaves the political wars to be fought by big contributors and powerful interests.

On the other hand, the citizens who choose to exercise their franchise often are constrained by the alternatives available to them. Some individuals, such as the political "angels" who contribute money to competing candidates, feel that they can benefit from the outcome of an election regardless of who wins. Others anticipate rewards from the election of a particular candidate rather than of the opponent. But there is also a sizable proportion of the electorate that expect to lose from the election of either candidate.[31] This group is basically disenchanted with the political process and seldom donates funds to political campaigns.

For them, the vote either represents a net loss or a choice between "the lesser of two evils." As Levin notes:

> Assuming that any candidate who is well known and who has held public office for some time must be corrupt, the alienated voter tends to favor the less well-known and experienced candidate, simply on the ground that as an unknown quantity he may not be so bad as a known evil, at least at first. For the same reason, the alienated voter tends to favor the outs, on the assumption that it may take them some time to become fully corrupt. He also tends to vote against candidates who conduct opulent campaigns, because he is convinced that the opulence of a campaign indicates the degree to which the campaigner is obligated to contributors, rather than the public. For the alienated voter the ideal candidate is honest, sincere, nonpolitical, not heavily financed, "inexperienced," "nonprofessional," and not too well known.[32]

The analysis illustrates the problems inherent in any attempt to end political scandals by selecting "better people" for elective office. The choice of candidates with various characteristics is not likely to be either a satisfactory experience or a permanent solution to the corrupting influence of money in American elections.

Another method of achieving political reforms has been demonstrated by the experience of minority groups. As a result of intensive efforts to organize and to mobilize for political action, some groups, such as blacks, have achieved a sense of collective identity and pride. This "group-consciousness" and pride often has inspired blacks to record higher levels of political participation than whites at equivalent levels of social class.[33] On occasion, the vigorous attempts by minority groups to increase their influence upon government and to improve their social and economic status in society have been reflected in supposedly unconventional forms of political persuasion such as boycotts, picketing, protests, demonstrations, and violence.[34]

The motivations for political activity were revealed by surveys of white and black residents of Detroit that disclosed a precipitous decline of political trust in the black community between 1967 and 1971.[35] Furthermore, among whites the willingness to engage in conventional forms of political participation was "positively related to trust."[36] As whites displayed higher levels of confidence in government, they were more likely to vote, to contribute money to candidates, and to work actively in political campaigns. "For blacks, on the other hand, there was a general tendency for the distrustful to be the most active."[37] With the exception of financial contributions to campaigns, blacks with the least confidence in government were more likely to engage in both "conventional" and "unconventional" forms of political activity than their counterparts with higher levels of trust. As Aberbach and Walker noted,

> This is a significant finding because it indicates that distrust can be a spur to conventional as well as unconventional political action. The distrustful citizens of the black community were trying varied approaches to achieving their goals. They vote, go to meetings, contribute to and work in campaigns, in addition to their relatively high level of participation in protests involving picketing, boycotts, marches or sit-ins.[38]

The implication of this conclusion is significant since it means that many members of minority groups no longer have much confidence in government institutions and leaders but are determined, nevertheless, to achieve their own political goals. To this end, they are prepared to devote a relatively large amount of time and effort to the task of influencing public policies. Their actions comprise, in effect, a means of providing government with "one more opportunity" to satisfy their demands. It is unlikely, however, that such feelings can persist indefinitely. At some time, the cumulative impact of increasing distrust is apt either to be dissipated by the attainment of major objectives or to explode in a mounting wave of fury. Political institutions must be sustained by at least a minimal level of public faith and trust. If not, if minorities are unable to fulfill their aims, it is likely that such an absolute lack of confidence among significant segments of the American public could result in the collapse of the political system. The elimination of a feeling of alienation, especially among groups that have been denied full participation in American politics, will require fundamental changes in the institutions and values of the society.

Another example of the depth of estrangement felt by some minorities was provided by an additional study of the attitudes of black separatists, or persons rejecting racial integration, who lived in the neighborhood that was the major scene of the violence in Detroit during 1967. The survey revealed that most of the separatists favored violence and opposed such commonly accepted governmental policies and institutions as the antipoverty program and political parties. Yet, in response to a question that asked whether they would prefer a totally honest local government that provided few services to its residents or a government that offered numerous services but which dispensed occasional graft and payoffs, most of the separatists expressed a decided preference for public services, even at the expense of bribery and corruption.[39] Similarly, a national survey that asked respondents if corruption was a serious problem in their communities revealed striking differences between the perceptions of black and white citizens. While most whites denied the existence of corruption in their cities, a preponderance of black respondents said that local corruption was present but that it was "not a serious problem."[40]

The findings contain some important and far-ranging implications. To the vast majority of Americans, the idea of tolerating a blatantly corrupt or dishonest city government that supplied the needs of its citizens regardless of the costs, would be reprehensible. Overt bribes are clearly more repugnant to many people than the indirect pressure that is applied through campaign contributions and other uses of money in politics. Some segments of society, however, consider the attainment of crucial goals, the provision of needed services, and the opportunity to participate as equals in political decision-making as of higher priority than purity in government. Attention, therefore, must be devoted not only to obvious forms of graft but also to the systemic sources of corruption in American politics.

In many respects, attempts to reduce widespread feelings of disaffection and to provide alienated citizens with an opportunity to express their discontent[41] may be doomed. Any proposal to alter the means by which the public can exert its influence must be approved by the existing political system; and it is precisely this system from which many people are alienated. To expect those persons who have experienced a deep sense of estrangement to mobilize or to work toward structural reforms, therefore, is to ask them to contradict themselves, to engage in inconsistent behavior. Moreover, there are few other alternatives for the expression of political grievances. On occasion, the politically disaffected may engage in relatively unconventional forms of expression such as picketing, boycotts, protests, demonstrations, and even violence. For many individuals, however, neither the style nor the potential efficacy of these activities is compatible with their hopes and preferences. As a result, many citizens seem to be trapped in an irreconcilable dilemma: they are profoundly alienated from the existing political system, but they must work within and seek approval from that very system in order to change it.

This dilemma is perhaps nowhere better illustrated than in the use of financial resources to influence the vote in elections. Although all votes are presumed to be equal, the expenditure of vast sums of money in political campaigns is purposely designed to overturn that assumption and to provide large contributors, or political "angels," with more influence than the average voter or the part-time political activist. Moreover, there is considerable evidence to suggest that, in any comparison between money and time or activity, money is likely to emerge as the superior method of gaining political power. The rich and the poor might be theoretically equal at the ballot box; but, in any ultimate controversy, the rich will win and the poor will lose.

In a fundamental sense, therefore, the reluctance of many persons to devote money or energy to political activity may reflect a basic value judgment that the competition is unfair. Just as very few people would be willing to turn out for a rigged election, many persons are understandably reluctant to donate time or money to a political cause knowing that their meager efforts are almost certain to be overwhelmed. Only the most altruistic idealist might be willing to enter a contest he or she is bound to lose; self-interest provides the others with compelling reasons to withdraw from the fray.

Although there has been shockingly little discussion of the issue, these dual propositions—that contributors exert a disproportionate influence upon the vote, and that money is spent in campaigns to influence voters—seem obvious and undeniable. The use of money to inject inequalities in the voting power of citizens seems to be a fundamentally undemocratic idea, but most commentators have preferred to focus their attention upon the influence that political "angels" impose upon public policy. Thus, when one of the authors explained the concept of "weighted voting" on a television talk show, he was asked by a Los Angeles city councilman, who was also a guest on the show, if the author meant to imply that large contributors exercised disproportionate influence upon elected officials as well as upon other voters. The answer to that question was "Yes." The explanation of *that answer* is contained in the following chapters.

NOTES

1. Lester Milbrath, *Political Participation* (Chicago: Rand McNally, 1965), p. 19.
2. Sidney Verba and Norman H. Nie, *Participation in America: Political Democracy and Social Equality* (New York: Harper & Row, 1972), pp. 30–31.

:cording to a Harris survey reported on July 20, 1971, 65 percent of
ollege students believed that "working to elect better public officials" was
a "very effective means" of accomplishing "real improvement in the
problems facing the country." This response outranked other alternatives
such as writing or visiting public officials, as well as protests and violence,
by more than 35 percent.

4. Angus Campbell, Philip E. Converse, Warren E. Miller, and Donald E.
Stokes, *The American Voter* (New York: John Wiley, 1960); Angus
Campbell, Philip E. Converse, Warren E. Miller, and Donald E. Stokes,
Elections and the Political Order (New York: John Wiley, 1966).

5. V. O. Key, Jr., *The Responsible Electorate* (Cambridge, Mass.: Harvard
University Press, 1966), p. 7.

6. Richard Hofstadter, *The Age of Reform* (New York: Alfred A. Knopf,
1955), p. 9.

7. Ibid.

8. See James Q. Wilson and Edward C. Banfield, "Public-regardingness as a
Value Premise in Voting Behavior," *American Political Science Review*
58 (December 1964):876–887; Harlan Hahn, "Ethos and Social Class:
Referenda in Canadian Cities," *Polity* 2 (Spring 1970):295–315.

9. Murray B. Levin, *The Alienated Voter: Politics in Boston* (New York:
Holt, Rinehart and Winston, 1960), pp. 43, 63.

10. Murray B. Levin with George Blackwood, *The Compleat Politician: Political Strategy in Massachusetts* (Indianapolis, Ind.: Bobbs-Merrill, 1962),
p. 155.

11. Harlan Hahn, "Reassessing and Revitalizing Urban Politics: Some Goals
and Proposals." In Hahn, ed., *People and Politics in Urban Society,* vol.
6, Urban Affairs Annual Reviews (Beverly Hills, Calif.: Sage Publications,
1972), pp. 30–31.

12. David C. Schwartz, *Political Alienation and Political Behavior* (Chicago:
Aldine, 1973), pp. 13–16.

13. Hadley Cantril, ed., *Public Opinion, 1935–1946* (Princeton, N.J.: Princeton University Press, 1951), p. 584.

14. Levin, *The Alienated Voter,* p. 60.

15. Ironically, the best known literature of political science is silent on many of
these points. Hence, the authors have been compelled to develop these
theoretical considerations without the benefit of extensive references to
secondary sources.

16. Levin, *The Compleat Politician,* p. 235.

17. V. O. Key, Jr., *Politics, Parties, and Pressure Groups,* 5th ed. (New
York: Thomas Y. Crowell, 1964), p. 515.

18. *The Washington Post,* November 22, 1970, p. A 14.

19. Key, *Politics, Parties, and Pressure Groups,* p. 517.

20. William Riordan, *Plunkitt of Tammany Hall* (New York: E. P. Dutton, 1963), pp. 8–10.

21. Elihu Katz and Paul F. Lazarsfeld, *Personal Influence* (New York: The Free Press, 1955).

22. Key, *Politics, Parties, and Pressure Groups,* p. 497.

23. William C. Mitchell, *Why Vote?* (Chicago: Markham, 1971), p. 44.

24. Dan Nimmo, *The Political Persuaders* (Englewood Cliffs, N.J.: Prentice-Hall, 1970), pp. 194–195.

25. Herbert McClosky, "Consensus and Ideology in American Politics," *American Political Science Review* 58 (June 1964):361–382.

26. Schwartz, *Political Alienation,* p. 246.

27. F. Christopher Arterton and Harlan Hahn, "Political Participation," *Supplementary Empirical Teaching Units in Political Science* (Washington, D.C.: American Political Science Association, 1975), p. 37.

28. In fact, an unusually high turnout in an election or a referendum often is regarded as denoting the appearance of alienated voters. See Harlan Hahn, "Voting in Canadian Communities: A Taxonomy of Referendum Issues," *Canadian Journal of Political Science,* 1 (December 1968):483–495.

29. Levin, *The Compleat Politician,* p. 163.

30. See E. E. Schattschneider, *The Semisovereign People* (New York: Holt, Rinehart and Winston, 1960), pp. 1–18.

31. The general outline of this model was first presented by Murray B. Levin and Murray Eden, "Political Strategy for the Alienated Voter," *Public Opinion Quarterly* 26 (Spring 1962):47–63.

32. Levin, *The Compleat Politician,* p. 167.

33. Verba and Nie, *Participation in America,* pp. 149–173.

34. See Joe R. Feagin and Harlan Hahn, *Ghetto Revolts: The Politics of Violence in American Cities* (New York: Macmillan, 1973).

35. Joel D. Aberbach and Jack L. Walker, *Race in the City: Political Trust and Public Policy in the New Urban System* (Boston: Little, Brown, 1973), pp. 182–184.

36. Ibid., p. 206.

37. Ibid.

38. Ibid.

39. Harlan Hahn, "Black Separatists: Attitudes and Objectives in a Riot-torn Ghetto," *Journal of Black Studies* 1 (September 1970):35–53.

40. This finding is based upon a reanalysis of the data collected by Verba and Nie, *Participation in America*. Appreciation is expressed to the Interuniversity Consortium for Political Research for the opportunity to conduct this research.

41. For a cogent analysis of related efforts, see William A. Gramson, *Power and Discontent* (Homewood, Ill.: The Dorsey Press, 1968).

3

The Institutionalization of Corruption

IN A PERIOD OF HISTORY THAT HAS WITNESSED A MONU-
mental erosion of public confidence in political institutions and personnel, the steady and often unspectacular institutionalization of corruption
continues unabated and virtually unrecognized. Indeed, many political
analysts who purportedly influence the decision-making strategy of
campaign managers, the ad-making style of public relations firms, and
the determinations of money managers are unwilling to give serious
attention to the decline of support for political institutions that characterized public reaction to Watergate and other scandals.

Dramatic evidence of this loss of trust was revealed in a special
public opinion survey conducted by Louis Harris and authorized by the
Senate Subcommittee on Intergovernmental Relations in 1973. The survey found a reduction of public confidence in government institutions
and officials. In fact, the public displayed greater faith in the operators
of local trash collection services than in the people running the White
House (53 percent expressed confidence in the garbage collectors, only
18 percent in the White House people). Between 1966 and 1973, all
major political institutions of the United States government suffered a
serious loss of public trust. The most precipitous drop was reflected in
public attitudes toward the executive branch of the federal government,
which suffered a decline of confidence of 22 percentage points from 41
percent to 19 percent. The House of Representatives dropped 13 percent, from 42 to 29; the Senate, 12 percent, from 42 to 30; and the

Supreme Court, which enjoyed the highest level of confidence at the federal level, experienced a decline of 18 percent, from 51 to 33.[1]

An indication of the short-term impact of the Watergate scandal is provided by a comparison of identical questions asked in 1972 and 1973. In 1973, confidence in the executive branch of government declined by 8 percentage points from 1972; but, confidence in the Supreme Court, the Senate, and the House of Representatives *increased* by 5 percent, 9 percent, and 8 percent, respectively. Although the Watergate affair apparently produced a continuing loss of confidence in the President and his administration with a concurrent temporary slight recovery for Congress and the Supreme Court, those developments were part of a long-range trend that appeared to reflect a major erosion of public support for the political process. Between 1966 and 1972, confidence in all major institutions had plummeted by substantial margins ranging from 14 to 24 percentage points.[2]

Even more important, the surveys revealed that the public felt increasingly alienated and powerless, underscoring a deepening sense of frustration and distrust. In addition, a national survey conducted by the Institute of Social Research at the University of Michigan disclosed a serious loss of public confidence in elections. During the period of the Watergate crisis, the belief that outcome of elections "make the government pay attention to what the people think" fell dramatically. In 1972, only 7 percent of the public responded to this statement by answering "not much"; but, in the fall of 1973, the proportion of people reporting this negative reaction rose to 29 percent.[3] Apparently, the exposure of widespread corruption, which culminated in the Watergate affair, stimulated growing public doubts about political institutions as well as about the process by which its leaders were chosen.

In the face of this evidence, some researchers have persisted in providing optimistic diagnoses of the health of the body politic. Take, for example, a paper presented to the 1974 meeting of the American Association for Public Opinion Research. Based upon surveys in the San Francisco area during the summers of 1972 and 1973, it suggested that "despite the President's embroilment in the most explosive political scandal since Teapot Dome, citizens retained their confidence in the integrity of the political system."[4] This conclusion is exceedingly difficult to reconcile with the findings of the Harris survey. The results of the Harris survey were, to be sure, mitigated by findings that citizens were "eager to participate, to work for change."[5] The decline of support for both political parties seemed to indicate serious systemic problems.

From the perspective of professional politicians, the crisis reflected by those public attitudes has made office-holding more difficult and less enjoyable. Members of Congress who chose not to run for reelection generally agreed with the sentiments of retiring Congressman Howard W. Robison of New York: "It truly isn't fun anymore."[6] Still another measure of public discontent with political institutions was revealed by a Field Research Survey of California adults. While the respondents in this survey subscribed to the belief that young people should get into politics, they strongly resisted the notion that their own sons or daughters should pursue this path.[7]

Ironically, the discontent provoked by the loss of public respect for politics and political institutions does not seem to have produced changes in the life-styles of most politicians. More important, it does not appear to have influenced the behavior of those who seek to manipulate the political system for their private gain. After several years of steady exposure of corrupt behavior arising from the Watergate incident and the resignations of the President and Vice-President, some modification of conduct by politicians and interest-group spokesmen might be expected. Yet, there is little evidence that public attitudes have inspired any changes in those practices. In 1974 the opening three weeks of the Virginia General Assembly, for example, continued in the tradition of lavish wining and dining of state legislators by interest groups. It ended, in this instance, with a party hosted by the Virginia Agribusiness Council. This fete was financed by a $53,000 fund raised to promote several lobbying goals which, if adopted, would cost Virginia taxpayers many millions of dollars.[8] Similarly, less publicized lobbying has protected the escalating profit margins of giant oil corporations from the efforts of reformers to secure policies that are mandated by simple equity such as meaningful taxation of excess profits and foreign income.

The Role of Money

The root of the problem of such systemic corruption can be traced to the influence of money that has been used to finance lobbying activities, to pay the increasing costs of campaign management, and to subsidize the recipients of government favors. Although much of the debate on this subject has seemed to be inconclusive, the role of money—and especially campaign contributions—formed an integral and fundamental element of the controversy initiated by the Watergate affair. Airline, oil, and conglomerate executives contributed substantial amounts of corporation funds illegally to the Committee to Re-elect the President in 1972. Not only was much of this money contributed illegally, but in a number of instances the funds were spent for illegal and unethical purposes. Although these activities have generated considerable discussion, there is surprisingly little useful empirical evidence available on the impact of campaign contributions.

Much of the blame for this neglect can be attributed to social scientists. In an analysis of four leading introductory textbooks on American politics and four major books on political parties and campaigns, Delmar Dunn found that only minimal attention was focused on the crucial subject of campaign financing. To remedy these omissions, Dunn suggested that political scientists devote increasing attention to the campaign donors, the group that any candidate must please before aspiring to public office, as well as to the process of raising campaign funds as a continuous activity.[9] If monetary contributors and rank-and-file voters were treated as separate entities, and if fund-raising efforts were viewed as ongoing functions, several important issues and questions could be identified for further research. Neither recommendation would be considered novel by political practitioners, but they could be valuable to social scientists.

The failure of many prominent political scientists to consider the simple questions raised by Dunn has injected serious biases into the limited studies that have been conducted on campaign financing. In particular, they have neglected to examine seriously the barriers to candidacy for public office that are posed by the lack or shortage of campaign funds. Typical of conventional statements on this subject is the following comment by Nelson Polsby and Aaron Wildavsky:

> It is exceedingly difficult to get reliable information on an event that involves a decision not to act. Such an event would be a decision by a political candidate not to run because he could not raise the money. There is, of course, no literature on this subject. But there have undoubtedly been some men whose inability to raise the cash has proven fatal to their chance of being considered for the nomination. While this is most regrettable, a more important question concerns whether there has been systematic bias in favor of or against certain kinds of men that consistently alters the outcome of Presidential nominations. We can immediately dismiss the notion that the richest man automatically comes out on top. If that were the case, Rockefeller would have triumphed over

Goldwater, Taft over Eisenhower, and neither Nixon nor Stevenson would have been nominated.[10]

This assessment not only neglects the numerous cases in which candidates were forced by a lack of funds to withdraw from campaigns, but it also ignores the plight of many people who have been discouraged by financial considerations from even entertaining thoughts of running for public office. Instead, they divert attention from this fundamental problem by confining their discussion to the relative advantages of several affluent candidates for the presidency. By pleading that there is a dearth of evidence and by focusing on a narrower question, Polsby and Wildavsky avoid the basic issue of whether or not the lack of campaign contributions imposes a ban on candidacies for elective positions in America.

A similar orientation can be seen in efforts to ascertain whether or not large monetary contributions make a significant difference in the outcome of elections, which is one of the most crucial questions raised by the Watergate controversy. By focusing on the extent to which exceedingly rich candidates have an inherent advantage over moderately wealthy nominees, researchers have neglected the broader ramifications of this issue. In one influential study of campaign financing and the Watergate controversy, Ralph K. Winter, Jr., cited the opinions of Polsby and Wildavsky with obvious relish to reach the conclusion that "scholars generally agree that money is only one factor influencing elections and that its impact is not, on balance, either decisive or harmful."[11] Before this conclusion can be accepted, however, such an assertion requires careful empirical investigation.

There is little doubt that the weight of scholarly opinion supports the notion that money, while influential, is not determinative of election results. Yet, there are also cases in which the ability of a candidate to outspend rivals has emerged as a dominant factor in campaigns. An example of the massive power of money in elections occurred in the early stages of primary threat to Governor Marvin Mandel of Maryland in 1970. Mandel's opponent was no pauper, nor was he politically unknown. He was, in fact, Sargent Shriver, the former head of the Merchandise Mart and an attractive member of the Kennedy family. Shriver was obviously aware of the importance of money in politics, but as Richard M. Cohen, *Washington Post* reporter, concluded, "[Mandel] and his three foremost fund raisers . . . showed the state how to raise money. In a single night they took in more than $600,000 at a Baltimore fund raiser, leaving virtually nothing for any primary opposition."[12] Interestingly enough, Governor Mandel's subsequent landslide victory over Republican C. Stanley Blair purportedly cost 1 million dollars, precisely $600,000 more than Blair was able to spend.[13] Subsequently, on July 18, 1974, during the next campaign in the midst of what was allegedly a period of heightened public awareness resulting from the Watergate affair, another primary opponent of Governor Mandel's withdrew from the campaign. State Senator George Snyder acknowledged that it was "virtually impossible to reach the voters" in two of the most populous counties of the state of Maryland. Snyder reported that he had raised $10,000 for the campaign and had an organization of 500 volunteers. Mandel's campaign fund totaled $917,000 and included control of the major party organizations throughout the state.[14]

Many other prominent candidates have been compelled to abandon politics because of a lack of funds. At the presidential level, which was treated so parsimoniously by Polsby and Wildavsky, the aspirations of Senators Estes Kefauver, Paul Douglas, and Fred Harris provide examples of candidacies that were either limited or thwarted by massive opposition from most corporate and monetary interests and their political allies. The realization that campaign financing is an ongoing problem for candidates, therefore, yields abundant evidence that contradicts the opinions of those political scientists who attempt to limit or to minimize the importance of money in politics. Nor can it be argued by any careful student of the subject that financial donations are irrelevant to the outcome of elections. The candidate with no money faces almost insurmountable odds against victory; and, as was shown in Chapter II, the citizen who can contribute to campaigns is in a position to influence more votes than a counterpart who cannot afford to make such contributions. Although the effort to measure the precise impact of monetary donations upon elections is an admittedly difficult task, it may be a more appropriate endeavor than simply defending existing methods of financing campaigns.

Regardless of their motivations, the writings of several political scientists seem to be an effective apology for existing methods of financing political campaigns rather than a systematic, detached investigation of the subject. Their arguments are interesting and varied. The opinion of Alexander Heard, who conducted one of the first quantitative studies of private contributions to political candidates, is illustrative.

> And it has been repeatedly demonstrated he who pays the piper does not always call the tune, at least not in politics. Politicians prize votes more than dollars.

> Contrary to frequent assertions, American campaign monies are not supplied solely by a small handful of fat cats. Many millions of people now give to politics. Even those who give several hundred dollars each number in the tens of thousands.
>
> And the traditional fat cats are not all of one species allied against common adversaries. Big givers show up importantly in both parties and on behalf of many opposing candidates.[15]

Heard's statement appears slightly inconsistent with his major findings that Republicans usually receive more money than Democrats and that the amount donated by contributors of hundreds or thousands of dollars overshadows the sum provided by contributors of smaller amounts. This view of campaign financing betrays an implicit, unverified faith in the financial support that candidates can acquire, regardless of their political ideas, from the holders of the nation's purse strings. Such a belief in pluralist America is difficult to reconcile with the harsh realities of political fund-raising.

Another rationale is suggested by Polsby and Wildavsky:

> Although the difference in ability of the two parties to raise money is not in any sense a critical determinant of national elections, large sums of money are necessary to run campaigns. May not those who contribute or raise money in large amounts thereby gain influence not available to others? Aware that the answer to this question is not a simple one, we would say, "Yes, but not overly much." What contributors or fund raisers (the financial middlemen) get to begin with is access to centers of decision-making. Control over money certainly makes it easier to get in and present one's case. Men of wealth, however, are likely to have substantial economic interests which would provide them with good access whether or not they made contributions. If no significant interest feels disadvantaged by what these contributors want, they may well be given the benefit of the doubt. But in matters of great moment, where the varied interests in our society are in contention, it is doubtful whether control over money goes very far with a President.[16]

Skepticism about this position might be expressed not only as a result of events which have made campaign funding a salient national issue but also on the basis of abstract principles. Many people might realistically observe that, since access is one of the advantages of financial contributions, there would be little reason for wealthy persons to spend money for political purposes, for their status has already provided them with sufficient access to gain a favorable hearing. In any event, private donations clearly enlarge rather than reduce the inequities produced by wealth.

Others have argued that the influence of money in politics is unavoidable in an allegedly pluralistic society. Testifying before a Senate subcommittee on a measure to curb excessive private campaign spending, Herbert Alexander asserted that

> it is well to remember that the availability of money for a given campaign may be an inherent effect of our democratic and pluralistic system— either the constitutional right to spend one's own money or to financially support candidates with congenial viewpoints or a manifestation of popularity. This is not to say that monied interests do not sometimes take advantage of a candidate's need for funds, or that candidates do not sometimes become beholden to special interests. They do, but that is part of the price we pay for a democratic system in which political party discipline is lacking and the candidate (and some of the public) may value his independence from the party.[17]

Alexander's explanation of private campaign financing as an "inherent effect of our democratic and pluralistic system" essentially amounted to a rationale for this method of funding political activities. But David Adamany carried this approach to the interesting, albeit factually unsupported, conclusion of treating the present system of private campaign financing as a positive good:

> A sophisticated examination shows that by most measures Americans pay a small cost for the maintenance of an adversary political process in a complicated federal system with its many elective offices at a variety of levels of government . . . . Even the scholarly work on campaign finance tends to concentrate on the amounts spent, the sources from which the money is raised, and the uses to which the money is put. These data are all helpful, but they do not show the relationship of campaign finance to the political environment—to the kinds of party systems, the available channels of communication, and other political and social phenomena. Nor is money ordinarily viewed as a form of functional representation by groups in the community and as just one of the several ways in which groups may seek their policy objectives through the allocation of resources to the political process . . . . Yet much less attention is given to money as a form of functional representation than to the very infrequent instances in which campaign gifts are made for the purpose of procuring actions by public officials which would not have been forthcoming in the absence of contributions.[18]

The assertion that campaign donations constitute a type of "functional representation" is no more supportable than the view that they reflect an innate product of a supposedly pluralistic society. Obviously, under any form of "functional representation" based upon money, some members of the community—the poor—are certain to be unrepresented. This view simply comprises another rationalization of a system skewed by social and economic privilege. Furthermore, the claim that private campaign donations form only a "small cost" of the American political process hardly can be substantiated by available evidence. On the contrary, a persuasive case can be made that the expense of this method of financing campaigns to American taxpayers with low or average incomes is astronomical. Taxpayer subsidies to the Lockheeds of American industry are one of the systemic manifestations of this problem.

Perhaps the most distinctive feature of most prior examinations of money in American politics has been their inability, or reluctance, to find any faults in the existing system. In a discussion of the influence of the wealthy, which can best be characterized as cute and marked by dilettantism rather than by analytical rigor, Polsby and Wildavsky contend that

> the ability to raise money is not only a matter of personal wealth but of being able to attract funds from others. Does this mean that only candidates attractive to the wealthy can run? It might be said that the problem is not so much whether it helps to be rich but whether men who favor the causes of the rich have the advantage over those who favor the poor. There is little evidence to support such a view. Given the nature of the American electorate, no candidate would openly admit to being the candidate of the rich. Candidates holding a variety of views on economic issues—most of which are highly technical—manage to run for the nomination of both parties. If candidates are generally chosen from among men who differ but little on most substantive issues the reason is not because the rich are withholding their money from more radical candidates but rather because the distribution of opinions in the electorate renders the cause of such men hopeless. Our conclusion is that it is nice to be rich; some men who lack funds may be disadvantaged. From the standpoint of the total political system, however, the nomination process does not appear to bar types of men who are otherwise acceptable to the electorate.[19]

Ultimately, conventional treatments of campaign finance resort to a familiar excuse. These authors, like many others, seem to overlook the tremendous costs involved in publicizing an idea. Rather than acknowledging the defects in established institutions or forms of political activity, they ascribe the blame to the people.

Despite the gravity of the problems created by the influence of money in politics, Herbert Alexander and Harold Meyers concluded,

"If any reform is needed, it is not to restrict large gifts—which candidates obviously need—but to make disclosure more complete than it is now. Another desirable reform would be to make more television and radio time available to candidates at free or reduced rates."[20] In view of the evidence they already had collected by 1970 concerning the tremendous imbalance in private financing in the pending 1972 presidential campaign and the preceding 1968 presidential election, it is difficult to understand *their* unwillingness to restrict large private contributions.

The disclosures emanating from the Watergate investigation have not produced any major changes in the prevailing patterns of political finance. In fact, the tendency toward bigness in campaign contributions and expenditures continues to spiral. For example, the three dairy cooperatives, which contributed over 400 thousand dollars to President Nixon's reelection campaign in 1972, raised a staggering amount of money for the 1974 congressional and the 1976 presidential and congressional campaigns. It was reported in 1974 that the coffers of those cooperatives were being replenished at the rate of $2,200 per day with a cash balance of over $2 million available by the end of February 1974.[21]

The determination and effectiveness demonstrated by the groups comprising the dairy lobby indicated the overall response in microcosm of special interest groups to the Watergate crisis—to be more careful in their fund raising and dispensing activities, but to accelerate rather than to curtail private campaign finance activity. By early July 1974, special interest groups had raised 17.4 million dollars for the 1974 congressional election—more than twice the amount given to House and Senate candidates in 1972. Characteristically, private interest group funding activity escalates when major changes are pending in the policies in which those interest groups have a stake. Because national health legislation was under consideration, lobbying groups affected by the health professions dramatically increased their contributions over the level of campaign spending in 1972 from 844 thousand dollars to more than 1,800,000 dollars by July 1974. Labor union groups also increased the size of their war chests. Indeed, one small union, the Marine Engineers, which had a strong interest in possible maritime legislation, raised nearly 1 million dollars. Business committees also nearly doubled their funds over 1972 levels, and the National Education Association reported a ten-fold increase in its campaign funds compared with 1972. Such examples can be multiplied indefinitely. According to Common Cause's careful estimates, interest group finance funds grew to even greater proportions before the 1974 elections. Under existing campaign finance statutes there is no limit on the size and number of campaign contributions that these special interest groups may make.[22] Because *meaningful* limitations on such contributions and on total campaign expenditures were not seriously considered in most proposed campaign reform legislation, the impact of Watergate upon these activities has been virtually nonexistent.

Statutory Remedies and Judicial Responses

Although congressional action to correct the abuses arising from the role of money in politics has been either slow or imperceptible, the courts have taken aggressive action to eliminate certain inequities such as the barriers imposed by filing fees. The requirements of those fees, while generally a modest amount in most jurisdictions, have been utilized at times to exclude candidates of limited economic means. In Texas, for example, a filing fee was authorized by state law to pay the expenses of holding primary elections. The rather complex determination of the size of the fee was based on a variety of factors such as size of population of the jurisdiction in which the office was sought, the salary of the office, or the length of the term. The fee charged for filing was set for each election by the county executive committee of each political party. The filing fees, which were challenged in the courts, ranged from 1,400 dollars for the opportunity to run for the Democratic nomination for commissioner of the General Law Office to as high as 8,900 dollars for other offices.[23]

In a unanimous decision (Justices Powell and Rehnquist not participating), the Supreme Court invalidated this Texas statute in the case of *Bullock* v. *Carter*. The Court held that while filing fees ostensibly limit candidates, such arrangements also impose limitations on the options available to voters.

> The initial and direct impact of filing fees is felt by aspirants for office, rather than voters, and the Court has not heretofore attached such fundamental status to candidacy as to invoke a rigorous standard of review. However, the rights of voters and the rights of candidates do not lend themselves to neat separation; laws that affect candidates always have at least some theoretical, correlative effect on voters.[24]

The comments about the impact of the Texas filing system has important implications for other issues involving election campaign finance:

Many potential office seekers lacking both personal wealth and affluent backers are in every practical sense precluded from seeking the nomination of their chosen party, no matter how qualified they might be, and no matter how broad or enthusiastic their popular support. The effect of this exclusionary mechanism on voters is neither incidental nor remote. Not only are voters substantially limited in their choice of candidates, but also there is the obvious likelihood that this limitation would fall more heavily on the less affluent segment of the community, whose favorites may be unable to pay the large costs required by the Texas system. To the extent that the system requires candidates to rely on contributions from voters in order to pay the assessments, a phenomenon that can hardly be rare in light of the size of the fees, it tends to deny some voters the opportunity to vote for a candidate of their choosing. . . .[25]

The necessity for firm action to stop the escalation of campaign costs arises not only from formal institutional arrangements such as unusually high filing fees, but also from the practical conditions of campaigning that produce serious imbalances in the electoral process.

Another indication of the slight impact Watergate has had upon the everyday activities of practicing politicians was a significant institutional change passed "quietly" by members of Congress in late 1973. This provision exempted the cost of preparing and mailing political material under congressional franks from any future campaign spending ceilings. A blatantly self-serving section stated the following:

Notwithstanding any other provision of Federal, state or local law, or any regulation thereunder, the equivalent amount of postage . . . on franked mail . . . and the cost of preparing or printing such material . . . shall not be considered a contribution or an expenditure . . . of a member of Congress for the purpose of determining any limitation on expenditures or contributions . . . imposed by any Federal, state or local regulation . . . in connection with any campaign of such official for election to any office.

This clause obviously was drafted to further enhance the advantages that incumbents enjoy in congressional elections.[26] In view of soaring campaign costs and their almost complete dependence upon large contributors to assume those expenses, the persistence of corrupting influences among members of Congress may be easy to understand. But they cannot be excused. Legislation is needed to curb the abuse of money in political campaigns rather than to create additional loopholes and opportunities for corrupt or unethical practices.

The Exceptional "Evil" Man or Systemic Corruption?

Perhaps the most dangerous implications of the Watergate scandal and of the failure of Congress to adopt reforms that would alter existing methods of financing campaigns have been reflected in the widespread tendency to blame one man or a group of men for the problem. Oddly enough, the inability of American institutional structures to cope adequately with a serious crisis of public confidence has invoked praise among some scholars. In a widely discussed interview, for example, historian Daniel Boorstin stated:

> One of the things that we've witnessed which has not been sufficiently pointed out is the great advantage that the nation has at the moment in having a fixed term election. If this had been a parliamentary system the government would have fallen, there would have been criminal prosecutions. The problem would not have been dramatized as a political problem. . . .[27]

But the Watergate affair reflected institutional problems rather than narrowly defined partisan or "political" problems. In fact, the incident demonstrated that a great scandal early in a presidential term cannot be effectively corrected except by impeachment. And, as the resignation of President Nixon revealed, it is extremely difficult to invoke this constitutional alternative.

Curiously, his resignation stimulated a flood of commentaries that sought to explain the Watergate scandal as the result of the complex and malevolent character of Richard M. Nixon. However, the personification of the evils of Watergate in one man or one administration is a vast oversimplification. Placing the burden of explanation on a single cause overlooks the fundamental institutional factors that made possible the abuses of power committed by Richard Nixon, institutional factors potentially available to future violators. More important, it also fails to acknowledge the necessity of objectively and rigorously assessing the performance or nonperformance of personnel and institutions that are vested with the primary responsibility of protecting the integrity of the Constitution.

An instructive example of the propensity to overlook sources of systemic corruption is provided by a comparison of prevailing interpretations of the resignations of Agnew and Nixon. In the former case, the corruption of Spiro Agnew was widely attributed to his origins in the shady ethics of state and local governments in Maryland from which he rose to assume the second highest office in the United States. Some commentators felt that it would be almost impossible for a politician to resist the temptations offered by contractors, architects, and engineers, and the traditional system of bribes, favors, and kickbacks that characterized the environment of Maryland politics.[28] But few similar observations were made about Richard Nixon after he entered the White House. The new rich, the wealthy intent on purchasing an ambassadorial post, the corporate ideologues seeking an alteration of the economic and political system to promote both their immediate greed and their eventual desire to dominate workers and consumers, as well as similar figures surrounding the President were conspicuously omitted in most explanations of Nixon's downfall. Perhaps some Americans are reluctant to admit that their presidents are susceptible to the same sources of institutionalized corruption that afflict other officeholders. Or perhaps they have been unwilling to recognize the close connection between societal standards and political corruption. In any event, the tendency to personalize the evils of the existing system has done little to prevent their recurrence.

Responsibility for the failure to correct pervasive flaws in the American political process must be shared by Congress and by other government institutions. Action on the Watergate scandal in both the Senate and the House ended with a whimper. While the Senate investigating committee, chaired by Sam Ervin of North Carolina, contributed to increased public awareness of the scope of systemic corruption and uncovered significant facts, such as the existence of presidential tapes which ultimately led to Nixon's resignation, the committee signally failed in meeting its obligation to make "recommendations for new legislation."[29] Similarly, the impeachment hearings conducted by the House Judiciary Committee reflected several crucial weaknesses. Not only did this committee fail to insist upon original investigative work, but also failed to take the hard but necessary step of voting to hold President Nixon in contempt of Congress for his refusal to furnish the committee with pertinent evidence. The tendency of the Judiciary Committee to handle key issues gingerly created a dangerous precedent because of the implicit suggestion that the House does not have the authority, even in impeachment proceedings, to subpoena relevant material from the president. In the opinion of many observers, the timidity of the committee "grievously weakened the impeachment instrument for future use."[30]

Perhaps the most telling criticism of the committees and the Congress, however, was made by George F. Will. On the very eve of

President Nixon's resignation, he outlined both the constitutional and ethical case for impeachment rather than resignation:

> Resignation, the perennial Watergate panacea, is still a pernicious idea because it will leave Mr. Nixon in a position to merchandise his anti-constitutional and amoral view of politics . . . . So instead of egging Mr. Nixon on to resignation, Congress should do its duty, which involves more than just prying Mr. Nixon loose from his desk. Congress' duty is to pronounce final judgment against Mr. Nixon's conduct. Only that will cleanse the stain of Mr. Nixon and his men from our government.[31]

Rather than heeding the advice of perceptive social critics such as George Will, both political parties embraced Nixon's belated resignation with sentiments akin to outright gratitude. Their passivity established a historical precedent of turning the other cheek to blatant constitutional sabotage and villainy in the highest public office in the land.

Furthermore, the Watergate crisis and related incidents, which resulted in the resignation and discrediting of a president, a vice president, several cabinet members, and other high administration officials, revealed some serious weaknesses in the party system. Many of the men who were indicted and convicted of major offenses in this scandal played dual roles as White House and cabinet officials and as partisan officers of the Committee to Re-elect the President. Perhaps more important, the Democratic party also failed to exercise its influence effectively to remedy systemic bases for these abuses of power. The impact of Watergate, therefore, provided additional evidence that political organizations, as they are presently constituted, have not immunized American government from political movements and events that threaten to destroy the system.[32]

One of the most significant features of the Watergate scandal, besides the resignation and the subsequent pardoning of Richard Nixon, was the emergence of small portions of the news media as the only "loyal opposition" within the American political process. It was not the Democratic party that fulfilled the role of providing constant and meaningful constructive criticism. There was, of course, great variation in the performance of Democratic party leaders, as well as segments of the news media, with respect to Watergate. Indeed, in the beginning only a few highly independent media organizations actually supported the tough investigative reporting, which was best exemplified by the Carl Bernstein and Bob Woodward stories on the relationship between the White House and Watergate in *The Washington Post*.[33] By comparison,

the political parties were largely content to sit back and allow th
aggressive elements of the news media to perform the crucial fun
of investigation and constructive criticism. In fact, with the exceptio
several initial disclosures by the Ervin Committee and the long delayed
action on the articles of impeachment by the House Judiciary Committee, virtually every crucial action in the Watergate scandal was advanced by courageous investigative reporting by *The Washington Post*
or by the courts and Federal District Judge John Sirica. Neither the
political parties nor the members of Congress seemed capable of providing effective leadership to pursue an investigation of the Watergate
scandal to its ultimate conclusion.

As a result, many observers were unable to understand the
broader implications of the Watergate crisis. William Raspberry sum-
marized the dilemma of news commentators when he drew a distinction
between political opposition to the policies of former President Nixon
and some of the more ominous facts that were uncovered by reporters:

> What some of us slowly came to see were not just improprieties and
> repugnant policies, but an attempt to transform the system into something
> alien to the American tradition—an attack on the country from the inside.
> If we were outraged at the allegations of huge cash rip offs, we were truly
> frightened by the mind set of a national government willing to deal in
> enemies lists and secret police forces and subversion of official
> agencies. . . .[34]

Journalists and representatives of mass media were primarily concerned
with reporting the news; they were unprepared, either by training or
experience, to assess the impact of events upon American political
institutions. The initial inability or the unwillingness of many political
leaders and social scientists to interpret the meaning of the discoveries
made by reporters prevented many people from recognizing the actions
of the government in the Watergate scandal and other incidents as a
fundamental attack on democratic values.

Governmental Lawlessness

The stark reality of the Watergate exposures has tended to overshadow
other manifestations of governmental lawlessness. The recent publication of studies of official illegality such as Theodore L. Becker and
Vernon G. Murray's *Government Lawlessness in America,* [35] Jethro K.

Lieberman's *How the Government Breaks the Law*,[36] or Colman McCarthy's essays on "Governmental Lawlessness" and "The Cost of Injustice,"[37] documented a wide range of examples beyond the scope of Washington. Furthermore, the issues raised by William Dobrovir, Joseph Gebhardt, Samuel Buffone and Andra Oakes, which directly relate to Watergate and the executive office, contain a formidable number of serious violations enumerating and documenting twenty-eight counts against President Nixon and his associates.[38]

An important example of the dangers implicit in such practices—and of the lengths to which public officials will go in attempting to defend their acts—was reflected in two sections of a major revision of the U.S. Criminal Code introduced in the Senate by the Nixon administration in March 1973. Conceived as a direct response to the demands for "law and order" made by former Attorney General John Mitchell, former Vice-President Spiro Agnew, and then President Richard Nixon, the bill included several sections that sought to impose harsh punishments upon criminal defendants by making it a felony for any federal employee to disclose classified information to "unauthorized recipients"; by seriously limiting defenses based upon insanity; by making the death penalty mandatory for certain offenses; by curtailing the instruments of probation and parole; by restricting freedom of speech; and by permitting the wider use of wiretap evidence. But, where government lawlessness was involved, this administration bill, S. 1400, became a defense attorney's dream.

Two sections of this legislative proposal contain the most sweeping defenses of official lawlessness in modern legal history. Under the title of "Public Duty" Section 521 states:

> It is a defense to a prosecution under any federal statute that the defendant reasonably believed that the conduct charged was required or authorized by law to carry out his duty as a public servant, or as a person acting at the direction of a public servant.

Similarly, Section 532, entitled "Official Misstatement of Law," says:

> It is an affirmative defense to a prosecutor under any federal statute that the defendant's conduct in fact conformed with an official statement of law, afterward determined to be invalid or erroneous, which is contained in . . . an administrative grant of permission to the defendant . . . if the defendant acted in reasonable reliance on such statement . . . and with good faith believed that his conduct did not constitute an offense . . . .

The implications of these provisions of S. 1400 for the Watergate indictments and future transgressions by public officials were unwittingly revealed by the arguments in behalf of John Ehrlichman and of Egil Krogh (before he pleaded guilty) that they acted as "officers of the United States." Ehrlichman's attorney contended that President Nixon had specifically directed Ehrlichman to make known to Krogh, David Young, and Charles Colson that the investigation of Daniel Ellsberg was related to national security matters. On this basis, the attorney asserted, "The essence of the crime of conspiracy is . . . evil intent. The association of persons with honest intent is not a conspiracy, and the association of Ehrlichman with the others on a presidential assignment cannot be transformed into a criminal conspiracy." In the context of Watergate, which involved a plan that was originally a concerted effort to eliminate or seriously curtail a legitimate political opposition, the long-range impact of legislative acceptance of these two sections could be totally destructive of a competitive party system. The governmental officials assigned to such destructive activities could readily invoke these sections as a complete defense of activities to corrupt and undermine the institutions of American government.[39]

Although some have sought to defend the protection of government officials from criminal prosecution as a necessary means of combatting the danger of revolution, the Watergate crisis again seemed to raise the issue of whether or not a person can claim that merely acting under official orders or in accordance with his interpretation of public duty or governmental authority provides an adequate defense against criminal charges. This question emerged most prominently in the controversy over high officials in Hitler's Germany who were charged with unspeakable acts of bestiality and murder committed against millions of people, but it also must be considered in the assessment of activities that threaten to destroy a political system. As Associate Justice Robert Jackson stated at the Nuremberg trials, "One who has committed criminal acts may not take refuge in superior orders nor in doctrine that his crimes were acts of state. These twin principles, working together, have heretofore resulted in immunity for practically everyone concerned in the really great crimes against peace and mankind."[40]

The attempt to legitimize the illegal activities of government officials and to eliminate political opposition is not unprecedented in American history. Perhaps the earliest examples of such acts were reflected in the efforts of the Federalists to maintain a preferred social and economic status by curbing political dissent and by seeking to declare some forms of opposition illegal shortly after the adoption of the Constitution. Historian Paul Goodman has noted, ''Those who built the first political party system in the 1790's mistook parties for factions, assuming that those with whom they differed were disloyal to the nation and its ideals.''[41] Federalist judges invented a national common law jurisdiction that had not been provided for in either the Constitution or statutes. A Congress dominated by Federalists enacted the Alien and Sedition Acts. These moves enabled the courts to enforce these laws vigorously and to employ their charges to grand juries as a forum for denouncing those whom they deemed to be politically unsound.[42] The condemnation of citizens who dared to criticize government officials was designed not only to prevent the development of a meaningful political opposition, but it also sought to protect socially privileged segments of society from any attempt to correct the inequities of existing economic and political policies.

Efforts by government officials to stifle or to eliminate political criticism frequently have involved direct attacks on individuals or sectors of society to divert public attention from serious inequalities. Moreover, such attacks occasionally have sought to curtail the effectiveness of legitimate political opposition simply by depriving them of the right to vote. Thus when poor whites and poor blacks in the Reconstruction South succeeded for a short time in developing a political coalition to attempt to wrest some degree of economic justice from a system that was cruelly exploiting them, Bourbon Democrats effectively invoked the race issue to divide and defeat them. After regaining power, the representatives of upper-class interests constructed a complex system of legal and state constitutional barriers to political participation.[43] Many impoverished whites accepted those restrictions in the misguided belief that they were designed merely to disenfranchise blacks. But the evidence, such as the debates of the Virginia Constitutional Convention of 1905, indicates that the poll tax and other limitations on political expression also were intended to disenfranchise poor whites. Whether they involved suppression, disenfranchisement, or espionage, activities designed to reduce or to eliminate opposition to established officeholders have been an endemic source of corruption in American politics.

Persistent attempts to legalize practices that lend a sense of legitimacy to official actions that were previously illegal or are basically antithetical to democratic political competition have occurred in several eras in American history. Some ultimately failed, as did the Federalist plan to ensure political, social, and economic control by curtailing political criticism. Some—such as property qualifications for voting, the poll tax, and invidious and complex voter registration requirements—succeeded for long periods of time, substantially contradicting democratic values. In short, the tactic of seeking or securing legal authority or justification for hitherto illegal, corrupt acts has been a recurring and unsavory aspect of American politics. To date, these attempts have not permanently destroyed the political system. Yet, it is not clear that more concentrated efforts supported by institutional power and prestige might not ultimately succeed.

Conclusion

The lessons of history, as well as the Watergate scandal in the ill-fated second term of the Nixon administration, indicate that the corrupting influence of money and the desire to curtail political opposition through illegal acts has not been an unusual or an atypical feature of American politics. Perhaps the most remarkable feature of the Watergate crisis, however, was the reluctance or refusal of many observers to recognize its historical parallels or its dangerous implications. In his 1973 interview, for example, historian Daniel Boorstin tried to draw a distinction between Watergate and earlier American scandals including not only the actions of the Federalists and the Bourbon Democrats, but also the infamous Hayes election of 1876 and the Teapot Dome scandals in the 1920s. Although Boorstin acknowledged the threat to democratic norms posed by an administration in which "loyalty to the leader seemed to override everything else," he argued that prior incidents of corruption "have been distinct in that they tended to be connected with greed and with the desire of people to make something out of it."[44] He apparently disregarded or overlooked the questions raised by the campaign donations to the 1972 Committee to Re-elect the President, as well as the Watergate break-in and cover-up. By asserting that this episode was unique rather than similar to earlier scandals, Boorstin and others have failed to recognize the systemic sources of corruption in American politics.

Perhaps a major cause of this neglect has been the tendency of politicians and social scientists to embrace a relatively narrow approach to the role of money and improper influence in American politics.

Corruption involves more than the personal financial aggrandizement of public officials, direct bribery, conflicts of interest, and similar phenomena. When viewed from the broader perspective of de Tocqueville, there is a clear linkage between efforts to ensure monopolistic domination of the institutions of political power and attempts to perpetuate or extend economic influence unfettered by effective public regulation or control. The undermining of the norms and constitutional foundations of democracy, which was a central focus of de Tocqueville's study, has been a recurring characteristic of American politics.

Obviously, there is a need to widen the conceptual approach to the study of political corruption in several major respects. Initially, the notion of a social and economic threshold to office-seeking in America must be expanded. Under existing methods of campaign financing, aspirants for elective office are virtually restricted to individuals who either possess personal wealth or who have access to others with large sums of money. The implications of a political system dominated almost exclusively by the affluent, and by those who associate with the wealthy, are enormous. Although American political scientists have been reticent about dealing directly with these aspects of social stratification, the study of political candidacies as a manifestation of social class and status differentiation offers a fertile area of inquiry. In fact, it is conceivable that elective offices, which are conventionally discussed as reflections of Jacksonian democracy, actually have become the citadels of a subtle contemporary aristocracy.

Second, and perhaps even more important, increased attention must be devoted to the means by which economic influence is translated into political power. Existing methods of funding campaigns have provided the basis for a form of corporate state socialism that is in direct contradiction to the conventionally accepted free enterprise ideology of American business leaders. The development of this new version of the nineteenth-century elites, which was feared by de Tocqueville, fundamentally represents a combination of historic forms of aristocracy and a business-oriented technocracy. As Kingman Brewster, Jr., president of Yale University, commented in a 1969 address:

> The concentration of economic power, opinion power and political power creates a sort of closed loop. Politicians must raise money from corporations in order to pay the networks the enormous cost of television time. Corporate advertisers call the network tune. And the networks must curry favor with the successful politicians to assure their franchise. The

open society seems to be closing—not by conspiracy, but by mutual dependence.[45]

The interdependence between politicians, corporate executives, and the television industry is, of course, only one example of the reliance of the political process upon social and economic privilege. Writers Jerry Cohen and Morton Mintz offer an incisive, realistic, and somewhat broader account of how this system functions. The following statement from "The Politician as an Investment" provides a comprehensive summary of its operation:

> It costs money, more all the time, to seek elective public office. The money is obtained from where it's at, which is primarily large corporations and financial institutions. Their campaign "contributions" are really not that at all; they are investments in licenses to govern the government, or, if you prefer, to translate economic power into political power. Being prudent, the investors take out insurance by, for example, investing in both political parties at once. The investors get all that money can buy from candidates and parties, which is not to say they get everything they want. As compared with corporations, those who cannot afford such investments, or who are too unorganized to make them—the poor, the blacks, Puerto Ricans, Spanish-speaking and Spanish-surnamed Americans, Indians, workers displaced by advancing technology and retreating resources, much of the middle class, even professional men—generally get bad deals. "Under the circumstances, it is utterly amazing that the public makes out as well as it does," Senator Russell B. Long (D-La.) once said. "Even so, the Government pays out many millions of dollars in unnecessarily high interest charges; it permits private monopoly patents on over $12 billion of Government research money annually; it permits billions of dollars of Government money to remain on deposit in banks without collecting interest; it permits overcharging by many concerns selling services to Government; it tolerates all sorts of tax favoritism; it fails to move to protect public health from a number of obvious hazards; it permits monopolies to victimize the public in a number of inexcusable ways. It provides for too much tariff protection to some industries and too little to others."

To concentrate economic power is to magnify the power of giant corporations to make government behave in ways such as those deplored by Senator Long—to make a bad situation worse. One has but to think of the major oil companies, which have so rigged the tax structure as to pay federal income taxes at a rate comparable with that paid by a laundry worker. In the five years 1963 to 1967, for example, Standard Oil of New Jersey paid at an average rate of 5.2 percent, Texas 2 percent, Gulf 8.4 percent, Mobil 5.2 percent, and Standard of California 2.5 percent. In all, they paid $1 billion, or 4.9 percent on before-tax net profits of $21 billion. "They paid foreign governments more than five times as much," Ronnie Dugger has pointed out.[46]

In the light of this pattern, the erosion of public confidence in governmental institutions is not difficult to understand. The virtually total dependence of politicians upon private interest groups to finance their campaigns for public office has placed enormous tax burdens upon millions of middle- and low-income citizens. Indeed, American taxpayers probably have suffered a cost in the favors, concessions, and access granted to contributing special interests that is astronomical.

Despite the revelations of the Watergate investigation and the resignation of an American president, there is little evidence that this pattern has changed. An example of the perpetuation of these practices by powerful lobbying interests was the defeat of a comprehensive plan to abandon the costly forty-year-old sugar quota system and to replace it with a free-market economy.[47] Similarly, in September 1974, a coalition of lobbyists led by the United States Chamber of Commerce and the National Association of Manufacturers succeeded in defeating consumer protection legislation when the Senate refused to invoke cloture to end debate on the bill. Many of the costly special privileges accorded powerful interests probably would not remain on the statute books, if it were not for the interface between campaign financing and lobbyists in the legislative process. In short, the continuation of present methods involving private funding of electoral activities has inevitably produced detrimental consequences for the average citizen.

NOTES

1. Louis Harris and Associates, *Confidence and Concern: Citizens View American Government,* A Survey of Public Attitudes by the Subcommittee on Intergovernmental Relations of the U.S. Senate Committee on Government Operations, Part 1 (Washington, D.C.: U.S. Government Printing Office, 1973), pp. 8–12.

2. In fact, by January 1974, the public's rating of Congress fell below that of the President—negative responses totaled 69 percent to 21 percent positive for Congress and 68 percent negative to 30 percent positive for President Nixon. *The Washington Post,* February 12, 1974, p. A15.

3. *The Washington Post,* January 8, 1974, p. A7.

4. *The Washington Post,* June 3, 1974, p. A3.

5. Harris, *Confidence and Concern.*

6. *The Los Angeles Times,* February 3, 1974, part 1, p. 19.

7. *The Los Angeles Times,* February 3, 1974, part 1, p. 3.

8. *The Washington Post,* January 28, 1974, pp. C1, 2.

9. Delmar D. Dunn, "Contributions in the American Electoral Process," *American Politics Quarterly* 2 (April 1974):222–226.

10. Nelson W. Polsby and Aaron B. Wildavsky, *Presidential Elections: Strategies of American Electoral Politics,* 2nd ed. (New York: Charles Scribner's Sons, 1968), p. 39.

11. Ralph K. Winter, Jr., *Watergate and the Law: Political Campaigns and Presidential Power* (Washington, D.C.: American Enterprise Institute for Public Policy Research, 1974), p. 10.

12. Richard M. Cohen, "Marvin Mandel: Pols in Hand, Love in Bloom," *The Washington Post Potomac Magazine,* July 14, 1974, p. 24.

13. Richard M. Cohen, "Blair's Maryland Drive Hurt by Lack of Funds," *The Washington Post,* November 22, 1970, p. A15.

14. Fred Barbash, "Candidate Quits Maryland Race," *The Washington Post,* July 19, 1974, pp. B1, 5.

15. Alexander Heard, *The Costs of Democracy* (Chapel Hill: University of North Carolina Press, 1960), p. 6.

16. Polsby and Wildavsky, *Presidential Elections,* pp. 39–40.

17. Herbert E. Alexander, Testimony in Hearings on S. 372 before the Subcommittee on Communications of the Committee on Commerce, U.S. Senate, 93rd Congress, 1st Session (1973), p. 224.

18. David Adamany, *Financing Politics: Recent Wisconsin Elections* (Madison: University of Wisconsin Press, 1969), pp. 230–233, 244.

19. Polsby and Wildavsky, *Presidential Elections,* pp. 39–40.

20. Herbert E. Alexander and Harold B. Meyers, "A Financial Landslide for the G.O.P.," *Fortune* (March 1970), pp. 104–105.

21. Morton Mintz, "3 Milk Co-ops Build Campaign Fund," *The Washington Post,* March 24, 1974, p. M5.

22. Bob Kuttner, "Lobbies Amass $17.4 Million for '74 Races," *The Washington Post,* July 11, 1974, p. A7.

23. *Bullock* v. *Carter,* 405 v.s. 134 pp. (1972).

24. Ibid., pp. 142–143.

25. Ibid., pp. 143–144.

26. David S. Broder, "Franked-Material Costs Exempt from Vote Spending Limit," *The Washington Post,* February 28, 1974, p. A2.

27. Daniel Boorstin, "Effects of Watergate," *The Congressional Quarterly* (July 7, 1973), pp. 1796–1797.

28. For an interesting and useful analysis of Maryland politics, see John H. Fenton, *Politics in the Border States* (New Orleans: The Hauser Press, 1957).

29. Arthur S. Miller, "Watergate Cure: Constitutional Band-Aids," *The Washington Post Outlook,* July 21, 1974, p. C1.

30. Joseph Kraft, "Precedents for Future Impeachments," *The Washington Post,* August 8, 1974, p. A23.

31. George F. Will, "Impeachment, Not Resignation," *The Washington Post,* August 7, 1974, p. A15.

32. Walter Dean Burnham, "Political Immunization and Political Confessionalism: The United States and Weimar," *Journal of Interdisciplinary History* 3 (Summer 1972):1–30.

33. Carl Bernstein and Bob Woodward, *All the President's Men* (New York: Simon and Schuster, 1974).

34. William Raspberry, "The 'Liberal' Conspiracy," *The Washington Post,* January 25, 1974, p. A19.

35. Theodore L. Becker and Vernon G. Murray, eds., *Government Lawlessness in America* (New York: Oxford University Press, 1971).

36. Jethro K. Lieberman, *How the Government Breaks the Law* (New York: Stein and Day, 1974).

37. Colman McCarthy, "Governmental Lawlessness," and "The Cost of Injustice," *The Washington Post,* January 29, 1974, p. A18 and February 5, 1974, p. A18.

38. William A. Dobrovir, Joseph D. Gebhardt, Samuel J. Buffone, and Andra N. Oakes, *The Offences of Richard M. Nixon: A Guide for the People of the United States of America* (New York: Quadrangle/New York Times and Public Issues Press, 1973).

39. The analysis of S. 1400 from which our conclusion is drawn is based upon Richard R. Korn and Gregory B. Craig, "Making It All Perfectly Legal," *The Washington Post Outlook,* January 20, 1974, pp. C1–5.

40. Robert H. Jackson, *The Case Against the Nazi War Criminals* (New York: Alfred A. Knopf, 1946), p. 82.

41. Paul Goodman, "The First American Party System," in William Nisbet Chambers and Walter Dean Burnham, eds., *The American Party System: Stages in Political Development* (New York: Oxford University Press, 1967), p. 57.

42. John C. Miller, *Crisis in Freedom: The Alien and Sedition Acts* (Boston: Little, Brown, 1951), pp. 135–142; and James Morton Smith, *Freedom's Fetters: The Alien and Sedition Laws and American Civil Liberties* (Ithaca, N.Y.: Cornell University Press, 1950).

43. C. Vann Woodward, *The Strange Career of Jim Crow* (New York: Oxford University Press, 1955).

44. Boorstin, "Effects of Watergate," p. 1796.

45. *The Washington Post,* June 15, 1969, p. 3.

46. Jerry Cohen and Morton Mintz, "The Politician as an Investment," in *America, Inc.: Who Owns and Operates the United States* (New York: Dial Press, 1971), pp. 176–177.

47. Bob Kuttner, "Sugar Lobby Kills Free-Market Plan," *The Washington Post,* May 20, 1974, pp. A1, A4.

4

The Mutual Benefit Society: Financing Political Campaigns and Public Policy

THE NEED TO FINANCE ELECTION CAMPAIGNS BY PRIvate contributions has helped to nurture a close relationship between candidates and office holders and the individuals or organized interest groups with the resources available for investment in politics. At its best, this relationship tarnishes the credibility of all government officials in the eyes of the public; at its worst, it is a "mutual benefit society" whose policies serve the public only fortuitously. Unfortunately, politics at its worst has too often been characteristic of the American system of private campaign financing.

One of the principal reasons that many observers have failed to identify the major sources of political corruption in the United States has been the tendency to equate corruption almost solely with quid-pro-quo relationships. As such, unethical or improper behavior usually has been portrayed as a direct and immediate exchange in which a decision maker agrees to take a specific action in return for a pecuniary reward. As practiced in the United States today, however, such conduct seldom involves the elements of personal gain, direct payments, and immediate gratification that characterized corrupt practices in earlier eras. Instead, the exchange of favors often arises from an ongoing close relationship between officeholders and the agents of dominant economic interests, a relationship that entails indirect pressures and economic considerations. Thus a politician's campaign treasury or overall standing with regional or national economic elites is more significant than direct bribe taking.

The mutual benefit society, by definition, offers important advantages to both sets of participants. Political decision makers fulfill two fundamental needs through their association with major economic interests—the desire for social acceptance and the need for sufficient money to gain or keep official positions. Of course, many politicians publicly deny that they are motivated by such incentives. Thus, the frequently semiconfidential nature of their contacts with spokesmen for the wealthy and the influential is a means of rationalizing their behavior when they support the positions espoused by their benefactors. On the other hand, for those who wish to influence the decisions of public officials, the relationship is far less dangerous and considerably more profitable than direct bribery. Clearly, the need to provide payoffs or kickbacks for each decision made by a politician would be more costly. By employing indirect rather than direct forms of persuasion, they can also preserve the appearance—if not the substance—of propriety in their relationships with political leaders.

The nature of this relationship is familiar to the average person. In their everyday lives, most people benefit in a social or economic way as a result of actions taken by friends, relatives, or acquaintances. There are, however, several crucial differences between those relationships and the mutual benefit society that characterizes relations among representatives of the political and economic elite. Most rank-and-file citizens tend to be more honest and a good deal more candid in acknowledging the nature of their relationships with other people. Even if they are not in a position to repay those who have been of assistance to them in some way, they are frequently prepared to express their gratitude. Consequently, when politicians say that their decisions are not influenced or affected by the receipt of large campaign contributions or by friendship with the representatives of powerful economic interests, many members of the general public find those words difficult to believe and inconsistent with their own experience and personal values. The net effect of such statements by politicians probably increases the public's feelings of cynicism and alienation rather than enhancing their trust or confidence in political leaders.

Furthermore, citizens and politicians deal in vastly different types of favors. When the average person repays an obligation to someone, the effects usually have relatively little impact beyond the parties involved. The political decision maker, however, can take actions that could shape and influence the personal lives and the economic well-being of millions of people. Therefore, when a politician is influenced by the generosity or friendship of a benefactor who has subsidized his/her campaign, an act made on behalf of these special interests may have adverse consequences for a substantial segment of the general public.

Clearly, it is difficult, if not impossible, to contain all of the forces that may influence the direction of decisions of public officials. For example, the desire for social acceptance by persons who have gained prestige and respect as a result of their economic position seems beyond the ability of many officeholders either to recognize or control. The willingness of most members of Congress to accept Nelson Rockefeller's rationalization of his uses of money is, consequently, not very surprising.[1] Concurrent public opinion polls indicated that the public found these rationalizations less acceptable. This is not to say it is impossible to curb some of the influence generated by private financial contributions in the political system, but rather that the present method of financing campaigns to secure public office or to retain it has created a relationship in which decision makers are overwhelmingly dependent upon the favors of political "angels." It is exceedingly difficult for anyone who is in a dependent position to make *independent* decisions. Given the existing structure of American politics, politicians are forced to nurture relationships with wealthy benefactors, relationships that virtually insure that corrupting influences will emerge. The impact of private money in political life is the principal source of systemic corruption in America today. Both the increasing need for campaign money and the continuing close relationship between economic and political interests create circumstances in which the potential for widespread corruption is immense.

Most of the efforts to restrain the corrupting forces in American politics have failed, largely because they were based on a restricted concept of corruption that conceived of graft primarily as an immoral *direct* exchange of favors rather than as a product of continuing relationships and of *indirect* pressures. There are numerous national, state, and local laws that forbid bribery, kickbacks, payoffs, and similar forms of collusion between public officials and those who stand to benefit from government policies. Yet, in modern American politics direct bribes—the payment of money for favorable action on a pending issue—have been neither profitable nor particularly prevalent in American politics. The far more common form of corruption has been the transfer of money to a campaign fund, which is not disallowed by most laws. Thus laws outlawing direct forms of bribery have not been particularly effective because of secrecy, the costs entailed in such transactions, and resultant enforcement problems.

Another factor that has contributed to a misunderstanding of modern political corruption may be related to a misreading of the primary goals of organized interest groups. As Robert Sherrill observed:

> The primary effect of the friendships and overlapping interests among members (of Congress) and industry is that nothing is done. Most industries do not send their lobbyists to Washington to seek profitable legislation; they send them to Washington to block legislation that might control or cost them more in taxes. The major goal of the Washington lobby is not to pass legislation but to maintain the status quo. And from all appearances they are quite successful.[2]

Examples of such tactics abound in Washington, D.C., but the activities of the American Medical Political Action Committee (or AMPAC) in opposition to increased government participation in the health field illustrate the point. Because it is against the law for a tax exempt group such as the American Medical Association (or AMA) to contribute campaign funds to candidates, the AMA in 1961 set up AMPAC. Prior to this time the association had been successful in its lobbying efforts to defeat all proposals for some form of national health insurance, including those first presented during the Truman administration. In 1961, pressure was building for some form of government-backed medical plan for the aged, and AMPAC was created to counter the movement. In addition to massive direct lobbying efforts, the group contributed extensive amounts of money to individuals who were "pro free-enterprise medicine." In addition, it gave special attention to those who had some direct control over the passage of legislation such as committee chairpersons and members of committees before which legislation was pending. Throughout the struggle, the primary objective was to defeat legislation rather than gain approval for alternative plans. The latter strategy was adopted only after it appeared certain that some program would be adopted by the Congress in 1965.[3] This is not to suggest that special interests do not seek special favors. One need only look at the tax laws to see the result of such efforts. Nevertheless, Sherrill's observation that the major goal is to maintain the "status quo" does seem most accurate.

A further signal failure has arisen from the attempts to eradicate corruption by abolishing political patronage and placing most government jobs under so-called merit systems and civil service requirements.

Although serious questions can be raised about effectiveness of patronage either as a reward for votes and services or as a means of disciplining party mavericks, there is not much evidence to indicate that some forms of patronage have been eliminated. Positions that are still basically political in nature include a large number of officials at all levels of government including ambassadors, executives, administrative staffs, the members of various special and permanent commissions, judges, bankruptcy referees, the guardians of estates, and the personnel, as well as the offices of banks in which public funds are deposited.[4] Many of the individuals who occupy such positions, which frequently are lucrative or prestigious, are major contributors to political campaigns. For example, Herbert Kalmbach, Nixon's personal lawyer and one of his leading fundraisers, pleaded guilty to a charge of promising federal employment as a reward for support of Nixon's candidacy. In this particular case, Kalmbach promised J. Fife Symington, then ambassador to Trinidad and Tobago, a more prestigious European ambassadorship in return for a $100,000 contribution to be split between Republican senatorial candidates and Richard Nixon's campaign.[5] This was not exactly a unique incident. *The Congressional Quarterly* reported that of thirteen noncareer ambassadors appointed after the 1972 election, eight had donated an aggregate of $706,000.[6] The Senate Watergate Committee found that over $1.8 million in presidential campaign funds was attributable solely to ambassadorial appointments.[7] Instead of eliminating patronage, therefore, lawmakers have transferred it from the ranks of those with little education, few skills, and in need of a job to those already enjoying high social status. Thus modern patronage is accessible only to upper-middle and upper-class benefactors or those donors who wish to aid their economic and social pursuits with direct financial involvement in the political process.

Although the civil service system presumably removed most federal positions from the grips of patronage, evidence suggests that various administrations have devised numerous ways to subvert the system and place "loyalists" in positions. Although most presidents have attempted to manipulate the system, the Nixon administration advanced the technique to a near science. A White House personnel office was set up to place favored personnel in both career and noncareer jobs. It produced a hundred page "primer on how to dodge federal personnel laws . . ." and a *Federal Political Personnel Manual,* which provided a thorough review of civil service regulations and instructions on how they could be avoided.[8]

When Nixon took office, he had 1,200 key agency jobs that could be filled in a political manner. Individuals seeking such positions or who were considered "politically sensitive" were evaluated on a special form entitled "Value of Placement to the President Politically." The following categories were used:

1. Highest Political Value (Must Place)
2. High Political Value (Place if Possible)
3. Moderate Political Value (Handle Courteously)
4. Little Political Value (Handle Routinely)[9]

There also were 8,000 "super-grade" positions available, but only 600 were genuine political positions. In addition, the administration attempted to influence the appointment of some of the roughly 200,000 new civil servants hired each year and the 500,000 positions filled by promotions, transfers and reassignments.[10] They also developed a program to remove "undesirables" with the techniques detailed in a section of the manual entitled "Techniques for Removal Through Organizational or Management Procedures."[11] In short, the Nixon administration was able to subvert the civil service system and to place its "loyalists" throughout government. This had been done previously, but not to the same extent. Experience during this period indicates clearly that political patronage continues to be a part of politics in Washington even though most federal positions are supposed to be filled on the basis of competitive examination and under the guidelines of the civil service system.

Other Types of Contributors and Their Motives

Obviously the reformer must not neglect or ignore graft, bribes, and payoffs but must aim the strongest efforts at the subtler forms that most contributors to political campaigns employ. As one political scientist with practical political experience observed:

> It is a truism that everyone who makes a substantial contribution to a political candidate expects something in return, whether it be personal psychological satisfaction; ideological commitments from the candidate, straightforward economic benefits, or a combination thereof.[12]

The psychological dimension or ego gratification that emanates from private campaign contributions may be the least costly to the public. In other words, the direct cost of a personal call from a candidate, the cost of the time spent massaging the ego of contributors at private lunches, meetings, insuring proper seating arrangements at political functions, and the like, may be low in dollar terms. (According to one prominent California politician, however, "The people who take your time in order to salve their egos may be the worst aspect of campaign finance.")[13] These short-term costs are, of course, heavily outweighed by the long-range costs created by a system that resembles a modern aristocracy based on the nurturing of friendships among elites.

The second type of return that must be understood is the quid pro quo. As pointed out previously, the payoff usually is not made in cash, but rather takes the form of contracts, zoning variances, lax regulatory policies, official positions such as judgeships, or other financial benefits resulting from governmental actions. At the federal and state levels, the income tax laws that are written to provide loopholes for the wealthy offer perhaps the best illustration of this type of return to contributors.

Obviously, the existence of this quid pro quo system is sometimes difficult to document, but the pattern of contributions by large corporations and wealthy individuals to presidential candidates in the period from 1960 to 1972 provides some rather convincing evidence. For example, the Republican party and its candidates traditionally have been the beneficiaries of the greatest amount of money from such sources. But this pattern was reversed in 1964, when the percentage of funds contributed by "angels" to Democrat Lyndon Johnson's campaign exceeded 80 percent of the total. Four years later, the old pattern was reestablished as the large contributors returned to their home in the Republican camp, where they have remained so far. According to Congressional Quarterly, the campaign contributors on record among the 1,013 officers and directors of the 25 largest industrial corporations listed in the Fortune Directory in 1968, favored Republicans nearly 6 to 1. A similar pattern existed in 1972.[14]

Further support for this analysis was provided after his losing campaign for governor of California in 1970 by Jess Unruh, who described the motives of large contributors—primarily businessmen—who had deserted the Democratic party.

> Most of them came into the Democratic Party when we had a Democratic Governor and a Democratic President. They came in as supplicants . . . and now today they're simply marching to a different piper. It's the same magic though. And the music is the one that jingles in your pockets as you walk along.[15]

Another category of contributor is ideologically motivated. These individuals have many of the characteristics of the old-fashioned evangelists. They frequently assume a moralistic posture and pursue their favored cause through the campaign of a particular candidate. Such individuals usually ascribe lofty motives for their actions as they proceed to empty their pockets to the deserving candidate. The ritual of candidates for the 1972 Democratic presidential nomination flocking one after another, again and again, to Beverly Hills and West Los Angeles, California, New York City, and other bastions of wealthy Democrats, suggests the influence of this group in the Democratic Party.

An item in *The New York Times* in 1975 indicates the practice has continued. A Democratic fund-raising event in New York City was described as follows.

> The Democratic party raised about $400,000 amid red-white-and-blue streamers, helium balloons and lavish seafood platters last night as great and small party men gathered with *wealthy contributors* [emphasis added] for a dinner dance in Pier 90, at West 50th Street.[16]

Commenting on the event, Mayor Beame observed to his press secretary, ". . . within that room is the next President of the United States."[17] The practice of placing the wealthy next to possible presidents is practiced by both parties and all of their various ideological wings. The fund raising of conservative United States Senator James Buckley in New York suggests a similar pattern at the other end of the political spectrum.

Regardless of the motivations of contributors to political campaigns, the goal is the same: they want something for their money. In terms of the implications for democracy, it really does not matter whether the object is a change in foreign policy or domestic policy. In both cases, the action reflects the will of an aristocratic mutual benefit society nurtured and developed on a diet of big money for campaigns. Former Senator Paul Douglas summed up the distinction between the mutual benefit society and traditional graft in these words:

> Today the corruption of public officials by private interests takes a more subtle form. The enticer does not generally pay money directly to the public representative. He tries instead by a series of favors to put the public official under such a feeling of personal obligation that the latter gradually loses his sense of mission to the public and comes to feel that his first loyalties are to his private benefactors and patrons. What happens

is a gradual shifting of a man's loyalties from the community to those who have been doing him favors. His final decisions are, therefore, made in response to his private friendships and loyalties rather than to the public good. Throughout this whole process, the official will claim—and may indeed believe—that there is no causal connection between the favors he has received and the decisions which he makes. He will assert that the favors were given and received on the basis of pure friendship unsullied by worldly considerations. He will claim that the decisions, on the other hand, will have been made on the basis of the justice and equity of the particular case. The two series of acts will be alleged to be separate as the east is from the west. Moreover the whole process may be so subtle as not to be detected by the official himself.[18]

This close overlapping relationship between special interests and government is not just a modern phenomena. As was shown in chapter 1, the development of the then western region of the nation shortly after the Revolutionary War, the federal subsidization of railroads, and countless other cases are illustrative of the long-standing close relationship between government and private interests.

For example:

No one got more from the government than the railroads. Between 1850 and 1871 they were given public land totaling more than the area of Texas. The generous politicians argued that if the railroads were induced with free land to build their lines across the country, farmers and merchants would follow them, and the general populace would be close behind. It was done in the name of "building" America.[19]

The direct grant, however, was not the end of the use of government by railroads to achieve economic and political objectives.

But like most commercial "builders" the railroads took advantage of their favored position. Within a few years it was a railroad system (to use the description of Norman Pollack) in which discriminatory charges had eaten away all prospects the farmer had for breaking even, a railroad system which gave preferential treatment to favored shippers, dominated state legislatures, blackmailed towns into issuing bonds, held large tracts of land off the market and refused to assume a proper share of the tax burden.[20]

This pattern of activity by economic interests continued to flourish in one form or another as government became more involved in the economic sector. With the creation by Congress of regulatory agencies, and the establishment of regulations for various business activities, which began in the nineteenth century, the relationship between business and government was nourished. This pattern continued with passage of Franklin Roosevelt's New Deal program, World War II, and was further stimulated after the war as the role of the federal government in the post-World War II period has substantially increased the potential for corruption. A study of the cost of federal subsidy programs by the Joint Economic Committee of Congress released in 1974 reported that between fiscal years 1970 and 1975 the total cost of federal subsidies grew 55 percent to $95 billion. During the same period, various kinds of federal tax subsidies grew to approximately $60 billion, or almost two thirds of the total value of federal subsidies. The extent of government activity is clear when benefit-in-kind subsidies or those that result when government provides something to individuals or communities at less than the cost of production, and other types of subsidies such as direct cash payments to large farmers, are added to the $95 billion.

The study also provided a revealing picture of the sectors of the economy receiving the largest share of federal subsidies. Not surprisingly, commercial ventures are the largest recipients with benefits worth an estimated $21.5 billion in fiscal 1975.[21] When the actions of state and local government are added to those of the federal government, Senator Douglas' observations are of even more concern. For this situation indeed "gives to the relatively few involved a powerful incentive to corrupt government in order to influence the decisions which must be made."[22] The potential for corruption from this interaction is obvious and occurs in such situations as the following:

> (1) When the government lets huge contracts, the terms of which can make fortunes for the contractors. (2) When it collects very large sums in taxes from individuals and corporations and hence offers a temptation for bribes in exchange for tax reductions. (3) When it grants loans . . . or permits plant and equipment to be amortized out of taxes over a short period of time instead of the customary twenty years or so. (4) When it fixes rates, as in the case of railroads, electric, and gas industries, and, in periods of "hot" and "cold" war, the prices of a wide range of commodities. Under these conditions, when prices are fixed not by the impersonal forces of competition but by state fiat, the managers of the dominant firms feel it necessary to control government in order to protect their own interests. (5) When the government has the power through the issuance or denial of certificates of convenience and necessity to select those who shall and who shall not be allowed to enter an industry, as is

now the case with radio, television, interstate trucking, and aviation, or locally or on state levels for various professions or trades. (6) When the power to allocate raw materials is placed in the hands of the government. (7) When subsidies are paid either openly or covertly by the government as was formerly the case with tariffs and land grants and is now the case with the silver and sugar industries, the Merchant Marine, the airlines, and with the carrying of newspapers, magazines, and advertising matter by the Post Office.

It is in these "action-laden" areas that venality operates. There the men in private industry have frequently both the incentive and wherewithal to corrupt and here the temptation for the government officials to succumb is great.[23]

In addition to those organized interests seeking to expand their share of governmental generosity through additional tax breaks, direct subsidies, and so on, it is common for interest groups to adopt a strategy maintaining the status quo and their privileged position in it. As Edgar Lane has observed:

The development of political interest groups has been accompanied by gradual but cumulatively significant changes in the uses and objectives of private political action. As groups realize their objectives, their political preoccupations are often subtly transformed. Group goals tend to become protective rather than acquisitive; that is to say, while they stand ready to accept whatever they can get from governments that still have much to give, many well-established groups want mainly to be left alone . . . . The relative circumspection of present-day group activity . . . may be even more significant as an index of past political success; not only are relatively satisfied interests no longer able to corrupt entire legislatures with virtual impunity, but they no longer have sufficient reason to try. Capitalizing on the procedural lacunae of the government process, on their access to decision-making vantage points in legislatures and administrative agencies, on their electoral power, and on the institutional sluggishness that Truman has immortalized as the "defensive advantage," major groups increasingly play a quiet politics of stalemate, attrition, and delay to head off threats from competing groups whose interests lie in upsetting equilibria. Such tactics are inherently less costly, less disruptive, and less visible than overt action in behalf of positive objectives, and they are also inherently less susceptible to the requirements of disclosure statutes (as these are ordinarily interpreted).[24]

It really does not matter whether the objective of special monied interest groups is to increase their share of the take or simply to protect the status quo. The key to their success is participation in the financing of political campaigns. Because the cost of running for political office in the United States "has climbed to such dizzy heights in recent years . . . ,"[25] it has become evident that "the interdependence between special interests, wealthy individuals and politicians and government has become nigh total."[26]

The escalation of the cost of campaigns is most apparent in the table on pages 100–101.

The most important factor in the steady escalation of campaign costs has been the increased use of television. Although television is not used in all campaigns, in the case of presidential, senatorial, and gubernatorial campaigns, television and radio may well account for 50 percent or more of the total cost.[27] Herbert Alexander found that television and radio costs in presidential general elections from 1952 through 1968 increased dramatically. The Republican total expenditure for radio and television rose from $2,046,000 in 1952 to $12,598,000 in 1968. The total figure for Democrats went up from $1,530,000 in 1952 to $6,143,000 in 1968.[28] Perhaps as a response to this trend, the Federal Election Campaign Act of 1971 limited the amount candidates for federal office may spend on media advertising to a total equal to 10 cents multiplied by the voting age population of the area in which the election is held, or $50,000, whichever is greater. The law also requires that no more than 60 percent of the money may be spent on broadcast media. As a result, the overall limit for presidential media spending in 1972 was $14.3 million, with $8.5 million the limit for broadcast spending.[29] Probably as a result of the limitations, spending in the 1972 presidential election was approximately 50 percent lower than in 1968. All presidential candidates spent a total of $14.3 million on broadcast media in 1972 compared with $28.5 million in 1968. Nevertheless, the total amount spent on radio and television by all candidates for public office in 1972 was $59.6 million, or an increase of approximately 1 percent over the previous record 1968 total.

Although spending on broadcast media declined in 1972, the same pattern of escalating total costs of campaigns continued. According to Congressional Quarterly:

> The 1972 presidential campaign was the most expensive in American history. Precise figures on total spending are hard to come by; illegal contributions by individuals and corporations, and the money that flowed into secret funds may never be fully totaled up. . . .
>
> In July, 1974, the Senate Select Committee on Presidential Campaign Activities (Watergate Committee) reported that: President Nixon's and

TABLE 1: Campaign Financing—1954, 1958, 1962, 1966 and 1970

The table below shows reported campaign spending included in reports to the Clerk of the House for the midterm campaigns since 1954. Numbers on the committee line indicate the number of groups reporting.

Committee Spending Reported Nationally

	1954	1958	1962	1966*	1970*
Republican Committees	27	14	11	21	17
Receipts	$ 5,380,994	$ 4,686,423	$ 4,674,570	$ 7,640,760	$11,754,305
Expenditures	5,509,649	4,657,652	4,637,586	7,863,092	12,702,215
Percentage of Total Spending	53.5%	53.7%	39.4%	41.5%	45.3%
Democratic Committees	13	7	8	8	19
Receipts	2,168,404	1,733,626	3,699,827	4,055,310	3,809,883
Expenditures	2,224,211	1,702,605	3,569,357	4,282,007	4,263,722
Percentage of Total Spending	21.6%	19.6%	30.3%	22.5%	15.2%
Labor Committees	41	32	33	42	54
Receipts	1,882,157	1,854,635	2,112,677	4,262,077	5,290,822
Expenditures	2,057,613	1,828,778	2,305,331	4,289,055	5,235,173
Percentage of Total Spending	20.0%	21.1%	19.6%	22.7%	18.7%
Miscellaneous Committees	15	11	26	44	89
Receipts	517,804	492,710	1,313,959	2,123,868	5,603,790
Expenditures	514,094	486,430	1,271,214	2,545,080	5,817,494
Percentage of Total Spending	5.0%	5.6%	10.8%	13.3%	20.8%
TOTALS					
Receipts	$ 9,949,359	$ 8,767,394	$11,801,033	$18,082,015	$26,458,800

Congressional Campaign Spending Reported

	1954	1958	1962	1966	1970
Republicans	$ 1,596,031	$ 1,670,933	$ 3,475,847	$ 2,230,835	$ 5,968,080
Percentage of Spending	52.4%	50.9%	52.5%	34.8%	41.5%
Democrats	1,436,576	1,600,117	2,950,552	4,081,685	6,653,648
Percentage of Spending	47.2%	48.7%	44.9%	63.6%	46.3%
Third Party and Independents	13,333	2,605	172,622	103,764	1,746,307
Percentage of Spending	0.4%	0.4%	2.6%	1.6%	12.2%
Total Congressional Spending	3,045,940	3,283,655	6,620,627	6,416,284	14,368,035
TOTAL REPORTED CAMPAIGN COSTS	$13,351,507	$11,959,120	$18,404,115	$25,395,518	$42,386,639

*The 1966 and 1970 expenditure figures are "less transfers"—i.e., lateral fund transfers between national-level committees have been deducted.

SOURCE: Reports filed with the Clerk of the House and Secretary of the Senate. Reprinted from Editors, *Dollar Politics* (Washington, D.C.: Congressional Quarterly, 1971), p. 60.

Senator McGovern's campaigns compiled total expenditures of over $100 million. The unsuccessful campaigns of others seeking nomination spent millions of dollars more. [30]

It should be noted, however, that broadcast media are not the only reason for escalating campaign costs. In addition to broadcast costs, the new media politics has produced an additional, expensive group of political experts including, among others, the pollsters, consultants, direct mail specialists, advertising agencies, and experts on the selling of candidates over television. As was observed by Congressional Quarterly:

> The costly services of these experts has added to the mounting costs of campaign spending on mass media and has provided wealthy candidates and contributors with opportunities to spend large sums on what are considered the most effective campaign methods. [31]

Thus the mutual benefit society has been aided by the escalation of the costs of campaigns as officeholders and candidates go to the financial "angels" for the funds presumed necessary for election. In short, the effort to finance campaigns for public office in an era of weak parties and media-oriented politics inevitably creates a close relationship between public officials and those seeking public office with individuals and organized groups that have substantial financial resources.

In short, the system of financing political campaigns is a potentially corrupting factor for *all* individuals holding or seeking public office at *any* level of government. The financial returns from a greatly diminished patronage system, the small contributions of party loyalists and individual candidates, and the personal financial resources of most candidates simply are not adequate to finance most campaigns in this era of media politics. The frequent professions of large contributors that they offer politicians financial support "for the national good" or some equally lofty motive is of no concern. Whatever the donor's declared motivations, it is our view that the necessity for large contributions inherently corrupts the system because the candidate remains dependent on a particular wealthy individual or collection of such individuals, or organized interests, for campaign resources. This is true even if the contributor does not directly make policy demands or requests for special favors. Clearly, the potential for undue influence is always present.

Furthermore, the existing system effectively precludes success for candidates who do not have access to such funds. As a result, the need for large contributions to meet exorbitant campaign costs really is a perversion of the democratic electoral process. Congressman James Wright (D., Texas) underscored this point most directly.

> The price of campaigning has risen so high that it actually imperils the integrity of our political institutions. Big contributors more and more hold the keys to the gates of public service. This is choking off the well springs of fresh men, and thought, and severely limiting the field of choice available to the public. I am convinced, moreover, that the intellectual quality of political campaigns is deteriorating as a result.

> One curious by-product of big money in politics is the slick, shallow public-relations approach with its nauseating emphasis on "image" at the expense of substance. In the arenas where Lincoln and Douglas once debated great issues, advertising agencies last year [1970] hawked candidates like cornflakes.[32]

Campaign Money: Business and Labor in Action

The corrupting influence of money to nurture the mutual benefit society also is evident from the variety of subterfuges that individuals and groups have taken to get around the few weak laws related to campaign finance. The Tillman Act of 1907 banned corporate gifts of money to candidates for federal elective offices or to committees supporting candidates, and the federal Corrupt Practices Act of 1925 broadened the prohibition to cover contributions of "anything of value." Yet, as President Dwight Eisenhower observed in 1968:

> [corporations] lend office equipment and the services of their public relations experts and lawyers; they make it easy, through bonuses and expense accounts, for executives to contribute substantial sums; and they buy advertising space at ridiculously high rates in political pamphlets and brochures.[33]

Richard Harris has described this process in detail:

> A frequent device used by companies is for an officer's fund to be administered by some committee. The officers and employees make contributions to this fund, sometimes even by an automatic payroll deduction plan. Such contributions are sometimes indirectly coerced through intra-corporate memos by superior officers pointing out that they have made contributions and inviting action memos from subordinates. Sometimes

the voluntary contributions are encouraged by the corporations' providing some other fringe benefit of significant value, such as group life insurance. Sometimes employees are encouraged to pad expense accounts as a device for reimbursement for their "voluntary" corporate contribution. Devices which are illegal and clearly prohibited but difficult to detect are sometimes used by corporations. Examples of these are donations of stamps to candidates with the expense hidden in the general corporate expenditures for postage. Sometimes loans are made which are subsequently written off as uncollectible. This activity for banks is clearly prohibited and would be immediately suspect. Another device sometimes used is for advertising agencies to render bills for services . . . to the candidate's campaign and sending the invoice to the corporation without specific detail for what services were rendered. Similarly, printing, printing bills, or in some cases, even lawyers' fee bills are used. A frequently used device is the loan of employees or other facilities of the corporation, such as duplicating facilities, computer facilities, telephone networks, and the like. In addition to contributions of postage stamps, [there are] often contributions of envelopes or other products of a company which might be usable in the campaign, such as lumber for signs, stationery, or other paper . . . . All of the foregoing probably constitute a prohibited expenditure, though indictment and prosecution are infrequent.[34]

In addition to such "in kind" donations, companies and unions have used front committees through which money is funneled to candidates. Examples of such practices gained prominence during the Watergate controversy. *The Washington Post* discovered groups such as the League for Concerted Action, the Committee for a Better Nation, the Organization of Community Volunteers, and others had been established solely to "funnel" campaign cash into the Nixon reelection campaign. For example, the dairy industry sent $2,500 to 68 such committees in just *one* phase of its contributing to the Nixon campaign.[35]

Labor unions use somewhat similar methods in their political activities. Most international unions have created committees such as the Active Ballot Club of the Retail Clerks International or DRIVE which translates Teamsters. Unions also provide manpower, equipment, offices, and a variety of other "in kind" contributions. However, the total value of direct business contributions to Republicans exceeds considerably that of labor to Democrats by at least five times.[36] Although some money, most notably that of the Teamsters, goes to Republicans, the greatest share goes to Democrats.[37] The process differs further in that union constitutions and bylaws, and federal laws related to labor unions, place a number of restrictions on the raising and giving of money to political campaigns. Although the individual member's contribution to political funds sometimes resembles a virtual assessment given under substantial pressure, theoretically the contributions are voluntary. Even though organized labor's political donations are nowhere near as large as those from the business community, they are large enough to incur substantial obligation on the part of the recipient.

The type of interest group or the differences in the size of their total contribution is not really the critical question. It is quite simply whether the pattern of past activities has changed. The evidence gives every indication that overall interest group spending has continued to increase. For example, the Congressional Quarterly reported in 1974:

> A total of 526 groups representing business, labor, agriculture, doctors, educators and other interests reported expenditures of $15.3 million by August 31. About $2 million of this was simply transfers of cash between national groups and their state committees, however. In addition, the same political committees reported another $12.9 million in cash on hand ready for use before the November [1974] elections.[38]

Because of the loopholes in the 1974 reform law, it will not be difficult for special interest groups to raise and spend as much or more on politics in 1976.[39] In fact, a survey of 514 political committees set up by labor unions, corporations, professional associations and the like, conducted by *The Washington Post,* reported that as of June 30, 1975, the groups had cash balances totaling $12,518,731.[40]

There appears to be another difference between business and labor involvement in politics, namely in terms of enforcement of laws related to such activities. For example, in the 62 years following enactment of the Tillman Act of 1907 on campaign financing, the Justice Department successfully prosecuted only three business concerns for violation of the ban on political gifts by corporations.[41] Although there has been more active enforcement since 1970, the fact remains that unions and union officials traditionally have been far more likely to be prosecuted than business firms and executives. In neither case, however, has the government vigorously attempted to uphold and enforce the laws. In neither case have many convicted violators gone to jail. V. O. Key's characterization of past statutes as more declaratory of "righteous indignation about huge expenditures rather than restrictive of behavior" is most accurate.[42]

NOTES

1. This is discussed in greater depth later in the next chapter, "Angels and Their Agents" that follows.

2. Robert Sherrill, *Why They Call It Politics,* 2nd ed. (New York: Harcourt Brace Jovanovich, 1974), p. 128.

3. George Thayer, *Who Shakes the Money Tree* (New York: A Touchstone Book by Simon and Schuster, 1973), pp. 211–212.

4. For a discussion of this pattern at the federal level see Editors, *Dollar Politics: The Issue of Campaign Spending,* Vol. 2 (Washington, D.C.: Congressional Quarterly, 1974), pp. 15, 69–89.

5. Ibid., p. 15.

6. Ibid.

7. Ibid. In addition to the Congressional Quarterly see the *Reports and Hearings* of the Senate Select Committee on Presidential Campaign Activities, 1974.

8. Arthur Levine, "I Got My Job Through CREEP," *The Washington Monthly* (November 1974), p. 36. See the article for examples of how to fill positions and how to fire people covered by civil service.

9. Ibid., p. 42.

10. Ibid., p. 40.

11. Ibid., pp. 36–37.

12. Robert Goodman, "Media and Money in a California Campaign," unpublished paper, University of Southern California, October 1971, p. 16.

13. Ibid.

14. Editors, *Dollar Politics,* Vol. 2, p. 4.

15. Goodman, "Media and Money," p. 19.

16. Mary Breasted, "Democrats Raise $400,000 Here," *The New York Times,* June 13, 1975, p. 38L.

17. Ibid.

18. Paul H. Douglas, *Ethics in Government* (Cambridge, Mass.: Harvard University Press, 1952), p. 44.

19. Sherrill, *Why They Call It Politics,* p. 232.

20. Ibid. Also see Peter Barnes and Larry Casalino, *Who Owns the Land* (Berkeley, Calif.: The Center for Rural Studies, 1972).

21. David T. Cook, "U.S. Subsidies Often Not Money Well Spent," *The Christian Science Monitor,* October 18, 1974, p. 8. For a thorough discus-

sion of the subject see Philip M. Stern, *The Rape of the Taxpayer* (New York: Random House, 1973).

22. Douglas, *Ethics in Government*, p. 22.

23. Ibid., pp. 22–23.

24. Edgar Lane, *Lobbying and the Law* (Los Angeles: University of California Press, 1964), p. 180.

25. Editors, *Dollar Politics*, Vol. 1, p. 1.

26. Joseph Goulden, *The Superlawyers* (New York: Weybright and Talley, 1972), p. 32.

27. Herbert Alexander, *Political Financing* (Minneapolis, Minn.: Burgess Publishing, 1972), p. 4.

28. Ibid., p. 10.

29. Editors, *Dollar Politics*, Vol. 2, p. 60.

30. Ibid., p. 64.

31. Editors, *Dollar Politics*, Vol. 1, p. 2.

32. *Report of the Committee on Standards of Ethics*, United States House of Representatives, December 2, 1971, p. 176.

33. Editors, *Dollar Politics*, Vol. 1, p. 6.

34. Richard Harris, "Annals of Politics: A Fundamental Hoax," *The New Yorker*, August 7, 1971, p. 50.

35. Morton Mintz, "Three Milk Co-ops Build Campaign Fund," *The Washington Post*, July 11, 1974, p. A7.

36. Harris, "Annals of Politics," p. 53.

37. For a discussion of the union totals see David W. Adamany, "How Shall We Finance Our National Elections?" Paper presented at the Western Political Science Association Convention, Denver, Colorado, April 4–6, 1974, pp. 25–28.

38. Editors, *Dollar Politics*, Vol. 2, p. 55.

39. Bob Kuttner, "Pressure Groups Adjust to Election Law," *The Washington Post*, November 5, 1974, p. A10.

40. Stephen Isaacs, "Interest Groups Amass $12 Million Despite Laws," *The Washington Post*, and printed in *The Sacramento Bee*, September 21, 1975, p. A4.

41. Editors, *Dollar Politics*, Vol. 1, p. 6.

42. V. O. Key, Jr., *Politics, Parties, and Pressure Groups* (New York: Thomas Y. Crowell, 1964), p. 513.

5

Angels
and
Their
Agents

IT HAS BEEN SUGGESTED THAT INDIVIDUAL BIG CON-
tributors represent for the most part the ruling class quietly funding the
electoral process.[1] Although social scientists and others debate the
validity of such assertions, there is little disagreement that the money
given by the very wealthy plays a significant role in politics in the United
States. It is important in terms of total amount, but it is perhaps even
more influential because of the fact that such individuals are courted by
all factions of both major political parties. Such contributors assume
even more importance and exert even greater influence than organizations contributing comparable amounts because they provide the early
money, particularly for nonincumbents. By being able to provide much
of the funds so necessary to start a campaign, the very wealthy can have
a great influence on who even runs for political office. This is particularly the case for those seeking a presidential campaign because it is the
early money that is available for primary and preconvention activities
that governs access to a party nomination. As Alexander Heard pointed
out, "Here, persons with access to money find their greatest opportunity
to influence the selection of public officials."[2]

The importance and influence of the very wealthy also are enhanced by the methods of soliciting large contributions. As David
Adamany observed:

> The large contributor has noteworthy advantages in exercising his
> influence within the political system. He is generally solicited for funds

by someone close to the candidate or officeholder . . . and he is thus recognized at the center of power as having given vital assistance. A group of small contributors . . . , even though they may give in the aggregate the same amount, are likely to be solicited by lesser persons who are farther from those who hold ultimate decision-making authority.[3]

In view of the importance of wealthy contributors to political candidates and their campaigns, an appropriate term for such individuals is angel. Probably because of the attitude of the public toward politicians and money in politics, candidates today seldom wear openly the labels of their angels, as was the case earlier in American history. Another change in the political scene has been that all segments of the political continuum—left, right, center or whatever—attempt to influence public policy through campaign contributions rather than primarily the corporate sector as used to be the case. There is no intrinsic difference between the activities of a W. Clement Stone, who attempted to promote what he labeled a conservative approach to government, and those of the "liberal" Stewart Mott, Jr., who sought to influence or purchase his own brand of public policy. The implications of such activities for the public and the entire political system are simple—a substantial perversion of the one-person, one-vote theory. Under the present unregulated system, can a politician afford to give equal consideration to the policy preferences of one voter who casts one ballot, and to those who possess vast financial resources in addition to their vote?

Let us examine the influence of our "equal citizens" in the light of the one-person, one-vote theory. Mr. Mott and his associates played a significant role in raising the $11 million spent by Eugene McCarthy in 1968, with Mott alone contributing at least $210,000. When the McCarthy efforts failed, Mott and his anonymous associates communicated a proposal to Hubert Humphrey that he adopt McCarthy's approach to foreign policy in return for desperately needed campaign funds. The letter from Mott to the former vice-president, which is reprinted in full in *Financing the 1968 Election* by Herbert Alexander, described Mott's efforts to influence policy positions. Mott pointed out how he personally had purchased twenty-one full pages of advertising for the Rockefeller campaign for the Republican nomination for president in 1968, and had spent over $90,000 of his own money on that campaign.[4] The letter also outlined Mott's capacity for additional generosity, noting that he and his group—not named—had raised $3 to

$4 million for McCarthy. After bemoaning the fact that Humphrey had not even contacted any of the members of the Mott group, the letter ended with the advice that if the group was "turned on" and "enthusiastic" about Humphrey's campaign, they had the capacity to give $1 million and raise more than "twice or three" times that amount. The only catch for the then money-short candidate was the promotion of a policy to end the Vietnam war that was more to the liking of Mott and his wealthy friends.[5]

How did Mr. Stone's operation differ? He also wanted to influence the course of history. The following article which appeared as an "exclusive to *The Los Angeles Times* from *The Chicago Daily News*" vividly described an attitude and approach similar to that exhibited by Mott.[6]

Millionaire Tries to Buy
Victory for Republicans

by Robert Billings

Chicago—We should all know by now the old familiar story: How the only son of a widowed seamstress with a craving for peppermint sticks and dill pickles was forced to drop out of high school. How he, undeterred, changed his name from Billy to W., raised a pencil-thin moustache, taught himself to tie a polka-dot bow, found a magical ring for his finger, and while chanting "I am! I can! I will!" went out to sell, sell, sell, and became Clement the Millionaire. . . .

W. Clement Stone, 68, lights one of his pre-Castro Cuban cigars and smiles a greeting.

He is in his sixth-floor office of his combined insurance company wearing a suit of dark, conservative brown mohair, set off by a light brown bow tie. . . .

He wants to change the world.

"It's very seldom that a private citizen can affect the course of history for the better," he says in explaining his entrance into politics. . . .

"I'm looking to '72. That's why I felt I had to get into state and county elections.

"We've got to give the President a Republican Congress and legislature to give the President a chance to really do the things that have to be done.

"I feel strongly about good government and law enforcement and I want to see these things brought about intelligently."

Toward that end Stone keeps rolling. He reportedly is spending $1 million in an effort to return Ralph Smith to the U.S. Senate and to elect Republicans to offices in Illinois and elsewhere.

The vault is always open in the interest of law and order. Stone is one of four Republican businessmen who united to buy nationwide time to telecast the major portion of the President's September 16 speech at Kansas State University in which he attacked campus violence.

There is a story that Stone met Mr. Nixon through their mutual association with the Boy's Club of America. It was after Mr. Nixon's defeats for the Presidency in 1960 and the governorship of California in 1962.

They met and W. Clement Stone, a supersalesman gave Richard M. Nixon, unemployed lawyer, a copy of his book, "Success Through a Positive Mental Attitude."

Stone doesn't deny it. In fact, the reference delights him. He laughs like a one-note siren.

There was talk that Mr. Nixon would name Stone secretary of health, education and welfare to give the whole country a powerful shot of PMA (positive mental attitude).

"I can do more good reaching different people through many organizations. When I get the idea, I can always call one of the secretaries of one of the departments. . . .

"I am in contact with the President."

"When?"

"Well, he called to thank me for my help after the election. He called me at Christmas.

"In fact, during the last convention he called to ask me what I thought about Mr. Agnew as his running mate."

Just like everyone, Stone said, he asked the President, "Spiro who?"

"But I thought his not being well known could be an asset. So I got out a book on him so people could know him."

"Come to think of it maybe we ought to reissue that book. Thanks for reminding me."

Stone took a pen from his desk set and made a note in his neat hand on his desk calendar. . . .

What can be concluded from the activities of the two angels? Stated very simply, one-person, one-vote, when confronted by the concentrated power of big money is a myth in the electoral and policy-making arena.

In his analysis of the Democratic party, G. William Domhoff aptly described the situation and the consequences.

It is not a pretty picture, but it is inevitable as long as the under classes find difficulty in pinning their hopes on a party containing both fat cats and plain Democrats. Until the unlikely day when millions of blue and white collar workers put aside their racial and ethnic differences and show themselves to be genuine democrats by contributing $10 to $20 a year to the support of anti-big property candidates, American politics will remain with few exceptions, a staging area for egotists, timid idealists, and the usual array of favor seekers, tax dodgers, and outright embezzlers. The essence of power elite politics is bamboozlement, and no group should be disappointed to find itself continually left out in the cold by sweet-talking Democrats who are bought and paid . . . .[7]

The response of a majority of Democrats in Congress to most aspects of the Watergate scandal supports Domhoff's severe critique of the Democratic party. As noted previously, the critical role of loyal opposition throughout most of the episode was performed by elements of the news media rather than by the Democrats.

Nelson Rockefeller recognized this stance on the part of Congress, specifically the Democratic members, when he observed that if Congress could be persuaded to act swiftly on his vice-presidential nomination, he would be protected from the kind of critical analysis that a truly effective loyal opposition should provide at such crucial times. Rockefeller promptly turned to the Congress and called for immediate hearings before the November 1974 election. The congressional committees considering his qualifications had authorized an FBI investigation as a requisite for confirmation. In the process, the agents discovered that a dummy corporation had been created to provide a conduit for money from Nelson's brother Laurence Rockefeller to a conservative book publishing house (Arlington House) to publish an anti-Arthur Goldberg book during the height of the 1970 gubernatorial contest between the former Supreme Court Justice and Nelson Rockefeller. A flood of commentary and criticism appeared in the news media, but few elected officials were critical. Indeed, most limited themselves to exceedingly guarded statements about whether the controversy might hurt Rockefeller's chances for confirmation.

In the course of the hearings on Rockefeller's nomination, it also became known that he had given large gifts to crucial politicians and influential journalists that would be deemed bribes if bestowed by Mafia leaders, but so muddled is the systemic conception of politics and ethics of some of our current political elite that the Rockefeller largess was initially treated as rather commonplace.

The magnitude of the Rockefeller bestowals of money has not been thoroughly revealed. Nevertheless, a partial picture emerges with the acknowledgment of $25 million in what Rockefeller referred to as educational and charitable contributions, plus over $2 million in direct personal gifts, and more than $20 million in political contributions over a seventeen-year period. The personal gifts elicited the greatest amount of controversy because several were to individuals who held key roles as gatekeepers or controllers of Republican politics, had significant roles in the news media, or held other opinion-molding positions. Rockefeller stated in a letter to Senate Rules Committee Chairman Howard W. Cannon that the gifts and canceled loans were made to "friends and associates to assist them in meeting the kind of pressing human needs which all people have from time to time." Some of the gifts, however, were not tied to any clearly defined personal need—$50,000 to Henry Kissinger, $550,000 to aide William Ronan, substantial sums to two former New York state Republican chairmen, Judson Morehouse, and Fred A. Young, and $150,000 to Emmet Hughes, a presidential advisor in the Eisenhower administration, and a loan of $100,000 to Democrat Tom Braden as well as a gift of $10,000 to his wife, Joan. In addition, several of the "charitable" donations were related directly or indirectly to political matters that were of prime importance to a potential presidential candidate.[8]

The biography of former Supreme Court Justice Goldberg authorized by Laurence Rockefeller was indeed a tawdry and inexcusable act made possible by great personal wealth. Moreover, as was illustrated by the tendencies and actions of Richard Nixon, such acts are not limited to just the very opulent, such as the Rockefellers. Nevertheless, Nelson Rockefeller's failure to "accept a real limitation on the use of his financial power . . . to achieve his political goals" does indeed suggest "that reaching for a checkbook can corrupt the holder of public office as much as putting a hand out for a payoff."[9]

Perhaps the most telling commentary concerns the political service performed on Rockefeller's behalf by William Ronan. As columnist Joseph Kraft described it:

> A very special case in point is the case of William Ronan, a longtime Rockefeller aide. Mr. Ronan received a gift of $550,000 in the form of a canceled debt. He lives well enough to list in "Who's Who" membership in eight different clubs. He has peremptorily refused to answer questions as to what he did with the gift money.

> It happens that Mr. Ronan played a key role in a power play critical to the Rockefeller fortunes in New York. That was the absorption of the Tri-Borough Authority by the Metropolitan Transportation Authority.

The upshot of that deal, as indicated by Robert Caro in his superb book, *Power Broker,* was the political extinction of a chief Rockefeller rival, Robert Moses.

The hinge of the deal was a provision whereby the Chase Manhattan Bank agreed to transfer millions of dollars of debt from the Tri-Borough Authority to the Metropolitan Transportation Authority. The transfer was arranged by Gov. Rockefeller for the state, and his brother, David Rockefeller, acting as head of the Chase Bank. The terms have been kept secret to this day. Mr. Ronan, who was chief of the Metropolitan Transportation Authority at the time, is the only living outsider involved. The Congress should certainly look into his role, and indeed that whole transaction, before passing on the governor as Vice President.[10]

But perhaps the most serious, albeit muted, issue involving the Rockefeller behavior in the American political system involves the elitist ideological implications of the behavior that Nelson Rockefeller exhibited in his vigorous pursuit of the presidency for more than a decade. It is an ideology that permits one to treat individuals and groups as pawns to be used, purchased, and manipulated at will. It differs little from that of Senator Nelson Aldrich, son-in-law of John D. Rockefeller, Sr., a thirty-year power in the U.S. Senate. Aldrich openly argued in the nineteenth century that geographic representation in the Senate was old-fashioned. He advocated a new type of Senate manned officially by representatives from the great business "constituencies"—steel, coal, copper, railroads, banks, textiles, and so on.[11] Although Senator Aldrich was not successful in his efforts to change the *formal* representation in the Senate, Governor Rockefeller's ancestors hardly would be displeased with the current political scene in the mutual benefit society.

"Shingle for Hire"

Another aspect of money and politics in our mutual benefit society involves the role and activities of some members of the legal profession. The role of lawyers in politics has long been documented.[12] For example, a study by the Congressional Quarterly reported that eighty-one members of the House of Representatives wore two hats—as legislators and lawyers.[13] Of the eighty-one who received $1,000 or more from law practices, nine received at least $5,000 in 1970. It is of interest to note that The American Bar Association Code of Professional Responsibility for lawyers states, "A lawyer who is a public officer, whether full or part time, should not engage in activities in which his personal or professional interests are, or, foreseeably may be, in conflict with his official duties."[14]

But questions remain: what constitutes a conflict, what defines an "active and regular" law practice, and, is the ABA ruling justifiable? As Representative Howard W. Robison (D. N.Y.), one of those who earned more than $5,000 in 1970 stated, "I don't see why lawyers need to be singled out as involved in a conflict of interest because we maintain some contact with a law firm."[15]

The point is not one of singling out lawyers, but rather of adding them to the list of those with financial and business relationships in the mutual benefit society that do pose the potential for conflict of interest. That the potential is real was made clear by the late Drew Pearson and his associate Jack Anderson in a chapter of *The Case Against Congress* called "Shingle for Hire."[16]

It also seems reasonable to raise questions as to why some law firms associated with the nation's lawmakers seem to attract so many important corporate clients. A classic example of this type of arrangement involved the hometown firm of the late Republican Senator Everett Dirksen of Illinois—Davis, Morgan and Witherell.

> The lineup of corporations that retain Davis, Morgan and Witherell is impressive. In addition to Panhandle and Eastern Pipe Line, there are International Paper, Pabst Brewery, Pepsi-Cola Bottling of Peoria, Illinois, State Farm Insurance, Mid-States Steel and Wire, Keystone Steel and Wire, Brass Foundry, National Lock and some two dozen others. They span manufacturing, oil and gas, timber, mining, utilities, and the savings and loan, banking and insurance industries. The fact that these corporations went all the way to Peoria to seek legal counsel may simply speak well for the talents of the firm. Yet the question of what the law firm, through Dirksen, can do for these clients is inescapable. Invariably Dirksen has sided in the Senate with the interests that his law firm represents.[17]

A more recent study of fifty law firms with partners serving in Congress revealed a rather remarkable similarity of clients, namely the vested interests of the United States. For example, forty of the fifty law firms represented banks, thirty-one represented insurance companies, eleven represented gas and oil companies, and ten represented real estate firms.[18] When some of the largest corporations in the nation are represented by firms in Nicholasville, Kentucky, and Pascagoula, Mississippi, the implications are quite clear.

The shingle is useful not only in a personal sense to the lawyer-legislator, but also can serve the moneyed interests in the Congress and in other governmental institutions at all levels. It is the key to the process whereby money is channeled, normally anonymously because of the hallowed lawyer-client relationship, to those seeking or holding public office. The fee or retainer for "services rendered" is simply increased by an amount earmarked previously for a particular candidate, party, or fund-raising committee. Some individual member of the firm, frequently a new and relatively unknown member, through his (and the firm's) "sense of public spirit," then makes the money available to the candidate by a direct contribution, frequently and certainly most preferably in the past, in cash. There are few successful politicians (or their employees) who have not endured the lunch, small-talk, and obscenity of this transaction. If the state has a provision for public disclosure of campaign contributions that require filing the name of the donor, the records probably will indicate the name of the lawyer and not that of the actual source of the funds.

In order to protect fully the interest of their clients, the law firm, if it is a large one, in many cases will be involved with both candidates in an election and both political parties. O'Melveny and Myers, one of the larger, and certainly one of the most politically influential law firms in California, is a classic example of climbing to the top of the financial and influential heap. During the 1970 election in California, members of O'Melveny and Myers were involved with both candidates for governor, three candidates for the position of United States senator, and one candidate for state attorney general.[19] Because of the secretive nature of the lawyer-politician relationship, it is not possible to determine how many candidates for lesser offices received assistance from one or more of the more than 130 lawyers associated with the firm.

Lawyers also pursue their clients' interests after the ballots are counted and the winners are ceremoniously installed in office. Joseph Goulden and others have illustrated vividly the nature of activities by lawyers to influence public policy decisions in the nation's capitols. Similar, though perhaps less sophisticated, operations exist in city halls, courthouses, and state houses throughout the nation. As Goulden pointed out, the expansion of government at all levels has contributed to the bank accounts of individual lawyers and firms as clients seek advice not on how to destroy the governments' programs, but how to benefit from them. This view was stated succinctly by one of the founders of what is perhaps the most influential law firm in Washington, D.C.,

Covington and Burling. When asked his views of the New Deal by a reporter, Edward P. Burling stated, "I disagreed with the New Deal strongly, but it was a great benefit to lawyers because so many businessmen all over the country began squealing about what was happening to them and had to hire lawyers. And when you ask me about bureaucracy, I say, 'Oh, I'm for it. How would I eat otherwise?' "[20]

In short, with the growth of government, lawyers have played a key role in the transformation of the United States into a corporate state. As Goulden observed, a corporate state is one in which the overlap of government and industry is "nigh total."[21] This state of affairs combined with the present system of financing campaigns is almost ideal for those who seek to influence the public policy-making process. Any effort to sever this fully developed and mature tie between economic power and political power must reflect an awareness of the intimate relationship of many members of the legal profession to the mutual benefit society, and their role in insuring its continued existence.

The role of a legal elite has rather serious implications for the principle of equality as well, as was suggested by the resignation of Leon Jaworski from the appointed office of special prosecutor on October 12, 1974. Jaworski had served in that post since November 1, 1973, succeeding Archibald Cox who had been fired by President Nixon. Although Jaworski directed the special task force that ultimately produced the indictments of seven former members of the Nixon administration, he also struck the plea bargain for former Attorney General Richard Kleindienst and was in charge when the special force determined that the questionable ITT settlements were not the products of bribes. Jaworski's resignation before the completion of legal proceedings on the seven defendants was greeted with surprise but also with a great many accolades. Senator Charles Mathias, a Republican member of the Senate Judiciary Committee, stated that "the republic owes a great debt to Leon Jaworski."[22] Mathias' invocation of the republic was unintentionally ironic because Jaworski's behavior and the manner in which he imperiously decided that most of his responsibilities to the public had been discharged denotes the behavior of an aristocrat who is above the ordinary obligations that other citizens feel duty-bound to fulfill. The wrong was compounded by the status of the eighteen nonaristocratic jurors and their families (twelve jurors and six alternates) chosen by Judge Sirica for the Watergate trial. The standards of public duty applied to them were to say the least, rather severe. Following the usual lengthy course of legal actions of this sort, these eighteen ordinary citizens were expected to listen to weeks or months of testimony, including hours of tape recordings. At a more personal level, they were put behind locked doors for several months. As a *Washington Post* editorial written at the time of Jaworski's resignation pointed out:

> They [the jurors] will spend Thanksgiving together, away from their families. They may spend Christmas and New Year's together. They will spend many hours just waiting—for the lawyers to argue points of law out of their presence—for the next day's session of court to begin. Their impartiality was maligned by high officials even before they were selected and their verdict, whatever it may be, will be criticized. Their only reward will come in the knowledge that they have done their duty as citizens and that they have shared the ultimate responsibility in one of the most important criminal trials of our times.[23]

The contrast between the obligation of the Watergate jurors and alternates and that of former Special Prosecutor Leon Jaworski is striking. In a sense, it parallels the double standard that characterized much of the Watergate sentencing and the Agnew plea bargain. No ordinary citizen convicted of similar offences could hope to get off as easily. We should ask ourselves how long will the ordinary citizens, asked to make sacrifices as jurors, maintain a sense of citizenship obligation while those in more aristocratic status unilaterally determine for themselves where civic obligation begins or ends? But what was reflected in the entire Watergate issue, namely, the resignation of President Nixon, and most clearly exemplified in the controversy over the pardon, was the prevailing norms and mores or values that govern the conduct of political affairs in the United States.

To some observers of the Washington scene, the charges against President Nixon and others represented highly pardonable offenses.[24] From their perspective, President Nixon was not guilty of any major crime or serious wrongdoing, he had merely been unfortunate enough to get caught. In many respects, therefore, the pardon may have been simply an unconscious reflection of the ethics and values that permeate so much of politics in the United States. Since far too many other politicians had either contemplated or committed similar offenses, it seemed only natural to pardon and to excuse the highest ranking public figure when he was threatened by the processes of the criminal justice system. Washington political leaders in both parties are, after all, members of the same club, and it is not surprising that they react instinctively to defend one of their own who has, in their view, unjustly suffered because of a breach of ethics that is regarded as unrealistic and little understood. In this circle, members of the general public are considered outsiders. The elite also often views them as alien or unwelcome intruders on their private domain, government.

It also is revealing to compare the treatment accorded various individuals involved in Watergate and related events who have been processed through the judiciary. The most obvious beneficiary of lenient treatment is the exiled former president who receives a large government pension and resides in the upper class setting of San Clemente in a house improved with government money. There is also the question of the $148,000 promised but not paid back taxes for 1969. The treatment of Nixon obviously reflects what James Reston has called "a tolerance for lawlessness . . ." on the part of the elite.[25]

There also is the case of former Attorney General Richard Kleindienst, who pleaded guilty to one count of refusing to testify accurately and fully about the ITT case. He was given a one-month suspended sentence and has since been employed as a $120,000 a year representative to look after Algeria's interests in the United States.[26] Of course the primary beneficiary of the protection afforded to the nation's wealthy elite is perhaps C. Arnholt Smith. He masterminded one of the nation's largest embezzlement of funds and was convicted of giving illegal campaign contributions and yet received a suspended brief jail sentence.[27]

Regardless of the notices that may have inspired it, the issuance of a pardon to Richard Nixon is a dangerous precedent. Not only may it tempt future presidents to use the loophole in the Twenty-sixth Amendment (naming their successor without holding a national election) but it also might be employed to justify the decision of any elected official who resigns in exchange for an explicit promise of immunity from criminal prosecution. The constitutional provisions that permit presidents to resign without calling a new election, to appoint important government officials, and to pardon anyone accused of a crime, bestow awesome powers, powers that could be used to further their own political ambitions and those of their friends and allies. It is no longer inconceivable that a person could use the nation's highest office simply to enlarge his personal fortune and power without any fear of punishment. By allowing Nixon's resignation to prevent a full discussion of the Watergate scandal in the House and the Senate, congressional leaders virtually negated the effectiveness of the impeachment process as a means of removing high-ranking corrupt officials from public service. Hence, there is an urgent need for a major restructuring of the political process both to correct these constitutional defects and to insure greater accountability of the elected representatives to the people.

The Lobbies and the Mutual Benefit Society

The inability of students and observers of the political system to come to grips with the influence of wealth on the public policy-making process certainly has been a crucial factor in the continued failure of reform efforts. Since most of the reforms have not been directed at the heart of the problem—the relationship between economic power and political power—they are doomed to failure. Thus, the move toward "professionalism" in Congress and state legislatures has been for the most part a failure.

Reformers have repeatedly asserted—but without supporting evidence—that a primary effect would be to make representatives and senators less dependent on the various special interests, interests that traditionally share with many elected officials a joint occupancy of Washington, D.C. We have called this the mutual benefit society. Certainly, no one could object to such an admirable objective, but what has occurred? *The Los Angeles Times* characterized the state of affairs in Congress in 1970.

> At least 60% of the members of the House of Representatives have substantial financial interests in companies which do business with the federal government or which are regulated by federal agencies. What this means, at the very least, is that a serious potential for widespread conflicts of interest and abuses of the public trust runs through the Congress.
>
> How widespread actual instances of legislating for private gain may be we don't know. Under House rules the details of outside financial interests and the full extent of nongovernmental income do not have to be publicly reported. That information instead is turned over to the Committee on Standards of Official Conduct in sealed envelopes. There it stays unless it is needed for some subsequent investigation of a congressman who has gotten into trouble.
>
> The small amount of information that is required to be made available for public scrutiny is nevertheless revealing. It shows that 102 congressmen—almost one fourth of the entire House membership—hold office or own stocks in banks or financial institutions . . . .
>
> These, we could emphasize, are only the visible sources of interest conflicts. There may be many others that the rules of the House permit to remain hidden; for example, investments of less than $5,000 don't have to be reported. But what we can see is disturbing enough.
>
> We don't know how often how many congressmen might be swayed in their votes on the floor or their work in committee by a concern to protect

or further their outside interests. Probably most try most of the time to be conscientious about keeping private business separate from public duty. But is it merely a coincidence that so many of the outside investments and interests of so many congressmen are in areas over which they can directly or indirectly exert some influence?

It all looks bad, and it may smell worse. Can anything be done about it? Well, the House has made clear it has no serious interest in policing itself, so that leaves it up to the voters. The first step would be to demand full accounting from those who seek office of what their outside business interests are, and, if these interests are in any way regulated or supported by the government, whether they are prepared to divest themselves of them if they gain office.[28]

Clearly—with such a large number of the members of Congress continuing to have substantial financial interests in companies doing business with the federal government, subject to its regulation, or receiving financial benefits from its policies—the objectives sought by reformers have not been achieved. Of course, one cannot simply assert that all of the members who subsidize their already substantial salary income with such arrangements always neglect the public interest while performing their duties in Congress. With so few barriers against conflict of interest, however, the extent to which it occurs is not surprising. As former Senator Robert Kerr (D., Oklahoma) pointed out, "If everyone abstained (from voting) on grounds of personal interest, I doubt if you could get a quorum in the United States Senate on any subject."[29] A good example of direct conflict of interest is the case of a congressman owning a broadcasting station and sitting on the subcommittee that has jurisdiction over the industry. Perhaps a more direct illustration is the case of the late Congressman Robert Watkins from Pennsylvania who, as chairman of an interstate trucking firm, also was chairman of the subcommittee with legislative responsibilities for the same industry. The bankers on the banking committees, truckers on the commerce committees, and owners of oil interests on the tax committees, are illustrative of the types of conflicts that are common in Washington.

Recent events related to oil, wheat, milk, and antitrust policy, to name only a few examples, indicate the impact of the intimate relationship. Fortunately, in spite of the secrecy that surrounds the subject, enough information exists to cast more than a shadow of doubt on the claims of apologists for the present system. For example, prior to 1975 a majority of the Congress certainly had not substantially shifted their policy with regard to petroleum. Although the previously sacrosanct oil depletion allowance was reduced from 27.5 percent to 22 percent in 1969, the oil *lobby* is not depleted. The exercise of political power by the oil industry is a striking contrast to the movieland image of oilmen as tough, independent operators, fiercely individualistic, dependent on no one and accepting no interference—or handout—from the government. Spencer Rich presented a far more accurate image.

> But that is not the picture emerging from a series of hearings on the petroleum industry held by Senator Philip A. Hart's Senate Antitrust and Monopoly Subcommittee. There, a battery of oil industry spokesmen has pleaded that the vast system of government subsidies . . . must be maintained . . . .
>
> That the industry profits handsomely from the 27.5% depletion allowance has long been known. What has not previously been etched so sharply is the extent to which domestic oil companies reap subsidies from an additional system of economic aids generously provided by the U.S. Government and the states.[30]

Or, as conservative economist Milton Friedman asserted, "Few industries sing the praises of the free enterprise system more loudly than the oil industry. Yet few industries rely so heavily on Government favors."[31]

One of the reasons for the unparalleled success of the oil industry in shaping public policy is the immense and unmatched size of its reservoir of financial resources available for political purposes—in short, campaign contributions for "friends of oil."[32] This effort was revealed several years ago in the industry publication, *The Oil and Gas Journal,* which Jack Anderson labeled the "holy writ of the oil industry." The spokesmen for the industry evaluated the 1966 elections and concluded, "Oil Wins Big in Off Year Elections." Anderson described the situation as follows:

> It has been a triumphant campaign for champions of oil indulgence. . . . The *Journal* noted that "the Senate's most articulate critic of percentage depletion, Senator Paul H. Douglas . . . was defeated." Oilmen were almost as elated to hear that the "voters silenced this year's most persistent gadfly in the House—Representative John R. Schmidhauser." Both were replaced by pro-oil legislators.[33]

Although a few members of Congress continue to confront the political and economic power of the oil industry, and even though the Congress that was elected in 1974 could take an approach more in the public interest, events surrounding the so-called petroleum shortage in 1973 do not create an air of optimism. But in the end, the activities of this industry only illustrate the most effective use of economic power to purchase the political power needed to turn public policies to its own interest. Some five thousand other registered lobbyists—and who knows how many unregistered—representing every conceivable business and labor interest, and the recently emerging "citizen's lobby" groups, perform in a quite similar manner. The groups represented include a newly formed National Association of Professional Bureaucrats, whose motto is "When in Doubt, Mumble."[34] But as Jack Anderson and Carl Kalvelage observed ". . . they are still hired, in the final analysis, to sell their clients' special interests."[35] One way to accomplish this is through campaign contributions.

No less authority on the subject than Senator Russell Long of Louisiana stated candidly:

> The government pays out billions of dollars in unnecessarily high interest rates; it permits private monopoly patents on over $12 billion of government research annually; it permits billions of dollars to remain on deposit in banks without collecting interest; it permits overcharging by many concerns selling services to the government; it tolerates all sorts of tax favoritism; it fails to move to protect public health from a number of obvious hazards; it permits monopolies to victimize the public in a number of inexcusable ways; it provides for too much tariff protection to some industries and too little to others. Many of these evils are built-in effects of American government resulting from the way we finance our political campaigns.[36]

In view of the way in which the mutual benefit society continues to operate in the United States, it should not be a surprise that efforts to persuade citizens to become involved more actively in politics have been met by the blanket response, "They're a bunch of crooks." Politicians and political scientists often respond to this remark with a look of incredulous exasperation, as well as a fleeting thought or two about the ignorance of ordinary people. Yet, there is hardly any solid evidence to refute the public's assertion. By refusing to restructure the existing electoral system, by not divulging the full story of major scandals, such as Watergate, and by constantly asserting that their decisions are unaffected by the receipt of huge financial donations to their electoral campaigns, politicians have succeeded in straining the credibility of the American people to the breaking point. By refusing to meet criticism directly, by constantly proclaiming pious but incredible statements that politicians' votes and decisions are not influenced by campaign contributions from special interests, both politicians and political scientists have contributed to the undermining of American institutions. As the following chapter shows, halfhearted reforms that have been enacted at various levels of government have had little impact on the mutual benefit society.

NOTES

1. David Nichols, *Financing Elections: The Politics of an American Ruling Class* (New York: New Viewpoints, 1974), p. 54.

2. Alexander Heard, *The Costs of Democracy* (Chapel Hill: The University of North Carolina Press, 1960), p. 321.

3. David W. Adamany, *Financing Politics* (Madison: University of Wisconsin Press, 1969), pp. 212–213 and cited in Nichols, *Financing Elections,* pp. 53–54.

4. Herbert Alexander, *Financing the 1968 Election* (Lexington, Mass.: D.C. Heath, 1971), pp. 263–265.

5. Ibid.

6. Robert Billings, "Millionaire Tries to Buy Victory for Republicans." Reprinted with permission from *The Chicago Daily News.* The article appeared in *The Los Angeles Times,* October 16, 1970, part 1A, p. 13.

7. G. William Domhoff, *Fat Cats and Democrats: The Role of the Rich in the Party of the Common Man* (Englewood Cliffs, N.J.: Prentice-Hall, 1972), p. 176.

8. William Greider, "Rockefeller Asks Prompt Hill Hearings," *The Washington Post,* October 16, 1974, pp. A1, A13; William Greider, "Rockefeller Lists $2 Million in Gifts," *The Washington Post,* October 12, 1974, pp. A1, A8; Spencer Rich and William Greider, "Rockefeller Gave Charity $24.7 Million," *The Washington Post,* October 20, 1974, pp. A1, A9.

9. David S. Broder, "Rockefeller: A Politician on the Give," *The Washington Post,* October 16, 1974, p. A24.

10. Joseph Kraft, "Gov. Rockefeller's Generosity," *The Washington Post,* October 15, 1974, p. A21.

11. Thomas R. Dye and L. Harman Zeigler, *The Irony of Democracy* (Belmont, Calif.: Wadsworth, 1970), p. 74.

12. See John R. Schmidhauser and Larry L. Berg, *The Supreme Court and Congress: Conflict and Interaction, 1945–1968* (New York: The Free Press, 1972); Justin J. Green, John R. Schmidhauser, Larry L. Berg, and David Brady, "Lawyers in Congress: A New Look at Some Old Assumptions," *The Western Political Quarterly* 26(3) (September 1973):440–452;

Harlan Hahn, *Urban-Rural Conflict: The Politics of Change* (Beverly Hills, Calif.: Sage Publications, 1971); David Gold, "Lawyers in Politics," *Pacific Sociological Review* 4(2) (Fall 1961). Also see chapter 1 of this volume.

13. *The Los Angeles Times,* June 8, 1971, part 1A, p. 8.

14. Ibid.

15. Ibid.

16. Drew Pearson and Jack Anderson, *The Case Against Congress* (New York: Simon and Schuster, 1968).

17. Ibid., p. 114.

18. Jack Anderson, "How to Bribe a Congressman," *Parade,* May 6, 1973, p. 6.

19. Warren Hinckle, "The Law Firm That Runs California," *Scanlan's Monthly,* September 1970, p. 49.

20. Goulden, *The Superlawyers,* p. 36.

21. Ibid., p. 38.

22. Morton Mintz, "Jaworski Is Resigning: Says Task Is Completed," *The Washington Post,* October 13, 1974, p. A1

23. Editorial, "The Watergate Trial Jury," *The Washington Post,* October 13, 1974, p. C6.

24. One apologist would be William Safire, "Nixon Never Did," *The New York Times,* January 5, 1975, p. L37.

25. Anthony Lewis, "A Tolerance for Lawlessness," *The Sacramento Bee,* September 12, 1975, p. B7.

26. Robert Gruenberg, "Kleindienst Serving Algeria as Lobbyist," *The Los Angeles Times,* November 2, 1974, part 1, p. 9.

27. "C. Arnholt Smith Charged by U.S.," *The Los Angeles Times,* January 1, 1975, p. 1.

28. Editors, "Monkey Business in the House," *The Los Angeles Times,* May 28, 1971, part 2, p. 6. Copyright 1971, *The Los Angeles Times.* Reprinted by permission.

29. Mark Green et al., *Who Runs Congress?* (New York: Bantam Books, 1972), p. 139.

30. Spencer Rich, "The Power of Oil," *The Progressive,* September 1969, pp. 19–20.

31. Ibid., p. 23.

32. See Erwin Knowll, "The Oil Lobby Is Not Depleted," *The New York Times Magazine,* March 8, 1970, p. 27.

33. Jack Anderson, "Tax the Oil Companies," *Playboy Magazine,* August 1967, p. 93.

34. Richard D. Lyons, "Lobbyists Shifting Quarters to Capital," *The New York Times,* June 8, 1975, p. L51.

35. Jack Anderson and Carl Kalvelage, *American Government Like It Is* (Morristown, N.J.: General Learning Press, 1972), p. 30.

36. "Paying to Get Elected," *The New Republic,* October 16, 1971, p. 7. For a new and refreshing approach to the problem see Theodore K. Becker, *Your Country Tis of Thee: Making a Constitutional Revolution* (Boston: Allyn & Bacon, 1975), part IV.

6

Lobbying, Money, and Legislatures: The Case of California

NOWHERE ARE THE CONSEQUENCES OF THE FAILURE OF political observers in the United States to examine corruption within the broad framework described here more evident than in many state and local legislative bodies throughout the nation. In the past, most of the reformers concerned primarily with corruption sought to insulate the individual legislator from the undue influence of special interests and lobbyists. Some also wanted to enhance the capability of legislative bodies to perform as effectively as possible in the public policy-making process.

The reform efforts aimed at the individual legislator were designed primarily to discourage, if not preclude, an individual from using an office to accumulate personal monetary gain. The underlying rationale for this approach to corruption appears to involve providing sufficient resources to attract a "higher quality" individual and to make it less likely that the legislator would accept the financial largess of interest groups and wealthy contributors. Thus, Lester Velie in his now classic article describing the success of California's most famous lobbyist, Artie Samish, made the increase of salaries one of his more important reform proposals.

> Increase the legislators' salaries. When $5,000 has to be spent to win a $1,200 a year job, it's hard for a legislator to resist offers of legal fees, insurance and other business patronage with which lobbyists wheedle favors.[1]

This view of the legislative process has many adherents among the public and among scholars. However, if recent revelations are indicative, the problem remains. Reformers—old and new—have attacked symptoms rather than diseases. Past efforts have centered on streamlining legislative procedures rather than on eliminating the fundamental causes of the problem of corruption.

Charles Garrigues, writing in the mid-thirties, provided the following description of corruption in the early part of the century:

> The popular picture of the politician of twenty years ago [1915] was that of a fat, gross, repulsive creature smoking a black cigar and wearing a sparkling diamond. The picture was correct in symbolism, if not in fact, for the politician of the period, having found things too easy for him, had grown fat in head if not in body. Bribery was practiced almost on the floor of the legislative chamber with no more attempt to conceal it than the modern official [1936] *makes to conceal its indirect bribery of the public.*[2]

It was this popular image of corruption that reformers sought to remedy with limited disclosure laws, increased pay, expanded staff help, and similar measures. They did not attack the source of the problem; namely, the relationship of alliance between so-called respectable businesses and politicians.[3] As the activities of government continued to expand, the importance of the alliance for vested interests increased.

Reform and State Legislatures in the 1970s

Reform proposals advanced more recently continue to embody concern with the satisfaction, effectiveness, and honesty of the individual legislator. However, there does appear to be the added concern with the efficiency and effectiveness of the institution.

As one political scientist stated:

> Much of the reform attention paid to state legislatures has been with structural (or housekeeping) aspects, In arguing that state legislatures must do a better job if more power is not to drift to the federal level of government, methods for strengthening those legislatures are proposed, and they often lean heavily toward providing more staff, salary, and office space. . . .[4]

As such, state legislative bodies should be smaller than the United States Congress and thus more manageable. The proceedings should be open for public and media scrutiny with rules and procedures designed to foster individual and collective accountability. There should be a limited number of committees. The legislature should have substantial budget and subpoena powers with as few as possible constitutional restrictions of its policy-making authority. It also should have substantial power of oversight of other governmental agencies. Rather than the traditional brief legislative session held every other year, which has been the prevailing practice in many states, there should be unrestricted annual sessions. As is the case with the United States Congress, it should be possible to carry a bill over to the second year. Thus the practice of killing a measure at the end of the first session, thereby forcing the time-consuming and costly reintroduction and rehearing process would be eliminated. In addition, legislators should have sizeable and qualified staff resources and a comprehensive public records and information system. Also, members of state legislatures should be *highly paid* so that they can devote full time to their legislative responsibilities.[5]

Such reform proposals, if implemented, do not and cannot guarantee effective performance. Rather, they would eliminate some of the excuses for failure to act effectively in the policy-making process. How responsive have the states been to the suggested reforms and how do the various states rank? The only systematic study which provides some clues was conducted by the Citizens Conference on State Legislatures which published its report in 1971. The researchers found considerable differences between the best and worst legislative bodies with many judged to be inept, understaffed, poorly paid, and in disarray. The states were ranked as follows:[6]

How They Rate

1. California	11. New Mexico
2. New York	12. Alaska
3. Illinois	13. Nevada
4. Florida	14. Oklahoma
5. Wisconsin	15. Utah
6. Iowa	16. Ohio
7. Hawaii	17. South Dakota
8. Michigan	18. Idaho
9. Nebraska	19. Washington
10. Minnesota	20. Maryland

21. Pennsylvania
22. North Dakota
23. Kansas
24. Connecticut
25. West Virginia
26. Tennessee
27. Oregon
28. Colorado
29. Massachusetts
30. Maine
31. Kentucky
32. New Jersey
33. Louisiana
34. Virginia
35. Missouri

36. Rhode Island
37. Vermont
38. Texas
39. New Hampshire
40. Indiana
41. Montana
42. Mississippi
43. Arizona
44. South Carolina
45. Georgia
46. Arkansas
47. North Carolina
48. Delaware
49. Wyoming
50. Alabama

What are some of the characteristics of those states ranked low? Wyoming, for example, allowed its legislature to meet only forty days every other year, and sessions could not be lengthened even if business was not completed. The legislature could not conduct studies between sessions, and not one employee was engaged in research to help the members. New Hampshire paid its lawmakers the least of all states, $100 per year, and had the largest and "most unwieldy membership."[7] Legislatures in three states—Kansas, Arizona, and Nebraska—were required to read aloud all pending bills. There are numerous other examples of ineffective and unreformed legislatures, but it is clear that substantial differences exist between the few states at the top of the list and those that follow. *Time* magazine observed:

> The net effect of such failings is that legislators are forced to cram much work into few days. Without staff help, they often have to rely on lobbyists to analyze what a bill might accomplish, to supply basic facts and often to write the very legislation. There is rarely any way to discourage a legislator from voting on measures that affect his own business or profession. The low pay makes lawmaking a part-time job in which the member's private interests may be his main reason for running.[8]

What does the legislature look like at the top of the ranking list? In terms of salary, members of the California legislature determine their own, and in 1975 the base pay was $21,120 with the total substantially increased to $23,232 in 1976.[9] In addition, legislators receive a tax-free $30 per day expense allowance while the legislature is in session, which is most of the year.[10] As a result, actual financial compensation averages approximately $30,000 per year. Furthermore, since legislators are not precluded from earning outside income, many maintain law firms, businesses, farms and other sources of income.

In addition to receiving a salary that is among the highest of any state legislature, California legislators receive a number of other amenities. For example, the state picks up most of the tab—90 percent of the monthly rental rate, up to a maximum of $225 for the assembly and $220 for the senate—for almost any type of car the legislator wishes to drive. Even though the trend nationwide has been to smaller cars, a survey of the capitol garage suggests that Cadillacs, Lincolns, Buicks, and other luxury models are still in vogue with legislators.[11] Along with the car, members of the legislature receive a gasoline credit card from a major oil company with the state paying the bill. If the member wishes to use the telephone, the state-provided telephone credit card will cover the expense. Each member of the legislature also may send extensive mailings to constituents. In addition, the legislator has access to a special recording studio from which emanates the self-proclaimed evaluations of the good work of today's modern lawmaking machinery.

The quality and quantity of the staff and supporting services and facilities provided for the California legislature for a number of years have consistently ranked number one among the nation's state legislatures. For example, in 1974 it cost the state approximately $22 million to employ 1,875 employees to serve 120 legislators. In order to keep up with the "increasing work load," the number of such employees increased by 25 percent between 1971 and 1974, with the payroll increasing by more than 50 percent during the same period.

Legislators are entitled to a personal staff to run the Sacramento office and at least one district office. Although each committee has a staff, the individual members and the institutions also have the services of two of the largest and most experienced legislative offices in the nation, the legislative counsel and the legislative analyst. The legislature also is served by the auditor general and a research organization headed by the Director of Research.

In short, the California legislature is the best example of a "reformed and professional legislature." It is unmatched in terms of salary, staff, office facilities, equipment and other resources that presumably better equip individual legislators to do their job, serve as an inducement for "qualified candidates" to seek the position, and shield the individual from the temptations of lobbyists.[12]

If a state legislator is unfortunate enough not to be reelected (in spite of the many obvious advantages of incumbency), he or she will not have to enroll in a retraining program or file for unemployment. The legislature approved a special retirement program to help maintain the standard of living to which its members become accustomed while on the public payroll. Retirement benefits are available for legislators at the age of sixty who have been reelected only once. Maximum benefits exceed $14,000 annually for legislators reelected more than once. The legislature has even been known to approve specially tailored retirement plans for what it regards as deserving legislators who were sufficiently appreciated by the voters. Indeed Assemblyman William T. Bagley, Republican nominee for state controller in 1974, acknowledged that he had engineered legislation in 1969 to ensure himself an early pension.[13] The legislature for some time had a program to permit lawmakers who were defeated at the polls in reapportioned districts to draw retirement pensions *immediately* (emphasis added), regardless of age, if they had been elected before 1970 and had served at least four years. This program was presumably in response to the special hardships of members who had the boundary lines of their districts changed substantially, or, as is true for some, had their district eliminated because shifting population patterns in the state required new boundary lines. Thus, the victims of the federal requirement that legislative districts reflect equal population in terms of one person-one vote were compensated by the state for their "misfortune." In addition to an early retirement program passed in 1965, which permitted lifetime pensions, such specially created benefits finally produced a public outcry in 1974. As a direct result, the legislature was forced to repeal the early pension program, as well as the special programs for those leaving office after reapportionment.[14] Accordingly, legislators now must wait until they are sixty to receive money from the still substantial state retirement system.

The financial compensation and other benefits received by members of state legislatures in California and New York as compared to that provided members in New Hampshire, Wyoming, and most other states is striking. Some perspective can be gained by comparing the following description by a veteran political reporter for *The Los Angeles Times* of the scene in Sacramento during the World War II era with the previous discussion. However, it should be kept in mind that the benefits provided at that time exceeded those of many states in the mid-1970s.

We were set for the long grind of the 55th session—the first legislative session of the Second World War, . . .

At least we thought in those days nearly 30 years ago that it was a long grind.

Except for the constitutional recess during February we knew we were going to be "stuck" in Sacramento until May, at least.

And we were. We didn't get out of there until adjournment sine die on May 5.

No one dreamed that a session ever would run a full year as did the one that ended last month.

The big worry as we headed for Sacramento was getting a room at the Senator Hotel. There were a few other hotels, but they had seen better days. So everybody headed for the Senator.

That's where, as it said on the matchbooks, "statesmen dine."

It was where Artie Samish, the kingpin lobbyist, headquartered; where most of the other powerhouse operators had suites and threw dinners for the legislators; where the deals were made, and where the lobby was the place to look when you had to find a legislator.

A memorandum written to me during the February recess by a fellow newsman in 1943 said:

"If I could locate an apartment for you and your family in Sacramento, I certainly would do so—if I had previously located one for myself.

"I guess you must be a humorist at heart. Count yourself lucky if you get back your cubbyhole in the Senator."

Legislators were being paid $100 a month, plus $10 per diem for expenses, during the session. My room bill at the Senator, including phone calls, was around $30 a week.

Old expense account records show dinner charges in such amounts at $2.50, $1.50, $1.45. Really living it up!

Bashore [Assemblyman Lee] got so angry he introduced a resolution (H.R. 37) in the opening days of the session charging that Sacramento hotel and apartment "keepers" had "forced" the legislators to spend a sum greater than their per diem compensation.

So, said the resolution, it was hereby resolved that "unless prompt action is taken" by said "keepers" to provide space on "just and reasonable terms," a constitutional amendment would be introduced to move the seat of government "to a place where living accommodations on reasonable terms can be provided."

It was adopted with argument.

The "keepers" got the message.
Two days later the resolution was rescinded.[15]

In spite of the accoutrements of their office, many state legislators still feel persecuted, overworked, and insufficiently appreciated by the public. They are troubled by the ambitions of challengers, and they do not believe that they have received sufficient esteem for the "sacrifices" they have made to enter public life. Such attitudes were reflected in a sanctimonious and self-righteous press release, which allegedly chronicles the rigors and sacrifices of a career in the state senate, prepared in 1974 by a staff member in the office of an Orange County [California] legislator:

> In a period when politicians rank near the bottom in public esteem according to the poll-takers, there is no shortage of candidates for public office. What motivates these thousands of citizens? What problems and expenses lie ahead for those who are successful? . . .
>
> No individual is typical, but the story of State Senator Dennis E. Carpenter, a Republican from Orange County, provides an example. A former FBI agent, lawyer and successful businessman, Carpenter is finishing his first full term in the State Senate. He had been a political activist and volunteer in both parties but never considered running for public office prior to his successful senatorial campaign in an August 1970 special election. . . . Urged upon to run, Carpenter met with a group of friends and supporters who formed a committee to back his candidacy. The original group of six has since expanded to 15 members, all of whom have been, and are, Carpenter's close friends and business associates. They call themselves the "Golden State Improvement Committee" because they believe state government needs vast improvement . . . .
>
> The group of supporters and Carpenter reached agreement on certain points that were considered important to his success as a state senator. These included:
>
> Carpenter would go all the way or not at all. If elected, he would serve a maximum of twelve years, then seek higher office or return to private life.
>
> His wife Madine would be totally and actively involved and would assist him in his public service. She would accompany him as much as possible.
>
> His children (four sons and a step-daughter) would be cared for in the best possible manner with minimum disruption to their lives due to his holding office.
>
> He would . . . maintain residences both in Newport Beach and in Sacramento. He and Madine would entertain in both residences.

The per diem expense of $30 per day while the Legislature is in session would not be adequate to cover the anticipated additional expenses of Carpenter holding office . . . .

Political and additional expenses would be covered in order to accommodate the job requirements and to enable Dennis to do the best job possible . . . .

In the three-and-a-half years from mid-1970 to 1973, the fifteen members contributed more than $42,000 through the Golden State Improvement Committee for Carpenter's added expenses and campaigning.

Madine and Dennis enjoy excellent reputations as hostess and host, due largely to Madine's efficiency and developed expertise in this area. . . . Friends, constituents, fellow political figures, other government officials and even lobbyists drop by for an hour or an evening, depending upon the invitation and occasion . . . . Other evenings, particularly when Madine is not in Sacramento, Carpenter may be host or guest at a home, political gathering or in one of Sacramento's restaurants . . . .

In all, the rent, telephone and utility bills on the Sacramento apartment amounted to $15,705.21 from mid-1970 through 1973. Additional expenses included food, furnishing and incidentals . . . . Besides the time and air miles involved, travel is not inexpensive. From his 1970 election through December 31, 1973, Carpenter's travel expenses amounted to more than $14,500 . . . . Members of the Legislature are provided automobiles under a basic lease agreement which covers the cost of a middle-sized sedan. If they desire, legislators may pay the increased cost and lease any type auto they want. Carpenter settles for practicality in the form of a Mercury station wagon which costs an additional $38 a month above the state's allotment . . .

All legislators receive a $30-a-day tax-free per diem allowance while the Legislature is in session. From 1971 through 1973, Carpenter's per diem amounted to $20,771 while the Sacramento apartment expenses and the salary of a housekeeper have totaled nearly $30,000 . . . . Before he was elected Carpenter made considerably more than his present $19,200 [1974] annual salary. . . . *Under the original agreement, contributions from the Golden State Improvement Committee make up the deficits in the expense account. . . .*

What has happened to the reformer's dreams of a professional legislator, informed, well-advised, and exercising judgment on behalf of his constituents? Money has happened. Campaign costs mar the dreams. Looking ahead to reelection at the end of a two-year term in the lower house of most state legislatures or a four-year term in the state senate, the individual legislators focus their attention on trying to raise the large sums of money necessary to finance the next campaign. To succeed, legislators cannot be divorced totally from those who have the money they need. Election costs have intervened in most states to spoil the finespun theory of the "professional legislator." In short, the old bribe of cash to the legislator has been supplemented—if not replaced totally—by the new, far more costly transfer of financial resources, cash and otherwise, to the campaign treasury. Although he was referring to the United States Congress, the problem for legislators at all levels was posed by former Congressman Emanuel Celler when he asked:

> . . . to what extent he [legislator] owes a campaign contribution to recognition of his qualities of statesmanship and to what extent it reflects approval of his particular past or anticipated action on a matter close to the contributor's heart. It begs the question to say that such contributions are proper when the purpose for which they are given is the election of the candidate and not the purpose of influencing his vote.[16]

It seems most accurate to suggest that both ends are served by contributions. As Garrigues pointed out in 1936:

> The necessity of collecting campaign funds of such size makes "advance bribery" of successful candidates almost inevitable. Campaign funds are necessarily collected from special interests seeking special privileges, and such interests, naturally, contribute only to those candidates whose records and connections assure them that the expected special privilege will be forthcoming.[17]

The relatively simple position of this chapter is that efforts to solve problems of corruption by increasing salaries, providing staff services, and related methods have been inadequate. A casual examination of politics, even in the so-called "reformed" state legislatures, suggests that, much to the consternation of well-meaning reformers, the efforts may well have increased the power of special interests by fostering a more direct relationship between big money and candidates by inadvertently contributing to the decline of political parties. Thus, rather than eliminating the cigar-puffing, overweight politicians of the old days, it has streamlined them. Or as one veteran political reporter observed:

> Now we're in a new generation of lawmaking.
> The sessions are longer, the staffs are bigger, taxes and budgets are larger, problems more complex than ever, jet trips to the capital have replaced leisurely train rides and lobbyists may not be as blatant.
> But has anything really changed that much?[18]

One of the striking facts about politics in state legislatures is how little basic difference there is from state to state in the actual interaction of the lobbyist and legislator. The pay of both may differ from state to state, and some of the policy issues may differ, but the common denominators are always present: the need for campaign funds, the availability of money from organized vested interests, the development of a relationship among the two groups, and the exchange process that follows. Conversations with those familiar with state capitols or examinations of newspaper accounts of state legislative activities suggest that the major difference is one of style. While some practices are regarded as crude or too blatant by legislators and lobbyists in the larger states such as California and New York, they are not eschewed, but rather practiced on a more subtle level.[19] In other words, although reforms have been of value in other respects, they have not eliminated corruption. Today's corruption may look different, may be more refined and less direct, but the result is basically the same: special favors for some, and cost for the public.

The remainder of this chapter is an examination of some of the facts of life in California legislative politics prior to the passage of the 1974 Political Reform Act. As will be pointed out in the chapter that follows, the reform act has brought about some changes in the California legislative system, particularly with regard to lobbying. Nevertheless, focusing on California as a case in point should provide a clear picture not only of what existed prior to the most recent reforms, but also some idea of what politics is like in most legislative bodies. In other words, if the discussion that follows portrays the situation of those states that have enacted many of the suggested reforms discussed here, what is the level of politics in those states that have not gone even this far?

Lobbyists and Legislators in California

The number and type of lobbyists and the issues of concern may differ from one state to another. However, in California there are basically four kinds of lobbyist:

1. The company lobbyist
2. The organization lobbyist
3. The independent lobbyist
4. The government lobbyist

The company lobbyist is often an officer of, or attorney for, the company represented. The company lobbyist is on the payroll of the company and is always identified with it. The job of the company lobbyist is to build and maintain good relations between the company and the legislators. This kind of lobbyist is almost always well-financed.

In contrast, the organization lobbyist may or may not be well-financed. He or she is hired by an organization with special legislative interests and, like the company lobbyist, is identified with the organization. Labor, medicine, teachers, farmers, dog and cat lovers, conservationists, lawyers, manufacturers, retail merchants, and others are all represented by organization lobbyists. Some, such as the California Medical Association in Sacramento, are highly professional and supported by ample financial resources. Others, such as the American Association of University Women, who choose a member living near the capitol in Sacramento and pay her expense money, cannot even afford to buy a round of drinks at the nearby Senator Hotel.

The independent lobbyist is an independent businessman or businesswoman who handles "accounts" and may represent a number of companies and organizations. Frequently, these individuals will, on a contract basis, handle the interests of a company or organization in a single bill before a legislature. Others handle accounts for a variety of interests and a wide range of legislative measures. One independent California lobbyist, a former member of the assembly, represents the malt beverage industry, the undertakers, the California Highway Patrolmen's Association, and a large race track in addition to other smaller accounts and "single-bill" jobs.

State agencies, city and county government, along with public school districts and public colleges and universities, are represented by lobbyists, most of whom are paid with public funds. Generally, those representing state agencies are members of the staff of the agency they represent and only provide testimony before committees of the legislature upon request. On occasion, they also do research for individual legislators on individual bills. The remainder, however, are generally hired by the governmental organization they represent and have fairly healthy "public relations" budgets. In Sacramento, the City and County of San Francisco, the City of San Diego, the City of Los Angeles, the County of Los Angeles, and the California State University and Colleges all maintain full-scale lobbying operations during each session of the legislature. Other cities, counties, and school districts are more limited, with the scope of their operations dependent upon population size and the number of specific legislative items in which they are interested.

Regardless of the type of lobbyist, the individual who is successful in Sacramento most frequently is the one who has been able to establish and cultivate friendships with anyone active in the decision-making process. It is through such friendships that the operation of a successful lobbyist is established. In the end, the lobbyist must depend on good personal relationships to gain access to legislators to get things done.

This is not to suggest that payoffs do not occur or that political pressure is not applied. For it is clear that the establishment and nourishment of the relationship between individual legislators and lobbyists requires the use of the age-old, ever-present ingredient, money. The nature of the interaction of this relationship in the California legislature was described by a former member and officer of the assembly in the following way:

> There are a number of unwritten rules which influence the process of nurturing the "friendships." For example, in Sacramento there is an unwritten rule that all discussion regarding legislation take place at the capitol and during working hours. "No formal lobbying after five o'clock" is a rule all successful lobbyists follow. However, the work that takes place at lunch and after five is what really counts. Each day of the week there is a big lobbyist lunch to which any member can go. The biggest is Moose Milk in the Sky Room of the El Mirador Hotel which is directly across the street from the capitol. This friendly gathering is sponsored by the best-financed company, organization and independent lobbyists. There is all the booze that any legislator wants and a gourmet buffet of infinite variety. Lobbyists and legislators have a good time together, get drunk together, eat together, and become "friends." No legislator really knows who paid how much for what, but he knows that the lobbyists he meets there are the ones with the money and are the ones footing the bill.
>
> Another gathering is Derby Club which meets in the back room of Posey's, a block from the capitol, on Tuesdays. Derby Club was a pet project of former Senate President Pro-Tem Hugh Burns and is for members only. The most influential lobbyists and members of both houses who are in leadership positions are members by invitation. When a lobbyist is asked to join Derby, it means he has made it. Similarly, many legislators are flattered when they are asked to join. Others, however, join because "I don't want my bills killed in the Senate." Derby is really an old guard Senate operation and the more powerful Senators regard turning down membership in Derby Club as an insult.

There are a number of smaller and less important lunches on a regular basis. But the established lunches aren't always the most fun. Besides, there are enough lobbyists at Frank Fats, the Senator Hotel, Posey's and El Mirador so that no legislator will ever have to pay for a drink or lunch for either himself or his friends. All a legislator needs to do is walk into one of these places and order. In a matter of minutes the bartender or waitress will come by to tell him that Jim or Joe has picked up his tab. Sometimes a lobbyist will stop at a legislator's table and ask, "Do you have a sponsor?" If no one has picked up the tab, the lobbyist usually will ask, "Please be my guest." Legislators count on finding such "pigeons."

Sacramento has one hundred and twenty legislators and over seven hundred lobbyists. Scratch the huge number who have no money and there are still enough to patrol all the favorite spots in Sacramento and pick up the tab for all the food and drink legislators can consume.

While food and drink are most important, so are the other forms of entertainment, such as trips to the San Francisco Opera, golf parties, gambling trips to Lake Tahoe, and hunting trips in Mexico.

Not all legislators accept lobbyist largess and not all are influenced. Certainly much money splashed around in Sacramento is wasted, such as a case of whiskey that once was left in my car in the Capitol garage. I still don't know who gave it to me.

In short, there are members who take [former Speaker of the Assembly and Democratic candidate for Governor in 1970] Jess Unruh's advice, "If you can't eat it or drink it at one sitting, don't accept it." And they try to remember another thing he said, "If you aren't man enough to eat their food, drink their booze and vote against them, you're not man enough to be here."

Through the distribution of so much happiness, the lobbyist is constantly building personal friendships he can use when he needs them. Friendships that will result in "getting things done" without fuss and without pressure.

One kind of lobbyist-legislator fun activity that still builds the lobbyists' "good guy" and "my friend" image is the poker game. But this is different and not so innocent. Nor is it so widespread as other activities. In poker games, when lobbyists lose to legislators they pay off. When they win from legislators, they make little effort or none at all to collect. This kind of "nice guy" behavior goes way beyond the lunch, dinner, drink or trip. This involves the closest thing there is to buying a legislator outside of an outright bribe. (And the direct bribe is, at least in the big states, considered "no class.") But this sort of thing is not necessary to a successful lobbying operation. Clearly, the lobbyists who can afford it spare no effort to build up good will among the legislators. To reap the benefit or the investment involves a second step. If, for example, a

lobbyist needs a "no" vote on a bill before a particular legislative committee, he or she drops by the office of those members of the committee
who are his or her "friends" and explains the bill in one or two sentences. The lobbyist asks if the legislator is getting any mail on the
subject, and wonders in a seemingly questioning way whether a "no"
vote would hurt the legislator back home. When it is clear that there has
been little or no mail on the subject (generally only a handful of bills in
each session generate the mail), the lobbyist says, "This one means a lot
to my principals. If I don't beat it, I'll lose the account (or my job). I'd
personally appreciate it if you can give me a vote. And I'll let our people
in your district know how helpful you've been to us and make sure they
give you some help [that's money] in your next campaign."[20]

If a legislator says that the desired vote will not be forthcoming,
there usually is no argument. "It will hurt me in my district," is most
frequently a final answer and taken as such by the lobbyist. After all,
argument may cost a "friendship," or may make it difficult, if not
impossible, to obtain a vote on other important questions that will
emerge in the future. Similarly, if a lobbyist is trying to round up "no"
votes, a legislator who must vote "yes" will be asked to be absent,
because that is the same as voting "no." If a legislator indicates that he
or she must vote and must vote "yes," the discussion normally is over.
Generally the lobbyist will thank the legislator and say, "I understand
your position, and I know you would help me if you could." (Thus the
lobbyist implants a sense of obligation on the part of the legislator.)

As is the case in Washington, some of the most effective lobbyists
seldom, if ever, appear before legislative committees. Their work is
done before committees even meet to consider bills in which they have
an interest. Lobbyists also watch the behavior of committees carefully,
even though they do not testify. The committee vote, which in most
cases in the past was a voice vote and hence unrecorded, is carefully and
accurately marked on a roll call card. The public probably never will
know how a particular member of a committee voted, but the lobbyists
always know.

There also is an unwritten law governing relations between legislators and lobbyists throughout the nation: "You never lie." Once a
legislator or lobbyist lies, effectiveness is gone forever. Consequently,
information given by lobbyists to legislators, whether cursory or
thorough, is always regarded as accurate. Similarly, a legislator's commitment to vote for or against a bill is considered binding unless the
individual asks to be released from a commitment.

What does this all mean?

First, the techniques of good salesmanship and public relations found in business also are used to exact desired actions from legislative bodies. Most bills introduced in the state legislatures generate only limited interest. As a consequence, most legislators find that they can comfortably vote either "yes" or "no" on large numbers of bills in each session. Why not give a vote to a friend who needs it? The choice is no tougher than choosing an item sold by a salesperson who is a friend over one sold by an unknown or unfriendly individual.

Second, when a legislator gives a vote to a lobbyist for a special interest group, it can generally be assumed that the vote will be applauded by those people in his or her district who have an interest in the legislation. Under these circumstances, legislators can rationalize their action and feel that they truly are representing the interests of their districts. Former Assemblyman Winfield A. Schoemaker described the process as follows:

> When I opposed attempts to remove California's fair trade laws on liquor, every owner of a "mom and pop" liquor store in my district applauded my actions. Many of them contributed to my next campaign and many of them did volunteer work as well. The only people in my district who cared about the proposed legislation liked what I did, and they let their friends know that I was the kind of legislator who really represented his district. Had all my constituents known that I chose to support small business and high liquor prices over big business and low liquor prices, I don't know what their reaction would have been. Anyway, the public never had to worry about that for they never knew about the issue. This sort of thing happens over and over again in each legislative session everywhere in this country.[21]

Lobbyists, in concert with legislators, communicate with interested constituents in different ways. One method that is quite popular is illustrated by a letter from a member of the California Senate to realtors in his district. The senator's letter was on one side of the page, and a letter from the lobbyist to the senator was on the other side.[22] (See pages 146–147.)

Third, legislators who have good relations with lobbyists build their own power in the legislature. Those who host lobbyist dinners or other lobbyist entertainment build followings among legislators similar to those of the host lobbyists. The friendships they develop in their own chambers are important in getting their own bills approved. When a legislator who has close connection with lobbyists (the "third house" of

California Real Estate
Association

DUGALD GILLIES
Legislative Representative

Executive Offices:
520 SOUTH GRAND AVENUE · LOS ANGELES, CALIFORNIA 90017
Telephone: AREA CODE 213·628-0551

Legislative Office:
1129 10th Street · SACRAMENTO, CALIFORNIA 95814
Telephone: AREA CODE 916 444-2045

May 3, 1972

The Honorable James Q. Wedworth
State Senator
State Capitol
Sacramento, California 95814

Dear Jim:

Let me thank you personally and extend the appreciation of the
California Real Estate Association for the continued active role
you play in the evolution of coastline legislation at this session.

Your persistent adherence to the principle that property owners
should be compensated when use of their land is taken for a public
benefit in the coastal zone, your opposition to a long-term
moratorium to freeze land use on unrealistic terms and your recognition for a need for balance in both use and conservation in the
coastal zone is applauded by us.

We are grateful, not only for your resistance of attempts to in-
corporate these principles in other measures now pending, but your
own authorship of SB 2 to apply a realistic solution to the environmental needs of the coast. It was a pleasure for me on behalf of
CREA to testify in support of the thrust of your SB 2.

Again our thanks and should there be any occasion in which I can be
of assistance, please let me know.

Sincerely,

Dugald Gillies
Legislative Representative

DG/bl

655

SACRAMENTO OFFICE ADDRESS
STATE CAPITOL
95814
(916) 445-2848

LEGISLATIVE OFFICE ADDRESS
8404 SOUTH CRENSHAW BLVD.
INGLEWOOD, CALIF. 90305
(213) 778-0604

CHAIRMAN
GOVERNMENTAL ORGANIZATION
SUBCOMMITTEE ON
AUTOMOTIVE SAFETY
GOVERNMENTAL ORGANIZATION
SUBCOMMITTEE ON RETIREMENT

COMMITTEES
VICE CHAIRMAN, INSURANCE AND
FINANCIAL INSTITUTIONS
GOVERNMENTAL ORGANIZATION
NATURAL RESOURCES AND
WILDLIFE
REVENUE AND TAXATION

JOINT COMMITTEES AND COMMISSIONS
JOINT COMMITTEE ON RULES
JOINT COMMITTEE ON LEGISLATIVE
BUILDING SPACE NEEDS
SUBCOMMITTEE ON CIVIL DISORDER
CALIFORNIA ADVISORY COMMISSION
ON MARINE AND COASTAL
RESOURCES
CALIFORNIA CONSTITUTION
REVISION COMMISSION

$\mathscr{S}enate$

JAMES Q. WEDWORTH
THIRTY-FIRST SENATORIAL DISTRICT

May 11, 1972

Dear Realtor:

I thought you might be interested in the attached letter from the California Real Estate Association thanking me for my help on coastline legislation.

When I drafted my own bill, SB2, and during the give-and-take of debate on other bills, I tried to maintain a sense of balance between the demands of the environmentalists and the legal rights of property owners and industries. A common sense approach to this problem is still my goal and I refuse to be threatened by the hysteria of the environmental crusaders.

You realtors are to be commended as a group with a fine legislative program and should take pride in your accomplishments and contributions to California's economic progress.

I am facing stiff opposition in this Primary Election mainly because of my position on coastline legislation. Now you can help me by working to re-elect me to the Senate to finish the job of protecting the environment while maintaining stability in employment and the general economy. Please contact my District Office, 8404 South Crenshaw Boulevard, Inglewood, phone 778-0604.

Sincerely,

JAMES Q. WEDWORTH

JQW:smh

Enclosure

the legislature) asks a colleague for a vote on a bill, the one being asked often assumes—quite correctly—that support for the position will be rewarded when election time rolls around. Furthermore, most legislators with real political muscle have that muscle as a result of some element of third-house support: labor, commerce, finance, medicine, manufacturing, oil, education, or the like.

Finally, this friendship system means that the public interest is seldom represented against special interest legislation, which sails through our state legislatures virtually unopposed. The idea that all interests are equally represented in our state capitals by lobbyists or legislative representatives is a myth. Only occasionally do two interests collide over a piece of legislation.

When a legislator or legislative committee comes up with legislation to cure a public ill, the next step is to round up as much support from special interest groups as possible. Without this support, the legislation has little chance of being enacted. For example, in 1968 the late Assemblyman Robert Crown of Alameda proposed legislation to provide funding for the San Francisco Bay Area Rapid Transit District. The money had run out. Work had come to a standstill with huge open trenches in the middle of Market Street in San Francisco. Assemblyman Crown's bill to provide funds passed the Assembly and went to the Senate where it was killed in the Committee on Finance. The committee chairman, the late Senator George Miller of Contra Costa County, was opposed to the bill. Crown charged Miller with "killing the proposal by working your committee against the bill." Miller replied that he did not kill the bill.

> Nobody was for your bill. The oil companies were against it. The cement companies were against it. The contractors were against it. Everybody was against it, but you say the public was for it. Who is that? I never heard from them, whoever they are. I didn't have to kill your bill. Nobody was for it.[23]

The second major aspect of the relationship between lobbyist and legislator is campaign money. Because most—if not all—legislators need, or believe they need, large sums of money for their election efforts, it is not difficult for the lobbyist to locate those in need. Study after study suggests the validity of this aspect of the relationship, commonly described as the "access explanation."[24] The niceties of social science notwithstanding, it can be described more accurately as a legally acceptable bribe.

Lobbyists and Money: The Scene in Even-Numbered Years

Another aspect of this mutual "friendship" system emerges during the even-numbered years. As campaign time approaches, lobbyists move through capitol halls passing out "easter eggs." A former assemblyman offered this description of the process.

> Just as I was entering my first re-election campaign, a powerful lobbyist in Sacramento stopped me in the hall and said, "Can I see you in my office for a minute?" We stepped through a door into the stairway and he reached into his breast pocket and pulled out a cashier's check made out to me for two hundred dollars. He wished me well in my campaign, and assured me there would be more "help" when the primary election was over.[25]

Because the lobbyist was an independent operator with a number of accounts, the source of the cash was not readily apparent. The lobbyist had not talked to the assemblyman about a bill and had never appeared before any committee on which the legislator served. The lobbyist was just building his own personal following with his anonymous client's money. Just as with the dinners, lunches, and booze, campaign money from the independent lobbyist often means that the legislator never knows the source.

Another approach taken by lobbyists is to give the legislator several one-hundred-dollar bills in an envelope. The generous donor is careful to point out that taxes have been paid on the money, which means that it can be used at the discretion of the legislator and does not have to be turned over to a campaign treasurer. The lobbyist emphasizes personal and company awareness of the fact that campaigns are a financial drain on the candidate, because certain necessary personal expenses arise that cannot be covered by campaign funds according to the California Elections Code. How much cash changes hands in such a manner is unknown.

The fact that it takes an ever-increasing amount of money to run a state legislative campaign in California makes it very difficult for a candidate to feel anything but good will toward someone who provides cash. Lobbyists are well aware of this as they make the rounds of the members of relevant committees to dole out the contributions. The amounts given to each legislator vary depending upon how "friendly" each has been, but usually most can expect at least a token gift from the lobbyist.

Some committees are much better cash generators than are others. Not surprisingly, these are called "money committees." Every legislator wants to be a member of at least one money committee, a fact made clear by a former assemblyman:

> During my first term I was on the Committees on Education, Natural Resources, Civil Service and Social Welfare, none of which was a money committee. Teachers came across with a little money as did conservationists and members of the State Employees Association, and because I had been a co-author of our Medi-Cal bill in the Social Welfare Committee, the medical profession was fairly generous. The California Medical Association supported the legislation and participated in the drafting of the bill. Two years later, however, I got nothing from them. This presumably was related to the fact that after having had a chance to see how the program worked in practice I had recommended drastic changes in the legislation and had publicly called the original legislation a license to steal.
>
> Two years later as Assembly Majority Caucus Chairman I had an ex-officio seat on the Rules Committee and had been appointed to the Ways and Means Committee. I had *a lot* of *new* friends. Money came in much easier and more friendly faces greeted me in the halls of the capitol and in my office with funds for my campaign. Such money committees are the key to the early money that the legislator does not have to solicit.[26]

When a state legislator sits down with his or her campaign finance committee to plan the campaign and make out a budget, a number of sources are considered and an estimate is made of how much can be raised from each of them:

1. A third-house taplist
2. An individual taplist
3. Fund-raising dinners and other fund-raising events
4. Groups who have supported the legislative positions that the legislator has taken
5. The party's legislative campaign committee and other party sources

The third-house taplist is a list of those lobbyists who have business before committees of which the legislator is a member and lobbyists whom the legislator knows well as participants in the friendship system. Many of these lobbyists will drop by with cash anyway, but others have to be reminded by the legislator.

The approach to the lobbyists' checkbook varies from legislator to legislator. Observations of the system, participation in it, and periodic disclosures in the press all suggest a general underlying tone that closely resembles a "shakedown." The following report, which appeared in *The Los Angeles Times,* is fairly typical of the system at work.

Senate Democratic leaders sent out letters reminding Capitol lobbyists they were expected at a $1,250-a-table fund-raiser in Beverly Hills as well as at a planning session in the back room of a local restaurant. . . .

Some of the lobbyists who received the letter said they objected to the "command performance" tone and definitely would not attend the dinner . . . in the Beverly Hilton or the planning session.

Proceeds from the dinner will go to pay campaign expenses of the winner of the . . . special primary election in the 27th State Senate District in Los Angeles County. . . .

The letters were signed by "Al, Randy, Merv and George."

They are Sens. Alfred H. Song of Monterey Park, chairman of the Senate Democratic Coordinating Committee; Randolph Collier of Yreka, committee treasurer; Mervin Dymally of Los Angeles, caucus chairman; and George R. Moscone of San Francisco, majority floor leader.

The letter text said:

"This is just a reminder that the Senate majority leaders are counting on your presence at 5 p.m., Wednesday, May 26, in Posey's Club Room (Posey's is a bar and restaurant located near the Capitol).

"During this brief meeting Sen. Mills (President Pro Tem James R. Mills, a San Diego Democrat) and ourselves will discuss the June 11 dinner and the part you can play to insure its success.

"You should confirm your attendance with Don Visnich (committee coordinator) in the caucus office by noon Monday. If you cannot attend personally, please advise Dan which of your colleagues will represent you. Many thanks."

A card noted the dinner will cost $1,250 per table, which was underlined in ink so it would not be missed.

"This whole thing is absurd," said an angry top lobbyist who did not want his name used.

"This is the second letter I've gotten from Song twisting my arm."

"I won't go to the dinner or the planning party, and a lot of others won't go either."

About 25 lobbyists showed up for the planning session and cocktail party . . . to discuss plans for the dinner.

Each one received an envelope containing a number of $125-per-person dinner tickets that they are expected to sell or absorb.

One lobbyist, who got 20 tickets or $2,500 worth, said angrily, "They're out of their minds if they think I'll get rid of this many tickets for this race."

It was recently disclosed that Song sent out letters to 28 lobbyists criticizing them for failing to buy tickets to his own May 1, $100-a-plate testimonial dinner in Los Angeles.

He followed this up with another letter advising lobbyists that he was joining a new Los Angeles law firm and their business would be appreciated.

Both of these communications caused considerable conversation in the Capitol corridors.

Asked for comment, Mills said . . . he saw nothing wrong with the latest letter, adding there would be "no hard sell" of dinner tickets at the . . . planning party.

"This is a matter of considerable importance," Mills said. "The committee is anxious to have a Democrat elected. It could mean losing control of the Senate."

Visnich said "several thousand" of the invitations were sent to Democratic Party contributors, lobbyists, and community leaders.[27]

The frequent occurrence of large fund-raising dinners in the posh hotels of Los Angeles and San Francisco suggest that it is a lucrative source of funds. Students and observers of political fund raising too often fail to understand the source of funds used to purchase those meals priced at $100 and up. The party faithful and the legislator's friends usually will purchase a fairly predictable number of tickets. However, the gala events are not aimed at these individuals, but rather at the interest groups and the lobbyists representing them in state capitals. In addition to the ever-present business and labor sources, the city, county, and public college and university lobbyists normally can find money for such events. But putting on a dinner does not involve just finding a hall, obtaining a speaker or entertainment, and sending out invitations. In addition to contacting the wealthy who will be "encouraged" to shell out a few hundred or even a thousand or more dollars, the real payoff comes from milking the carefully prepared list of all those interests that have benefited, or perhaps will benefit in the future, from legislation. They are the same interests and lobbyists that have nurtured the friendship system. Each interest is expected to come through with a predetermined amount. To avoid misunderstanding, the "assessment" is communicated in very plain and specific terms.

Those interests that have not been treated well by the individual legislator or by his or her party also are approached. Then, they frequently will contribute, believing that things could become worse in the next session. The lobbyists do not want the word to spread that a member of the club has been refused. Such contributions can be justified to the lobbyist's employers by telling them that the individual opposed them but did not "rough them up" in the press. This threat of publicity is an effective weapon for all participants in the existing fund-raising system. An old pro in the California legislature in response to a request for advice in obtaining lobby money described the process most vividly: "I tell them, there is a time for everything. There is a time to give and a time to receive. Right now it is your time to give. They understand and they'll be there."[28]

All the necessary money is not raised at dinners, and sometimes "cinch bills" are necessary. The "cinch bill" is a nasty device occasionally used in legislatures to spring tight money loose. It works in this manner. A big special interest has a great deal of money but has been less than generous. A legislator introduces a bill designed to regulate that interest so that it will cost them a sizeable sum. Rather than face the possibility of the bill becoming law, the interest becomes generous, and the bill is subsequently killed. Everybody is reasonably happy, with the exception of the public.

On other occasions "tree shaking," or further tapping of the "fat cats" is the approach taken to fund raising. This task is best undertaken by legislative leaders with substantial power. For example, Robert Moretti, former Speaker of the California Assembly, is an excellent "tree shaker," and when Jess Unruh was Speaker, he was the best. "Tree shaking" is the practice of going to members of the third house after the good times and fine fellowship, after the contributions and dinner tickets, after the lists of names to tap, and shaking more money out of the interests they represent. Members of the legislative campaign committee look over the legislation that has benefited certain interests during the preceding term and go after those interests for help. Whether or not their party helped those interests is not the question. After all, they reason, if the special interest did well, the party asking for money did not hurt them too badly. According to their logic, it should be rewarded. The "tree shakers" also look at the list of interests who did not fare so well and go after them. If they were more generous, perhaps they would do better in the future.

To be a good tree shaker, a legislator should be in a powerful leadership position. A speaker or president pro-tem has the power to be unfriendly to a large number of people who are not generous. Key committee chairpersons—those of the money committees—also make good "tree shakers," especially when discussing contributions with lobbyists who have business before the chairpersons' committees.

Jess Unruh, as chairman of the California Assembly Ways and Means Committee, and later as speaker, built his political power in Sacramento by this process of "shaking" money loose from the third house in sizeable amounts and then helping the election efforts of legislators who would be supportive. The former speaker, Robert Moretti, was the principal Democratic "tree shaker" in 1968 and 1970. In 1968 he was chairman of the Assembly Committee on Finance and Insurance, the number one money committee. In 1970, when the Republicans were in control, he still had a seat on the Finance and Insurance Committee and was chairman of the Committee on Government Organization, the committee that considered all horse-racing legislation, a position that certainly did not hinder his efforts at raising money in 1968, 1970, and 1974. In fact, the money he shook loose was a significant factor in helping the Democrats to regain control of the California Assembly in 1970. As the individual responsible for raising much of the money that helped his party members win control of the legislature, his election as the new speaker was practically a certainty.

Discussions with legislative leaders in other states suggest that their methods are quite similar to California's "tree shaking." It would be difficult to find a better description of the practice than that by one old hand in Sacramento rapturously describing Unruh at work:

> Jess sits those guys down and talks low and serious. Then, pretty soon he leads them to the top of the mountain, points toward the city, and says "this can all be yours, my son." Then he leads them down into the abyss and shows them the fires of Hell. Then you ought to see them trees shake loose money.[29]

Neither Unruh, nor Moretti, nor any "tree shaker" in the country of either party ever goes into a fund-raising session promising special favors. The only positive result members of the third house can expect is fair treatment if they are cooperative and generous. Lobbyists know that much of the money that is funneled through legislative campaign committees will go to people who oppose them. But they donate anyway because they do not want to face hostile leadership in either party or unfriendly committees in the next legislative session. Thus, some lobbyists frequently feel they are over a barrel, and they are. Campaign costs are rising at an alarming rate, and lobbyists receive increased pressure for contributions every election year.

Why do lobbyists give money in so many ways? Why not give only to individual legislative candidates and ignore the rest? The lobbyists must give to individual legislators. Otherwise they might alienate those who have the potentially needed votes. They also have to give to the leadership, or they may see nothing but hostile committees in the following session after new assignments are made.

Conclusion

How legislative campaigns are financed, and how lobbyists and legislators of both political parties interact in the state of California, which most observers agree is the most reformed and professional legislature in the United States, indicates much about the nature of the policymaking process in other states. Proposals for increasing benefits for legislators, expanding staff services, enhancing the power of the legislature, and many other such plans that are often presented cannot eliminate corruption at the national, state, or local level because they fail to sever the crucial relationship between economic and political power.

The preceding discussion shows that the practices of California really do not differ substantially from the "shake down" practices of so-called less reformed political environments such as those in Chicago.[30] Furthermore, state legislators, and most other elected politicians in the United States, operate in similar ways because they have a similar desire to remain in power; and they need money in ever-increasing amounts to do so.[31] What does this mean?

First, those individuals elected to office who want to do a job also want to be reelected. Very little can be accomplished in one term; in order to return, they need money in large amounts. Most would like to rely on money from friends and people who think as they do, but they cannot rely upon those sources exclusively because campaigns cost too much. Special interests, who have the money and who also want things done, offer legislators money. In addition, legislators ask them for it. Money, therefore, becomes directly related to the enactment of laws even if no votes are actually bought. Many, if not most, legislators are honest and have what they believe to be the public interest at heart. But too often they are put in awkward positions by accepting money from people seeking special favors and specific advantage. As one lobbyist observed, "You give money with no strings attached, but you know that sooner or later the recipient is going to be grateful."[32] It becomes easier and easier to let "little insignificant bills no one cares about" slip by or die to aid a big contributor or a prospective contributor. Most legislators remain true to themselves on the central issues in which they are interested. But it is "the little insignificant" things that are really the big issue. It is here that the public interest is not served, and the public loses.

Furthermore, most powerful special interest groups of all kinds have limited legislative goals. Generally, self-protection is the first goal. Special advantage is the next objective. They see their positions as just, and they are willing to pay to get done what they see as important. However, they feel burdened by having to increase their campaign contributions every election year, and they are beginning to complain.

In addition, the public is unhappy. Somehow, the rank-and-file voters know that they do not have the money to elect legislators who will serve their interests. The present system of campaign finance has removed legislators from direct responsibility to the people who elect them. Only when that direct responsibility exists can the public interest properly be served.

Finally, in spite of the existence of views such as those just presented, the move to reform and professionalize state legislatures has only recently been questioned by participants in the efforts.[33] A few individuals such as Jess Unruh, who was more responsible than anyone else for the reform in California, have done so publicly. The national implications for the preceding analysis are obvious. Alan Rosenthal observed that if the California legislature is not working very well, although it measures up to practically all the standards set by reformers, "it would seem that no other legislative body is working very well either."[34] In other words, if the analysis here describes the scene in the most reformed, most professional, most efficient legislature, what must be the level of corruption in other states? If California is an example of the success of reform efforts in dealing with corruption, the problem exists throughout the nation. The overwhelming approval by California voters of the Political Reform Initiative of 1974, which will be discussed in the following chapter, is clear testimony to dissatisfaction with political institutions and politicians who refuse to take needed corrective action. The measure also is a good indication of the people's willingness *and* ability to cope with the issue of corruption. Whether the measure will change significantly the present remains to be seen. It is clear, however, that the people of California were willing to address themselves to the issue and attempt to solve the problem; similar observation cannot be made about the legislature. The results support the contention that major structural reforms are needed to cope with the systemic causes of corruption.

NOTES

1. Lester Velie, "The Secret Boss of California," *Colliers,* August 1949, p. 64.

2. Charles Harris Garrigues, *You're Paying for It! A Guide to Graft* (New York: Funk & Wagnalls, 1936), p. 98.

3. Ibid., p. 99.

4. Stephen L. Wasby, *Political Science: The Discipline and Its Dimensions* (New York: Charles Scribner's Sons, 1970), p. 40.

5. For a discussion of the characteristics of a reformed legislature see William J. Keefe and Morris S. Ogul, *The American Legislative Process: Congress and the States,* 3rd ed. (Englewood Cliffs, N.J.: Prentice-Hall, 1973), p. 468.

6. "The States: Appraising the Legislatures," *Time,* February 15, 1971, pp. 16–17.

7. Ibid., p. 17.

8. Ibid.

9. The salary for members of the New York legislature—highest in the nation—was $23,500 per year in 1975. *The Los Angeles Times,* September 13, 1975, p. 1.

10. The tax-free status of the per diem has been challenged by the United States Internal Revenue Service, but there are indications that Congress will approve legislation to secure permanently the tax-free policy. See Leo Rennert, "Legislators' Tax: Lawmakers Plan Congress Appeal," *The Sacramento Bee,* September 11, 1975, p. 1.

11. See William Endicott, "Assembly Barely OKs Bill to Boost Legislators' Pay," *The Los Angeles Times,* September 13, 1975, p. 26.

12. Eugene Lee and Larry L. Berg, *The Challenge of California* (Boston: Little, Brown, 1975).

13. *The Los Angeles Times,* October 8, 1974, part 1, p. 3.

14. *The Los Angeles Times,* October 7, 1974, part 1, p. 3.

15. Carl Greenberg, "Politics, Poker and the Senator Hotel: The Legislative Session of 1943," *The Los Angeles Times,* January 3, 1972, part 2, pp. 1, 4. Reprinted with the permission of *The Los Angeles Times.*

16. Quoted in Keefe and Ogul, *The American Legislative Process,* p. 345.

17. Garrigues, *You're Paying for It!* p. 66.

18. Greenberg, "Politics, Poker and the Senator Hotel," p. 4.

19. *The Los Angeles Times,* October 7, 1974, part 1, p. 3. Also, for a good discussion of the transition from more explicit action of the past in California to the less direct modern approach, see "Money, Politics Link More Explicit in Era of Southern Pacific," *The Los Angeles Times,* January 6, 1974, p. 1.

20. The sources for the material on the California legislature were an unpublished article by a former member and leader of the California Assembly and discussions with legislators and lobbyists in California. For an account of similar practices in a rural, sparsely populated state, see Harlan Hahn, *Urban-Rural Conflict* (Beverly Hills, Calif.: Sage Publications, 1971), pp. 101–131.

21. Ibid.

22. Dugald Gillies, Legislative Representative, California Real Estate Association, letter dated May 3, 1972. Reprinted with permission.

23. See footnote 20.

24. For example, James Deakin, *The Lobbyists* (Washington, D.C.: Public Affairs Press, 1970), p. 401.

25. See footnote 20.

26. Ibid.

27. Jerry Gilliam, "State Senators Expect Lobbyists at Dinner, Four Democrats Write," *The Los Angeles Times,* May 27, 1971, part 1, p. 3. Copyright, 1971, *The Los Angeles Times.* Reprinted by permission.

28. See footnote 20.

29. Ibid.

30. For an excellent discussion of the practice in Chicago see Mike Royko, "Big Eddy's No Perle, but Parties Are Gems," exclusive to *The Times* from *The Chicago Daily News, The Los Angeles Times,* May 5, 1971, part 1B, p. 7.

31. For a discussion of corruption in cities see John A. Gardiner and David J. Olsen, *Theft of the City: Readings in Corruption in Urban America* (Bloomington: Indiana University Press, 1974).

32. Al Martinez, "Portrait of a Lobbyist: Power or Myth," *The Los Angeles Times,* May 26, 1974, p. 3.

33. Donald G. Herzberg and Alan Rosenthal, *Strengthening the States: Essays on Legislative Reform* (Garden City, N.Y.: Doubleday, 1972), pp. 10–11.

34. Ibid., p. 11.

7

Restructuring the Electoral Process

IMPORTANT CHANGE MUST BE MADE TO OVERCOME THE political disaffection of the American public. Perhaps the most important of these changes involves a significant restructuring of electoral institutions. The evidence is clear that a majority of people have lost confidence in their government.[1] Contrary to the views of many public officials and political observers, however, an increasing proportion of the American public is prepared to participate in decisions that shape society.[2]

There is a wide gulf between the political perceptions of the American people and the views of public officials, a gulf best seen in the distance between the opinions of the public and their leaders:

1. Officials are convinced that the "quality of life" in America has improved measurably over the last decade and credit government actions with the positive change. The people disagree and blame the federal government for having a negative impact on developments.

2. The public shows little respect for the attributes of men and women who run government at all levels; officials disagree.

3. Where a majority of Americans feel something has gone "deeply wrong" with their society, close to two thirds of the elected and appointed officeholders prefer the view that America "always has one crisis or another."

4. And when asked to make a hypothetical choice between putting government in the hands of the best and most expert leaders and giving them free rein, or insisting that official actions be subject to continual, close public monitoring,

Americans strongly prefer the latter alternatives. Officials ask, in contrast, for maximum freedom of action.[3]

This last view forms an appropriate basis for the consideration of structural changes. In fact, the absence of this view was the reason given for the failure of California's legislative reforms (such as increased salaries and staff assistance). Such laws did little if anything to foster a direct relationship between the people and elected officials. They did nothing to promote the fundamentally democratic notion that the people are the employers and the public officials are the employees. Indeed, this legislation probably contributed to the further isolation of the two groups by strengthening the political advantages of incumbency. In the wake of events since the Watergate scandal, proposed reforms must be evaluated in terms of their impact on the relationship between the people and public officials, which is vital to a democratic society.

The Resignation of a President

Perhaps the clearest example of the danger of corruption to the political system can be found in the events that brought about the downfall of an American president in 1974. Beleaguered by critics, confronted by a Supreme Court decision that forced him to surrender incriminating evidence, and faced with almost certain impeachment and conviction as a result of his complicity in the events surrounding the burglary of the Watergate headquarters of the opposition party, Richard M. Nixon was forced to resign as President of the United States.

This first resignation of an American president was obviously an event of major historical importance. But, in the wake of that traumatic event, many people were prepared to forget the entire incident. The predominant mood of Congress and other political leaders appeared to be relief that a cathartic episode in the life of the nation had finally ended. The incoming president, Gerald R. Ford, declared that the "nightmare is over" and pledged "openness, honesty, and candor in his administration." Many Americans told themselves that it had all been a bad dream, and they prepared to return to a comfortable slumber.

For a while, at least, it appeared that the system had triumphed. Initially, the actions of President Ford were remarkably free from partisan criticism, and approval of presidential conduct in office jumped from 26 percent during the final days of the Nixon administration to 71 percent in the first few days of the Ford Administration. The American people were displaying their natural open-mindedness and courtesy; they were prepared to give the new President a more-than-even chance to prove himself.

Furthermore, most public officeholders interpreted the apparent growth of confidence in presidential leadership as an opportunity to resume "business as usual" in Washington. Presumably, this meant a return to the wheat deals, milk deals, stock deals, and all of the other deals that traditionally characterized business-as-usual in that city. In the narrow view of many politicians, the political system had been rescued intact, and there was no need to change it.

Yet, in the transition from Nixon to Ford, several important facts had been overlooked. Initially, Gerald Ford was the first man in American history to gain the presidency by appointment rather than by election. Unlike other vice-presidents who had succeeded to this position after the death of a president, Ford had never appeared before the national electorate. In fact, the only voters who had ever been given an opportunity to determine his qualifications for public office were those who lived in a small and somewhat atypical congressional district centered in Grand Rapids, Michigan.

The succession of Ford, therefore, revealed an unrecognized defect in the Twenty-fifth Amendment to the Constitution. Under the unique circumstances surrounding Nixon's second administration, the amendment permitted the country's highest office to be filled by appointment without giving the people an opportunity to vote (although the thought of such a crisis repeating itself may have provoked shudders among some). Most people felt the probability too slight to seek reforms requiring a new election when a president leaves office.

The second major fact commonly ignored about Gerald R. Ford's elevation to the presidency seemed to be even less accidental. Ford was the fourth ex-vice-president to be listed among the six presidents who have served since the end of World War II, and he is the fourth former party leader in Congress to be included among the six vice-presidents who held office during the same period. A pattern of succession has developed that extends from a party leadership position in Congress through the vice-presidency to the office of president of the United States, a pattern not dissimilar to the hereditary bloodlines that control European monarchies.

There are several possible explanations for the emergence of these clear patterns of succession to public offices in America, the most disturbing one being that the positions of both vice-president and party leader in Congress are closely connected to the financial aspects of politics. As numerous aspirants to the presidency have discovered, one of the major functions of the vice-president—and an important task of anyone who seeks a presidential nomination—involves speaking at party fund-raisers and courting party "angels" throughout the country. This duty is often onerous, but always rewarding. It serves the allegedly important function of ensuring that almost all serious candidates for the presidency are contacted and subjected to the scrutiny of major donors who bankroll party activities and political operations in the United States.

Furthermore, in congressional posts, party leaders and whips often are required to cooperate and to negotiate with prominent lobbyists and the spokesmen for major economic interests. Through their interactions, which may extend over several years, party leaders have a chance to learn about the desires and the influence of important interest groups; and vice versa, the groups have an opportunity to observe the behavior of party leaders and to decide whether or not their presidential ambitions are worthy of financial support. If they are, the party leaders may receive donations not only from the lobbyists themselves but also from the associates and affiliates of powerful interests.

The party leaders in Congress and the vice-president, therefore, fulfill the important function of facilitating contacts between potential candidates and the "angels" who constitute the first portion of the "dual constituency" (of donors and voters), which must be wooed by any contender for high public office in America.[4] Similar lines of succession, which originate in legislative or law enforcement offices and lead to gubernatorial or senatorial positions, have emerged in many states.[5] In Washington, and in the state capitals, there is an interlocking network of legislative leaders and major interest groups, an insoluble bond of reciprocal favors and control. Frequently, the price of a politician's complicity in this arrangement is silence or the promise of immunity from exposure.

Thus, it came as no surprise, at least to those who retained a lively skepticism about the moral values that permeate American politics, when the President, within a month of Nixon's resignation, granted an open-ended, "full, free, and absolute pardon unto Richard Nixon for all offenses against the United States which he . . . has committed or may have committed or taken part in during the period from January 20, 1969, through August 9, 1974."[6] Although Ford's statement defending the pardon was laced with references to the Deity and to his own conscience, others found more sinister and disturbing motives for his action.

The reaction to Ford's announcement reflected varying interpretations. Some saw it as evidence of a dark conspiracy in which Ford had implicitly or explicitly exchanged the pardon for Nixon's resignation. Others saw it as a stupid error or even an honest mistake. Since many felt that Nixon had already suffered enough, there were also those who approved of Ford's action, ascribing its negative repercussions to bad timing. They, in turn, were attacked by spokesmen who argued that Ford's action established a double standard of justice; other citizens were simply baffled and overwhelmed by the fast-moving events. Relatively unheard amid the clamor was another view, one that forms a major theme of this book: to wit, an insidious form of corruption has permeated our entire political system.

Public displeasure with Ford's action was recorded in the first national survey conducted after his announcement. In this poll, 59 percent of the American people disapproved of the pardon, 26 percent approved, and 15 percent were undecided. The intensity of emotions on this issue was reflected by the fact that two thirds of those who disapproved of the pardon felt "very strongly" about their position, while only half of those who approved expressed equally strong sentiments. Among all respondents, general approval of the way President Ford was handling his job dropped precipitously. The poll also showed some support for the proposal to "pardon the other people indicted or convicted of Watergate-related crimes," a plan that was announced to be "under study" two days after the issuance of Nixon's pardon. Fifty-nine percent favored pardoning the others, 29 percent opposed it, and 11 percent were undecided. And the survey also revealed that most of the poeple who endorsed pardons for the other defendants were found among those who criticized Nixon's pardon.[7] The public again seemed to be lapsing into the mood of dwindling confidence and cynicism it had displayed throughout the Watergate affair.

Perhaps the principal concern affecting public attitudes toward the presidential pardon, as well as Nixon's subsequent reluctance to testify in court, was the deliberate and determined effort to conceal the truth from the American people. The major factor that crushed Richard Nixon was his repeated attempts to conceal the truth about the Watergate break-in, truths that were finally forced to the surface by a Supreme Court decision. President Ford's pardon seemed merely to compound the issue. As Senator Floyd Haskell says, "This is the final chapter of the Watergate coverup. . . ."[8]

Politicians seem reluctant to conduct their business in full view, or even within earshot, of the public and seem compelled to wrap their activities in a veil of secrecy.

A partial explanation for this fear may be found in the transcripts of presidential conversations, which were released during the Judiciary Committee investigation of articles of impeachment. Most readers approached this volume as a rare opportunity to examine the process of presidential decision-making and to observe the best minds of the country in action as they grappled with the weighty affairs of state. To many, however, the experience was disappointing. Even though the "good parts" were deleted, the tape recordings seemed to be nothing more than an account of simple, shabby, and frequently incoherent discussions of numerous immoral and unethical alternatives to serious problems.

The reading, therefore, raised a natural and inescapable question: "How many other politicians have considered similar options and committed similar offenses?" Speculation about the discussion of practices that border on illegality does not, of course, prove they exist. But, to many, actions such as the pardon and repeated attempts to conceal crucial facts in the Watergate case suggested that the politicians had something to hide. As President Ford himself admitted, the pardon was designed to close the consideration of Watergate or "to firmly seal and shut this book."[9] In the light of the controversy surrounding subsequent court cases and the confirmation of Nelson Rockefeller as Vice-President, it was clear that the action did not accomplish his purpose. So long as the country fails to adopt major changes in governmental institutions, American history is sentenced to periodic bouts of Watergate. And any attempt to prevent a full and comprehensive discussion of the issue of corruption is almost certain to become a political disadvantage.

The reactions of government leaders to the Watergate affair, however, indicate that few public officials are prepared to press for the major changes necessary to prevent systemic corruption in the American process.

This posture is in sharp contrast to the national needs as indicated in the final report of the Senate Investigative Committee. It was stated in the report that the "conduct of many Watergate participants seems grounded on the belief that the ends justified the means, that the laws could be flouted to maintain the present [Nixon] administration.''[10]

The reaction of political leaders to this report was remarkably mild. The political system was simply ill-equipped to examine incidents of government lawlessness as immense as the Watergate affair, and it was forced to rely upon newly created institutions such as the office of the Special Prosecutor to conduct its investigations. After Nixon's resignation, Congress refused to pursue the impeachment issue or even to continue its investigation of the Watergate scandal. The cancelation of impeachment proceedings deprived the American people of the potentially valuable opportunity to witness televised debates among their elected representatives on the floors of the House and the Senate. And finally, the pardoning of Richard Nixon, as well as subsequent actions by attorneys and the courts, seemed to represent an effort to prevent the public from ever learning the facts of the case.

It is our position that the sources of the Watergate scandal cannot be attributed to one man or to any group of men including President Gerald Ford, former President Richard Nixon, former advisors John Ehrlichman and H. R. Haldeman, former Vice-President Spiro Agnew, or former Attorney General John Mitchell. The cause must be ascribed to institutional defects in the American political system. The remedies for these defects have not yet been devised by Congress. Although many congressional leaders played a prominent role in the investigation of the scandal, they failed to enact legislation which would prevent its repetition. In fact, the events triggered by the break-in at the headquarters of the Democratic National Committee raised important legislative, administrative, and judicial issues which were not effectively resolved by any branch of the national government.

Can Congress Reform Itself?

A notable deficiency in the political response to the Watergate affair was the reluctance of Congress to move against the now clearly evident evils of election campaign practices. Although a provision for public financing in all federal elections was approved by the U.S. Senate, it was strongly resisted by members of the House of Representatives who feared that such a policy might threaten their legislative seats by encouraging challengers.[11] As a result, when legislation on campaign finances finally emerged from a conference committee of the two houses and was reluctantly signed into law by President Ford in 1974, it reflected the long-standing refusal of Congress to enact fundamental institutional changes in the electoral system.

According to the 1974 legislation, the principle of public financing is limited to presidential campaigns; the corrupting influence of private contributions is permitted to continue in congressional elections. The only innovative feature of the new legislative compromise and accommodation was the creation of an independent commission to administer the law. This body was granted civil enforcement powers. Although a great deal of attention has been centered on the monetary limitations built into the bill, it should be recalled that limitations of one sort or another have been in the statute books since at least 1970, and have rarely been enforced.

Among the major provisions of the law are overall spending limits for particular offices. They range from $10 million per candidate for presidential primaries, $2 million per candidate for national political conventions, and $20 million per candidate for the general election. Candidates for the House of Representatives are limited to $70,000 for primary and general elections, while the maximum expenditures for candidates for the United States Senate range from $150,000 to $1.7 million, depending on the size of the state's population. The public finance provision assures major party nominees $20 million for the general election, with minor candidates eligible to receive an amount proportionate to their party's strength at the polls. They must have received at least 5 percent of the vote for president in the preceding election to be eligible. If they receive 5 percent of the vote for president in 1976, the bill provides for some reimbursement of expenditures. The funds for the public financing provisions will come from the $1 checkoff on federal income taxes. Candidates for the office of president are not required to use public finances, but if private funds are solicited, the spending ceiling of $20 million applies.[12]

The 1974 law also establishes $1,000 as the maximum amount any individual can contribute to any one candidate in the primary, runoff, and general election, or a total of $3,000. There is an overall maximum contribution limitation of $25,000 for all candidates. Cash contributions of more than $100 are prohibited. Groups and organizations may not contribute more than $5,000 to any one candidate in each primary, runoff, or general election, or $15,000 overall. Significantly, the law places no limit on the total amount groups can contribute to all candidates. The law also provides for future increases on all limits,

based on the cost-of-living index.[13] Members of Congress also gener-
ously included a provision limiting themselves to $1,000 for each speak-
ing engagement or writing fee, with a maximum of $15,000 of such
income per year.

The creation of the enforcement commission is the major strength
of the law, but those hoping for substantial political reform probably
should not be overly optimistic. The eight-member body does have the
power to issue subpoenas and to seek civil injunctions and declaratory
judgments. However, criminal enforcement remains with the Department of Justice. In view of the department's record of almost complete
disinterest over the years in enforcing previous corrupt-practice laws,
the prospects of violators being prosecuted or being jailed for their
criminal deeds remain bleak. Optimism fades even more rapidly when
one recalls the alleged criminal activities of the two attorneys general
during the Nixon administration, who were preceded by long lists of
partisan but inexperienced politicians serving as the nation's top law
enforcement officers.

Another severe weakness of the law is that the power of purse for
commission staff and operating expenditures remains with Congress. If
the past record of Congress in providing funds for enforcement of civil
rights, antitrust and regulatory laws is any indication, the commission
will be relatively ineffective. All in all, the substance of the 1974 reform
law suggests that the lessons of Watergate have not been learned.

In fact, the Director of the National Committee for an Effective
Congress has held meetings with wealthy contributors to discuss their
plight. They were told that loopholes exist and an individual can give
more than the flat $1,000 contribution to a candidate. They also can
spend up to $500 to throw a party for a candidate and can spend $1,000
not in concert with the candidate, which means they can mail material,
put up billboards, etc. Jules Witcover went so far as to assert, ". . . the
sky is still the limit in political giving." Witcover also observed most
appropriately:

> So active is the desire of traditional large donors to continue to affect
> public policy through their checkbooks that seminars on how they can
> stretch the $1,000 limit are being held for them around the country by an
> expert in the giving business.[14]

Congress also created a substantial loophole in the provisions of
the 1974 law related to public financing of campaigns that will permit
contributing and spending limits to be exceeded. The law stated:

> Notwithstanding any other provision of law with respect to limitations on expenditures or limitations on contributions, the national committee of a political party and a state committee of a political party . . . may make expenditures in connection with the general-election campaign of candidates for federal office.

This amount is limited, but the total is about $3.3 million on a presidential candidate, $4.3 million on candidates for the House of Representatives and $1.1 million on Senate candidates, or a total of $9 million. In addition to $9 million of direct services and expenditures on behalf of federal candidates, the Chairperson of the Republican National Committee, Mary Louise Smith, estimated the Committee could spend another $9 million of private money on "party-building" activities such as training programs, computerized studies, polling and the like. Thus, these totals added to the amount available through public financing will probably make the 1976 election even more expensive than the 1972 election![15]

Still another serious deficiency of the 1974 law is that it is clearly an incumbent's measure. There is no doubt that the House of Representatives rejected public financing largely because it would stimulate election opposition.[16] In fact, members provided additional protection for themselves in which *The Los Angeles Times* pointed out in an editorial:

> . . . the limits in races for the House of Representatives—$70,000 in both the primary and general elections—are far too low, and would almost insure the reelection of incumbent members, whose challengers would have to spend far more than that to offset the formidable advantages of those in office. The House's rejection of public financing for its own elections, while voting to impress it on presidential candidates, is a further guarantee that incumbents would face only token opposition.[17]

Whether the spending limitation is too high or too low is subject to dispute. However, so long as federal and state reform laws do not establish spending limitations that are substantially lower for incumbents than for challengers, there will continue to be little more than token competition in most legislative races.

The need for lower spending limitations for incumbents is clear from examination of congressional election data. The turnover rate has not exceeded 26 percent since 1932, and it has been rare for more than 15 percent of those incumbents who actively seek reelection to be defeated.[18] As was pointed out in chapter 3, there is little evidence to suggest that lengthy tenure is conducive to responsive policy-making, or that it results in increased professionalism and higher ethical standards.

A second method that would increase membership turnover would be to limit the number of terms a member could serve. The length of time permitted might range from two to five terms in the House of Representatives and two terms in the Senate. A former member of Congress stated the case for this much needed reform when he observed:

> In fact, election is a goal so embedded in the folkways of Congress that many members have lost sight of why they are, or are not, elected or reelected. It is no surprise that this retards their ability to function as independent legislators and to resist domination by misguided presidents.[19]

Structural Weakness in Congress

The decline of the influence and effectiveness of Congress is due not only to the preponderance of elders, but the fact remains

> that the basic sources of Congressional power are controlled by men whose sole qualification for leadership is survival, chronological and political. No other ability is ever required to advance toward this influence. Perversely, the system operates so that those who do rise to power are the least likely to be responsive to their constituents, to the leaders of their house and party, to the President, to anyone. This mindless pattern is obstructive to law-making and demoralizing to the men and women who want to do it well.[20]

There are those who saw signs of change in the aftermath of the so-called freshman revolt in the House of Representatives in 1975. Indeed, the removal of several committee members and the revitalization of the Democratic caucus perhaps provide some support for this view. However, a more accurate interpretation was provided by James R. Polk in *The New Republic*: "The freshman revolt in the Democratic caucus swept out an aging chairman of the House Armed Services Committee and replaced him with *another feeble old man* [emphasis added]. . . ."[21]

An examination of Congressional reform action at the end of the first session indicates clearly that Congress is not willing to undertake a sorely needed internal restructuring. The members were confronted with a series of critical ethical issues, but action was not taken on a long list of proposed reforms. No action was taken to tighten rules on financial disclosure or to open the books on outside income, property holdings, and gifts of all federal officials. Nor were the members interested in cracking down on secret, private expense funds or adopting procedures to shed more light on lobbying. They also failed to enact the "Sunshine Act" which would open up to the public proceedings in Congress and in forty-seven federal agencies. It also is significant that the House Committee on Standards of Official Conduct continues to avoid its responsibilities. One observer offered the following description of the so-called ethics committee: "An ethics committee is among the most useless creations on Capitol Hill. Often it serves to delay, defuse and do nothing. The House group meets for maybe an hour each month and almost never gets to the end of the agenda."[22]

The response of Congress to the events of the 1970s is startling. Since 1970, payoff convictions have touched three senators' offices, four congressmen have been found guilty in the judicial system, and influence-peddling charges have been confirmed as high as the office of the Speaker. The record is clear that the further insulation of already secure members of an antiquated institution will delay additionally much needed structural reforms. For example, just prior to consideration of internal reform proposals in 1974, the prestige of Congress had fallen to the lowest point on record, 18 percent. Presumably immune to the public, members continue to reject proposals to streamline the institution. Thus, once again, members of Congress performed in accordance with the bankrupt philosophy that Majority Leader Thomas P. C. ("Tip") O'Neill summed up: "The name of the game is power and the boys don't want to give it up."[23]

Besides providing increased protection for themselves in the so-called election reform bill, and rejecting much needed internal reforms, members of Congress took other actions in 1974 to entrench themselves even more solidly. Before leaving for their month-long vacation before the 1974 election, members of the House approved without floor votes or public hearings a $9,280 increase in expense allowances, including a boost of $2,350, or a 53 percent increase, in their "stationery allowance." As Paul Steiger pointed out:

> The stationery allowance need not be used for stationery, but can be pocketed. Some members use it to help pay their taxes, others save it over the years for a retirement nest egg, and still others use it to finance political newsletters to constituents.[24]

In 1974, the direct subsidies provided to incumbents in six major categories totaled $25,840 a year, or 56 percent more than in 1973. The increases were for leasing office equipment, renting offices in home districts ($6,000), expenses for district offices ($2,000), telephone expenses in the home district ($2,400), postage stamps ($1,400 per year), and personal income tax deduction (the equivalent of a $1,700-per-year raise for those who pay taxes in the 39 percent bracket).[25] Of course, members already receive subsidized services such as life and health insurance, pensions, cut-rate barber shops and beauty parlors, subsidized dining rooms, a free gymnasium, swimming pool, paddle ball courts, saunas, and free potted plants. They also get free first class mailing privileges and employ sizeable staffs at public expense.

In view of the obvious advantages of incumbency, both in terms of dollars and personal well-being, it is something of a miracle (or perhaps at least a historical event such as in 1932, 1964 and 1974) that any challenger succeeds. In view of the isolation of members of Congress from the people, it becomes imperative that tenure be limited and that campaign expenditure ceilings for incumbents be set at a level far below that of challengers. The record suggests that Congress will not respond to these needs, and that is precisely why the proposed national initiative process should be established.

The 1974 reform legislation failed also to deal with the entire range of interest group political activity. These groups not only are involved in financing campaigns, but in a variety of other actions such as mobilizing employees and organization members. It is recognized by many members of the executive and legislative branches that producer interest groups are generally more influential than consumer groups. Congressman John B. Anderson provided a candid assessment of these influences.

> The influence of special interest groups in the political process should not be exclusively equated with their ability to make large campaign contributions. To be sure, Common Cause has shown that wealthy contributors and special interest committees provided more than $30,000 directly to congressional candidates during the 1972 campaign, millions more to party committees, and perhaps an equal amount to the presidential campaigns. But special interest groups have far more tools in their influence kits than mere campaign cash.
>
> Most important, they have the ability for effective political mobilization. Mancur Olson in his book, *The Logic of Collective Action,* incisively analyzes the fundamental dilemma of a large. heterogeneous industrial democracy: Producer groups of all types have an inherent advantage over consumers, the broad public and general taxpayers in affecting

the political process. In the first instance, this stems not from money but from a profound difference in incentives for political action.

The 2.5 million members of the building trade unions, for example, have a strong interest in the Davis-Bacon Act that assures them the highest union wage rate on each of some $40 billion in annual government contracts. It is commonly agreed that this law keeps construction wage costs considerably above the true market rate. But while economists have estimated that this distortion of the labor market costs the economy directly, and consumers indirectly, some $2 to $3 billion each year, it is the representatives of the building trades who are at the front door of the Education and Labor Committee when any threat to that particular policy arises. The "general public" isn't there.

Similarly, the hundreds of millions in additional income for dairy farmers represented by an increase in the support price from 75 percent to 85 percent of parity generates far greater incentives for political mobilization among producers than does the resulting few extra cents per quart of milk among the 60 million American households who drink milk. The life or death of the American shipbuilding industry, to take a final example, is vitally dependent upon the $300 million annual subsidy for ship construction. Yet, since that amount averages out to only about $3.50 per income tax return, it is readily understandable that the industry rather than the general public is mobilized when that program is subject to review or extension.

Most public policies have quite different effects upon different parts of the electorate. The incentives for political action are skewed in favor of producer groups who are hit hard rather than general consumers on whom each decision has only marginal impact.

Once activated, a series of further advantages accrue to producer groups. Since most are organized around a specialized economic interest or activity, they can frequently meet needs, offer services and provide tangible benefits to their members that provide an incentive for continued support of group activities.

Another advantage available to producer groups is their possession of effective communication networks. Most of the major lobbies and associations in Washington can mobilize their membership on literally an hour's notice when an urgent issue is at stake.

Still another advantage of producer groups is the financial capability to maintain professional lobbyists and staffs, which stems, of course, from their power to raise the dues and other revenues from their members needed to compensate professional employees. This is important because the federal government, or even Congress, is not a unitary monolithic institution but a complex and specialized social organism in which power is dispersed widely, depending upon the issue and concerns involved.

Finally, producer groups possess the ability to marshal specialized knowledge and expertise on the wide-ranging and often vexing problems which confront governmental decision making.[26]

Political Reform in California: An Alternative National Model

The failure of Congress to reform itself, to deal with the undue influence of special interests and lobbyists, to restructure the election process, and to open up the system, stands in stark contrast to the record of many states and local communities. For example, in June 1974, the voters of California overwhelmingly approved a measure known as Proposition 9 that had been placed on the ballot through the rigorous method of gathering signatures on petitions in the initiative process. This law, which was also called the Political Reform Act of 1974, asserted:

a. The people find and declare as follows: State and local government should serve the needs and respond to the wishes of all citizens equally, without regard to wealth;

b. Public officials, whether elected or appointed, should perform their duties in an impartial manner, free from bias caused by their own financial interests or the financial interests of persons who have supported them.

c. Costs of conducting election campaigns have been increased greatly in recent years, and candidates have been forced to finance their compaigns by seeking large contributions from lobbyists and organizations who thereby gain disproportionate influence over governmental decisions;

d. The influence of large campaign contributors is increased because existing laws for disclosure of campaign receipts and expenditures have proved to be inadequate;

e. Lobbyists often make their contributions to incumbents who cannot be effectively challenged because of election laws and abusive practices which give the incumbent an unfair advantage;

f. The wealthy individuals and organizations which make large campaign contributions frequently extend their influence by employing lobbyists and spending large amounts to influence legislative and administrative actions.

g. The influence of large campaign contributors in ballot measure elections is increased because the ballot pamphlet mailed to the voters by the state is difficult to read and almost impossible for the layman to understand; and

h. Previous laws regulating political practices have suffered from inadequate enforcement by state and local authorities.

The initiative measure was composed of major sections related to various aspects of political campaigns and state government. It can be amended only by a two-thirds vote of both houses of the California legislature. The law, which became effective January 1, 1975, contains the following provisions.

Fair Political Practices Commission

The commission will be made up of five members, with no more than three members of the same political party. The chairman and one other member will be appointed by the governor. The state attorney general, secretary of state, and the state controller will each appoint one member. The commission will have the power to subpoena records and witnesses, investigate violators, regulate campaign spending, and levy fines.

Campaign Disclosure

Campaign reports shall be audited by the Franchise Tax Board. All contributions of $50 dollars or more must be itemized. The statements must be filed 40 days before an election. Campaign statements will be required twice a year in years in which a public official is not a candidate. Anonymous or cash contributions will be disallowed unless the anonymous contribution is under $50. Any committee or other organization supporting or opposing candidates or ballot measures must also file under similar rules. A copy of any mass mailing must be filed as a public record with the Fair Campaign Practices Commission.

Limitations of Expenditures

Candidates for governor will be limited to an expenditure of 7 cents times the number of voters (at present this would be approximately $980,000 in a primary election) and 9 cents per adult citizen (approximately $1.26 million) in a general election. Candidates for secretary of state, attorney general, lieutenant governor, controller, or superintendent of public instruction are limited to spending 3 cents per adult citizen (approximately $1.12 million). Neither side in a proposition campaign can spend more than $500,000 more than the amount spent by the opposition. Statewide political party central committees are limited to 1 cent times the number of voters for each election (approximately $140,000).

Lobbyists

Lobbyists will be prohibited from making or arranging for campaign contributions and from making gifts to state officials of more than $10 per person in any month. Lobbyists are required to submit monthly reports detailing their activities in trying to influence legislation or the actions of state agencies. All lobbyists will be required to register with the secretary of state. The employers of lobbyists and any person or organization spending $250 within a month to influence legislation also must report their activities.

Conflicts of Interest

Public officials will be required to file annual conflict-of-interest statements. These statements must disclose investments and property owned in the state or local jurisdiction the official represents and all income received. Each state and local agency is given the authority to adopt a conflict-of-interest code governing its employees. Public officials may not participate in decisions that affect their personal financial concerns or interests. A public official will be considered to have a financial interest in a decision if that decision will affect any business or property in which the official has more than a $1,000 interest, or from which the official receives more than $250 within the 12 months before the decision, or in which the official holds a major management position.

Ballot Pamphlet Reform

The ballot pamphlet must be written in language that is clear, understandable, and easily readable. The analysis of ballot measures must be written in concise terms, avoiding technical language where possible so that "it will be easily understood by the average voter." The type size and page size will be increased. Any voter will be able to challenge in court the accuracy of the material within the booklet before the final version is published. The courts will be empowered to change any inaccuracies.

Incumbency

No legislator's newsletter or other mass mailing can be sent at "public expense" by an elected state officer after the officer has filed a declaration of candidacy for public office. The order of names of candidates on the ballot will be determined without regard to whether the candidate is an incumbent.

Auditing

In order to insure the accuracy and completeness of all reports filed in connection with this law, the Franchise Tax Board will make audits and field investigations with respect to campaign statements and lobbyist reports. Any violation of the law will be reported to the Fair Political Practices Commission and the state attorney general's office for consideration and possible further action.

Enforcement

Candidates, campaign treasurers, or other persons who violate the spending limits or any provision of the measure will be subject to fines up to triple the amount of the violation. In addition, the person found guilty of a violation can be jailed for up to one year. No person convicted of a violation of this law can be a candidate for elective office or act as a lobbyist for four years following the date of conviction unless a court orders otherwise. The Fair Political Practices Commission and the district attorneys or city attorneys of the counties or cities in which violations occur can bring civil action to stop violations of this act or to recover damages. If these officials fail to act, any private citizen can sue.

There is no reason why laws similar to those of California cannot be adapted for federal elections. Indeed, such a program for those elections might be far more restrictive on incumbents. The advantages of incumbency should be determined empirically, and appropriate restrictions similar to the California requirement that incumbents spend 10 percent less than others should be imposed. As a result, a member of Congress would have a considerably lower spending limit than the challenger. Incumbents also could be prohibited from using the franking privilege for a specified period prior to an election, and limitations could be placed on any number of the other benefits provided to officeholders.

There are many other campaign reform proposals that should be considered, such as the infusion of lay people into the governing bodies of professional associations such as those of lawyers. Moreover, California took this action in 1975 and increased substantially lay representation on the governing board of the State Bar. Indeed nothing short of sweeping reforms will cleanse democratic institutions and justify the political agonies of the early seventies.

Enforcement and Penalties: The Need for Jail Sentences

There remains, however, the critical question of enforcement. Reforms must be able to deal with the fact that a *corrupt act* violates responsibility toward a system of public order and is in fact incompatible with and potentially destructive of that system. Corruption has become institutionalized; democracy has been undermined; and, to a great extent, the people have grown aware of it. To remedy this situation, an approach is needed to the enforcement of the law and to the imposition of penalties for violators that will infuse integrity into the entire political system. Without proper enforcement procedures and the swift, certain administration of appropriate penalties, few positive results will emerge from any of the proposed reforms.

There are two alternatives for enforcement of these laws. (1) They can be regarded as conventional criminal statutes and enforced as such, an approach that seems to be more suited to the enforcement of laws concerning campaign practices. (2) They can be regarded as remedial in spirit. Under the latter interpretation, laws become less proscriptions of offensive conduct than attempts to inject certain values into the political process.

For serious violations of campaign laws, it is recommended that a system of mandatory minimum prison sentences should be imposed. This mandatory sentence should be a minimum period of six months, and judges should have the option of extending the sentence to a maximum of two years. This practice would represent a major departure from existing policies that rely upon fines, treble damages, and similar enforcement measures. The need for this approach is evident, as a review of the recent absurdity of cases shows in which corporation executives were fined $1,000 and corporations were assessed $5,000 for violations of federal campaign laws that involved policy benefits of substantially larger amounts to those businesses and individuals. There is no evidence to indicate that fines have ever deterred illegal acts in election campaigns. To act as effective deterrents, the fines would have to be so large that the authorities probably would be reluctant to impose them upon violators. Clearly, if the penalty has no deterrent impact, it contributes little to the objectives of the policy.

Prison sentences, of course, would be imposed only for such major offenses as the failure to report large cash donations. Minor and frequently accidental violations of campaign laws such as not listing proper addresses, telephone numbers, and similar errors should be handled in a manner similar to the existing procedures for other types of misdemeanors.

The evidence, however, suggests that imposition of mandatory sentences for serious violations of election laws would have a deterrent effect. Studies have shown that "businessmen abhor the idea of being branded a criminal. Society does not particularly care whether murderers and rapists like being branded as criminals; but businessmen, after all, form a large, respectable, and influential class in our society."[27] In short, it is generally accepted today that the fear of criminal prosecution is an effective deterrent to businessmen, professional men, and others who occupy a social position in the middle class or above. Because these types of people comprise the major party "angels," criminal sanctions ought to be effective in dealing with violations of the laws related to campaign finance and elections. Just as a respectable bookkeeper fears the social shame and the economic ruin involved in serving time for embezzlement, so might the business official, lawyer, or labor leader be deterred by the threat of conviction for violating campaign regulations.

In addition to mandatory sentences, other types of penalties might be imposed on certain convicted violators. Since guilds and associations traditionally have obtained the assistance of the state in the protection and furtherance of their economic interests, the state's licensing power should be used to deal with those groups found guilty of violating campaign laws. Any individual or group licensed by government that is convicted of a serious violation of such laws should automatically lose the *privilege*—and it is precisely that—to engage in their pursuits. If convicted, attorneys could not practice law, physicians could not practice medicine, certified public accountants could not prepare income tax forms, and credentialed teachers could not teach. Similarly, corporate charters should be revoked for flagrant violations of the laws.

To end the indifference that has characterized the response of politicians to earlier laws concerning disclosure and limitations on campaign spending, the people also need an advocate. It may not be sufficient to rely upon the good offices of the attorney general, the district attorney, the secretary of state, or any other elected official to enforce such measures. Perhaps national, state, and local governments should examine plans to establish the office of an ombudsman, which would be empowered to act as a representative of the people in the investigation of political corruption. This office should be *required* to investigate and to submit a public report on all complaints filed by citizens. Furthermore, if the evidence indicates that prosecution is warranted, the attorney general or the district attorney should be *required* to submit the case to a jury.

Individual citizens also should be encouraged—perhaps through the award of financial damages from the convicted—to form citizens' watchdog units in each electoral district to monitor the behavior of public officials, interest groups, political "angels," lawyers, and others who occupy critical positions at the junction of economic and political power. Every appropriate government official should be required by law to cooperate and to assist such groups in any activity that does not constitute an unwarranted invasion of privacy.

Thus, the imposition of minimum mandatory prison sentences, effectively monitored and enforced with certainty and swiftness, would deter violations of laws related to campaign finance, elections, and lobbying. Since the time of Beccaria, at least, it has been commonly accepted that the certainty of detection and punishment is a more effective deterrent to crime than the severity of the penalty. Hence, sentences need not be long, but they must be certain and inescapable.

There are those who question the impact of many of the proposed reforms and are skeptical of any enforcement proposals. The experience of California's first year of politics under the 1975 Political Reform Act and that of Oregon and other states offer contrary evidence. After passage of the wave of "open government" laws requiring financial disclosure, cries of invasions of privacy, warnings of mass resignations, and threats of noncompliance were heard. However, early evidence indicates that throughout the United States since the enactment of such measures, candidates and officeholders have complied, even if they were strongly opposed to doing so.[28] As the administrator of the Washington Public Disclosures Commission stated, "People want to comply with the law and are complying with the law. . . ."[29] Even the lobbyists have been forced to comply in California, and the Derby Club, discussed in chapter 6, has gone dutch treat.[30] In addition, the "watering holes" of California legislators and lobbyists also have dried up. A newspaper survey of restaurants and bars in Sacramento—discussed in chapter 6—found owners attacking the law as "stupid," "wrong," and bad for business.[31]

Although forcing lawmakers to foot their own bills is desirable, evidence indicates the California law has reduced somewhat the power of lobbyists. For example, during the 1975 session of the legislature the tax on beer was increased. Despite references to working people by rhetorical-minded legislators and intense lobbying by one of the most powerful lobbyists in the state, the measure was approved. This lobbyist pumped over $50,000 into the 1974 campaign, but the reform law stopped this practice. As one legislator observed, "He [the lobbyist] wouldn't have lost that one in those days [pre-1975]."[32] Discussions with legislators and staff in the legislature and interviews with members of the Fair Political Practices Commission and staff support the contention that the reform act has brought about some changes and will help to reduce the influence of lobbyists that has been based on campaign contributions.[33] A survey by the Council of State Governments concluded that generally the new requirements have won acceptance and are being conscientiously enforced.[34]

Campaign Financing and the Constitution

Some opponents of legislation to control or prohibit massive campaign contributions and to impose severe penalties upon those who violate such laws have attempted to use the Constitution in the defense of their position. They have contended that legal restrictions on campaign donations or expenditures comprise a denial of First Amendment rights to free speech and to petition the government for the redress of grievances. The following statement is typical of such arguments, which have been employed to oppose both public subsidies for campaigns and limitations on private funding.

> A limit on the amount an individual may contribute to a political campaign is a limit on the amount of political activity in which he may engage. A limit on what a candidate may spend is a limit of his political speech as well as on the political speech of those who can no longer effectively contribute money to his campaign. In all of the debates surrounding the First Amendment, one point is agreed upon by everyone; no matter what else the rights of free speech and association do, they protect explicit political activity. Limitations on campaign spending and contributing expressly set a maximum on the political activity in which persons may engage.[35]

A case that is frequently cited in support of this position involved a 1961 Supreme Court decision that refused to apply the provisions of the Sherman Anti-Trust Act against a "vicious, corrupt and fraudulent" public relations campaign funded by the Eastern Railroads Presidents Conference that was "designed to foster the adoption and retention of laws and law enforcement practices destructive of the trucking industry."[36] Indeed, Justice Black's majority opinion in this case contained dicta which seemed to oppose laws regulating campaign finance. Justice Black stated:

> It is neither unusual nor illegal for people to seek action on laws in the hope that they may bring about an advantage to themselves and a disadvantage to their competitors . . . . To disqualify people from taking a public position in matters in which they are financially interested would thus deprive the government of a valuable source of information and . . . deprive the people of their right to petition in the very instances in which that right may be of the most importance to them.[37]

Although these words might appear to elevate corrupt practices to the status of constitutionally protected behavior, there are sound reasons to believe that this has not been the intention of the Supreme Court in this or any other case.

Initially, the claim that regulations on campaign finances form a denial of First Amendment rights overlooks the fact that the Supreme Court has chosen *not* to decide the constitutional implications of prohibitions on corporate contributions as enacted January 26, 1907; of the law forbidding contributions by labor unions passed June 25, 1947; of limitations on individual contributions approved July 19, 1940, and amended in 1970; and of the restrictions adopted in 1971 on contributions by candidates and the families of candidates.

Most important, any judicial finding that laws regulating or prohibiting private campaign donations are unconstitutional would amount to a serious and massive violation of the rights of an overwhelming majority of citizens who seek to gain equality of political influence in state and national elections. Such a decision would serve only the cause of powerful organized interest groups attempting to preserve the status quo and their privileged position within it. As a result, the political system might be permanently biased in favor of established interests that wish to perpetuate the corrupting influence of private money in American government.

However, there is little reason to believe that the courts would embrace such a position. Often in the past, the judiciary has been willing to protect the political rights of citizens against the danger of aristocratic influences. Even in the dark days when the language of the Constitution was used to uphold the evils of slavery and the greed of unfettered laissez-faire capitalism, some justices frequently confronted harsh social realities to decide in favor of values such as freedom and equality. Manifesting this bent was the important dissent of Justice Gabriel Duvall in *Mima Queen and Child* v. *Hepburn*, in which he concluded, "It will be universally admitted that the right to freedom is more important than the right to property."[38] Hence, it appears unlikely that judges would display a callous disregard for the rights of millions of citizens who are expressing a demand for increased equality of electoral influence. By focusing exclusively upon the contention that laws controlling campaign finances are an unconstitutional deprivation of freedom of speech, the opponents of such legislation seem to be arguing that private campaign contributions should be elevated to a privileged status in the constitutional order.

Another line of reasoning that is worthy of far more consideration in a scheme of constitutional values is that the disproportionate influence exerted upon the results of elections by massive or unlimited campaign contributions constitutes a denial of the equal protection of the laws. The full implementation of this principle awaits further legal developments; however, a basis for the achievement of this goal was provided by the 1966 Supreme Court decision in *Harper* v. *Virginia Board of Elections*, which held that the poll tax in that state was unconstitutional. In this case, the Court declared:

> We conclude that a State violates the Equal Protection Clause of the Fourteenth Amendment whenever it makes the affluence of the voter or payment of any fee an electoral standard. Voter qualifications have no relation to wealth nor to paying or not paying this or any other tax. Our cases demonstrate that the Equal Protection Clause of the Fourteenth Amendment restrains the States from fixing voter qualifications which insidiously discriminate. . . . The principle that denies the State the right to dilute a citizen's vote on account of his economic status or other such factors by analogy bars a system which excludes those unable to pay a fee to vote or who fail to pay . . . . Wealth, like race, creed, or color, is not germane to one's ability to participate intelligently in the electoral process. Lines drawn on the basis of wealth or property, like those of race, are traditionally disfavored.[39]

Although this decision applied only to state laws, the doctrine of "equal protection of the laws" also could be used to challenge federal legislation permitting private campaign contributions or to defend public financing of national elections against the charge that limits on private donations comprise a deprivation of freedom of speech.

The courts increasingly have recognized the importance of the principle of equality under the law in both state and federal litigation. In *Bolling* v. *Sharpe* (1954), for example, Chief Justice Earl Warren offered an explicit discussion of the interrelationships between the equal protection clause of the Fourteenth Amendment and the due process clause of the Fifth Amendment:

> The Fifth Amendment . . . does not contain an equal protection clause as does the Fourteenth Amendment which applies only to the states. Both the concepts of equal protection and due process, both stemming from our American ideal of fairness, are not mutually exclusive. The "equal protection of the laws" is a more explicit safeguard of prohibited unfairness than "due process of law," and, therefore, we do not imply that the two are always interchangeable phrases. But, as this court has recognized, discrimination may be so unjustifiable as to be violative of due process.[40]

Subsequent decisions have consistently held that the due process clause of the Fifth Amendment may be applied against denials of equal protection by federal action in a manner analogous to the Fourteenth Amendment prohibition against denials by state action.[41] Because both federal and state legislation either implicitly or explicitly permits the expenditure of private campaign gifts in state or federal elections, the necessary basis for establishing governmental or "state" action in such constitutional cases is available. The appropriate doctrinal rationale is provided by the ruling in *Shelly* v. *Kraemer* (1948) that "whenever legal consequence is to be given to the activities of private parties, state action is thought to be present."[42] Indeed, such adaptations in another area of electoral litigation have been successfully argued.[43]

The first federal court rulings on the 1974 federal election reform act indicated the courts would uphold the measure. Citing the need to curb "the corrosive influence of money" on politics, the United States Court of Appeals upheld the major provisions of the law in 1975. The justices replied to those critics who expressed opposition to the law on First Amendment grounds that the government's interest in preventing abuses and restoring public confidence in the electoral process overrode "incidental limits on First Amendment rights." The justices pointed out that

> to the extent that prohibitions and restraints . . . work incidental restrictions on First Amendment freedoms, these constraints broadly considered are necessary to assure the integrity of federal elections.[44]

The court also stated most appropriately:

> It would be strange indeed if . . . the wealthy few could claim a constitutional guarantee to a stronger political voice than the unwealthy man because they are able to give and spend more money, and because the amounts they give and spend cannot be limited.[45]

In addition to federal court action, the reform measures of several states have survived constitutional challenges. In the case of laws in California and Washington, the provisions are more restrictive of individual activity than is true of the 1974 federal law. Washington state's pioneering law was challenged in state courts as a violation of the right to privacy and a hindrance to candidates running for office. The state supreme court ruled that the public was entitled to ". . . information which clearly and directly bears upon qualifications and fitness of those who seek and hold public office."[46] Decisions in California courts indicate that state's far-reaching law probably will survive in state courts.

The need to apply and to enforce restraints on the influence of private campaign money—and to adopt a measure requiring complete public financing of political campaigns—is justified on both constitutional and public policy grounds. As we have seen, large contributors exert a disproportionate influence upon the outcome of elections, as well as playing a decisive role in the selection of candidates for public office. Rank-and-file voters are forced to assume a subordinate and unequal status in their efforts to exercise electoral influence. As Joel Fleishman has pointed out, prior attempts to correct these inequities have failed.

> During virtually our entire history of attempting to cure the worst consequences of private financing of elections—now nearly seventy-five years, we have exclusively employed measures which constrain undesirable characteristics of the campaign process, such as limitations on the size and source of contributions and on the object and level of expenditures. Unlike many other countries, we have never utilized measures that support desirable characteristics in election campaigns, such as the public subsidization of political activity. Nearly all of the attempts to constrain election activity have been ineffective. This suggests that the basic method itself may be ill-suited to the task. Methods of election constraint inherently address symptoms of disorder, rather than the disorder itself. Only public support of elections . . . seems capable of coming to grips with the underlying problem, the financing of elections with private money.[47]

The Need for Public Financing of Campaigns

The task of eliminating private financial contributions and of implementing total public support of political campaigns must be granted the highest priority. In a democratic society, electioneering plays an indispensible role in acquainting the public with major public issues and with the qualifications and positions of the candidates. Without the information that is conveyed to them during the few months before an election, citizens would be incapable of making the choice between competing values that is required of them at the ballot box. As a result, the responsibility of communicating with voters is a *public* responsibility. As such, it should be financed by public funds rather than by private donations from a few self-selected and self-aggrandizing political "angels." Because the quality of the decisions that are made in an election have a critical bearing upon the fate of the nation for years to come, the content of campaigns should not be determined by the vagaries of private contributions. An investment of public resources to insure adequate dissemination of the messages of candidates seems to be a small price to pay for a vital public function.

Public financing of political campaigns would help to eliminate many of the existing inequities of the electoral process. It would remove the principles of the private marketplace, which allocate voting strength on the basis of the amount of resources that one has available to spend rather than on the basis of equality. It would abolish the practice of "weighted voting," which allows large contributors to exert an influence equal to hundreds or even thousands of votes in the outcome of elections. And, it would provide an opportunity for all citizens to share an equal investment in politics by eliminating the continuous influence of wealthy benefactors. In other words, public financing of political campaigns offers the promise of correcting some of the inequities in the present method of selecting candidates that have discouraged wide segments of the electorate from participating in the electoral process.

This proposal, of course, would little affect attempts to influence the outcome of elections that do not involve the expenditure of funds (e.g., working within political parties, distributing campaign materials, canvassing voters on behalf of the candidates, and other such activities). As a result, individual voters could continue to expand their political strength through activity to persuade others to support the candidates of their choice. Some inequities probably will remain because some persons obviously have more time to devote to political activism than others. But perhaps the principal impact of the public financing of electoral campaigns upon political action might be evident in the increased willingness of citizens to participate in campaign work and other types of political activities. Since activists could be assured that their efforts would not be canceled by a massive outlay of cash from large contributors, they might regain incentives to become involved in all phases of the political process. Hopefully, the electoral system could be infused with a fresh supply of new talent and energy from voters who previously had been unwilling to fight the overwhelming odds that mitigated against the success of their efforts. The benefits to be derived from this increased participation in political life both for the electoral system and for the development of a genuine sense of civic responsibility could be enormous.

Another plan that should be explored entails the provision of public service time on radio and television. There is no reason why the mechanisms of the private marketplace should determine the rates that candidates must pay for time and space in radio, television, or newspapers. If the messages of the candidates and the value judgments made by voters on the basis of those messages are taken seriously, it would seem appropriate that the time or space for political advertising be considered a public obligation to be determined by government regulation rather than by the practices of the communications industry. This proposal, therefore, would provide ample time in the mass media for major candidates to present their views to the voters. As an incentive to minor parties and candidates, similar opportunities would be provided to persons who won, say, 2 percent of the votes cast in the preceding election. A related proposal would involve provisions for a specified number of mailings in behalf of candidates for public office.

The various proposals for public financing should not be enacted if the amounts are so low that the bill becomes an incumbent's bill. Nor should they be approved if they work to the disadvantage of minor or potential new political parties. Even though we continue to hear reference to "the two-party system" the evidence suggests that the United States is not as solidly a two-party country as has long been assumed.[48] Polls that seek and measure party affiliation reveal that over 30 percent of the people disavow affiliation with either party, hardly an impressive confirmation of two-party politics. It also should be pointed out that there is a monopoly of the ballot by the two major parties. In short, the law is used to perpetuate their existence. This is done by laws that subject the entry of new minority party slates to extremely difficult burdens involving, for example, the number of signatures needed to qualify for the ballot. The courts also have interpreted such laws without regard to their prejudicial effect on small parties.[49]

As such, proposals for public financing must also be evaluated in terms of their impact on new or minor parties. In fact, the impact of any reform proposals on such parties should be of concern, and all prejudicial laws protecting the Republican and Democratic parties should be repealed. It has been observed:

> If politics is to have any meaning, if the political process is to regain any of its credibility with the American people, it must be opened to new ideas for solving the nation's ills. But new ideas all too often are not even debated because of the inherent fear they may jeopardize the outcome of an election. The development of new parties with access to the electoral process could change that. It is insulting to suggest that 200 million Americans are so intellectually and politically deficient that they can only come up with two closely similar approaches to the course their government should take.[50]

A National Recall and Initiative

In addition to public financing of all electoral campaigns, voters must be provided with improved methods of supervising their elected officials and of impressing their sentiments on public policy. Corruption cannot be eliminated simply by defeating discredited politicians. What the country requires is a restructuring of the electoral process that would increase the accountability of public officeholders. It is time for fundamental reforms rather than cosmetic ones.

It is appropriate for the people to reassert their rights to final responsibility for government decisions; ultimate authority is not, and should not, be delegated to *any* elected representative. Since most politicians cannot or will not take needed action, the people must be given the power to act directly on their own behalf. To accomplish this, the United States Constitution should be amended to enable the people, through the initiative process, to propose and enact any legislation that is deemed necessary. Furthermore, the people should be given the right to vote *directly* on the question of whether or not any elective federal official should be removed from office.

As long ago as 1911, Governor Hiram Johnson of California proclaimed in his inaugural address the urgent need "to restore power to the people." He asserted that "successful and permanent government must rest primarily on the recognition of the rights of man and the absolute sovereignty of the people." Johnson then took an oath that should be required of all public officials. He said, "I take it . . . that the first duty that is mine to perform is to eliminate every private interest from the government and to make the public service of the state responsive solely to the people." Although Johnson was only one of many progressive leaders who sought these goals, his ringing proclamation of the rights of the people prompted California to assume a position of leadership in the use of the initiative, the referendum, and the recall as a means of regaining public control of government institutions.[51]

Subsequently, however, these instruments of popular rule failed to fulfill the expectations of the early reformers. Special interests continued to exert a disproportionate influence on the adoption of important policies, and the results of public votes on various proposals often were a disappointment to those who had hoped that the people would use these tools to cleanse government of pernicious and self-serving influences.

The major flaws in the initiative, referendum, and recall may be ascribed to the same sources that have produced the systemic corruption of politics. The reformers had overlooked the fact that the tasks of placing a measure on the ballot, of presenting the case for a proposal to the public, and of publicizing the misconduct of an incumbent officeholder can be accomplished most effectively through the liberal use of money. Since there were few other groups with a sufficient investment in the outcome of a vote to justify the expenditure of massive funds, vested interests naturally absorbed the costs of many initiative, referendum, and recall campaigns. Consequently, a later governor of California, Edmund G. ("Pat") Brown, was forced to conclude that the initiative and referendum increasingly had been "used to turn the ballot into a field for jousting among public relations men wearing the colors of special interests."[52] City and state government agencies often have been placed at a major disadvantage in such campaigns by statutes that prohibit them from purchasing advertising to publicize their positions.[53] Nonprofit organizations or foundations have been prevented from endorsing a position on initiative, referendum, and recall votes under the penalty of losing their tax-exempt status.[54] As a result, the field for these campaigns was surrendered to special interest groups, which existed for the sole purpose of influencing public policy.

Proposals to eliminate the insidious influence of campaign contributions in American politics, therefore, offer not only a method of reducing corruption, but also a means of correcting some of the existing flaws in the initiative, referendum, and recall processes. Through a combination of public financing of political campaigns, the initiative, referendum, recall, and other plans, Americans would be in a far better position to launch total war against the whip of corruption that bleeds the political system.

In the light of the scandal-ridden Nixon administration, the most obvious need is for a constitutional amendment that would provide the people with the power to recall federal officeholders. This amendment would call for a vote of confidence to permit the removal from office of the president of the United States or any other elected national officer.[55] A petition for a vote of confidence on the president would be proposed by presenting a copy of the text containing a general statement of the reasons why removal is sought to the United States attorney general and to each secretary of state. It would qualify for the ballot when signed by qualified voters in number equal to a minimum of perhaps 8 percent of the total vote cast for president in the preceding presidential election. In case of the removal of the president from office, succession would be determined by the Constitution with the one exception that no person could occupy the White House unless he or she had been elected on a national ballot. There also would be the time allowed to collect signatures, and other technical provisions.

In the case of a vote of confidence for officials other than the president of the United States, the procedures would be similar. A petition would need the signatures of at least 10 percent of the total vote cast for the particular office in the previous regular election. In the event of removal, all candidates for the position would be filled by presidential appointment. The person appointed would act as caretaker of the office until the next general election and would be prohibited from being a candidate for reelection to that office. At least one term would have to elapse before that person could seek the office after having served as caretaker. The details of the process are similar to the recall provisions of California.

The second needed reform is a national initiative, which is simply a method of allowing the people to vote on a measure that has been either deadlocked or defeated in a legislature. The voters can adopt or reject the measure. If they should adopt, the measure takes its place in the statute books along with the laws passed by the legislature. The proposal for a national initiative, as well as for the recall of federal officials, already has been drafted by the People's Lobby, a grassroots organization based in California.[56]

An initiative measure could be proposed by presenting its text to the United States attorney general and to each secretary of state. It would be certified for the ballot when signed by electors equal in number to 4 percent of the votes cast for all candidates for president at the last presidential election. A period of twelve months would be allowed to collect the required number of signatures, and an expenditure limitation would be placed on the amount spent to obtain signatures to qualify an initiative for the ballot. If qualified, the initiative would be submitted to the voters at the next presidential election that is held at least 150 days after certification. Limitations also would be placed on the amount of money spent on the initiative campaign, and a prohibition would be imposed on initiative measures designed to amend the Constitution. An initiative could not embrace more than one subject. Special elections would be outlawed.

As Hiram Johnson observed— and as history has since confirmed—while the initiative and recall are not the panacea for all political ills, they do give the people the power of action when action is desired and provide the people with some means by which they can protect themselves. As political theorist Karl Popper observed, "We should like to have good rulers, but historical experience shows us that we are not likely to get them. This is why it is of such importance to design institutions which will prevent even bad rulers from causing too much damage."[57] The proposed system also would help to restore public confidence in government. The initiative and the recall are designed to foster the direct relationship between the people, public officials, and government, which other reforms have failed to do.

These proposals probably will not be received warmly by many social scientists, and they certainly will not evoke enthusiasm among most members of Congress. Too many persons in both groups seem to have accepted the elitist notion that only they and their peers really know what is best for the country.[58] A large majority of the public disagrees. They do not want to put government in the hands of the "best" and "most qualified" leaders and give them free reign. Rather, they prefer close and continuous monitoring of official actions. The initiative and recall would help to implement this relationship.

The overwhelming voter approval of the Political Reform Act of 1974—Proposition 9—in the California primary election stands as clear evidence of the ability of the people to act responsibly and independently to accomplish political reform. The measure was placed on the political agenda by numerous citizens groups and by several reform-oriented Democratic candidates for governor. The opposition to this sweeping structural reform consisted of a major share of the organized political power of the state—that is, most business organizations, much of organized labor, and most elected public officials. The politicians were soundly defeated, and the people enacted proposals similar to those the legislature was unable or unwilling to adopt.

Just as the California legislature had refused to enact most of the provisions of Proposition 9, Congress and other state legislatures have had a record of inaction on similar measures. In fact, the situation in Congress is worse than in the states. Whereas Congress has not acted on strong financial disclosure laws since Watergate, at least twenty-one states and a number of local governments took action in 1974. By mid-1975 the total reached forty. In fact, fourteen others had passed the laws even before Watergate.[59] This suggests that Congress and the powerful groups influencing its members are the real roadblocks to reform. The people are not.

There also are those who insist that the people are incapable of proposing and approving "good" legislation through the initiative process. In the eyes of some observers, California voters have approved a number of propositions that would support this view. However, the people do not monopolize the record for enacting "bad" legislation. Even a casual examination of much of the work of legislatures in many areas (campaign reform and taxes, for example) confirms this. Moreover, the authority to determine the constitutionality and legality of the actions of both the people and legislative assemblies remains with the courts.

There is not sufficient space here to answer adequately opposition to the concepts of direct democracy as embodied in the initiative and the recall processes. However, the record in California is strong supporting evidence. In fact, besides the 1974 Political Reform Act, many needed reforms such as the executive budget system, a quality state civil service system, an excellent state education system, and other programs stand as testimony to the viability of the process. Winston W. Crouch observed in his analysis of the California system that the initiative

> offers a procedure whereby a complete proposal may be put before the people for adoption or rejection without its having had to undergo crippling amendment and compromise that might have been its lot in the legislature. Admirable as the legislative process may be when it operates as it should, there are numerous occasions when a weary public must take an emasculated, compromised substitute measure produced by the legislature because it is the best that could be had at the time—the best that could survive the gauntlet of the lobbies.[60]

Reliance on the "best that lobbies will permit" simply is not adequate today or in the future. It is time to draw upon the experience of the states and to approve national initiative and recall amendments. Such action would reflect major progress in the long and difficult task of building an open democracy where the people, not special interests, are in charge.

Needed: Periodic Plebiscites

Each of the proposals we have offered previously was suggested as a means to attack the problem of corruption by reducing the influence of special interest groups and by granting the people an increased opportunity to monitor the activities of their elected representatives. There is, however, an additional plan that would help to secure these objectives and also would provide the people with another means of direct participation in the political processes, namely, periodic plebiscites. The plan is based on the assumption that a major cause of declining public confidence in the political process emanates from the discrepancy between the voting behavior of elected officials and the predominant wishes of their constituents. In such cases, legislators may simply be voting their own conscience, or repaying an obligation to a political "angel" or special interest. While there are those who defend a representative's right to decide an issue as he or she sees fit, this attitude also reflects a basic ambivalence about the concept of repositing trust in the people. In fact, the basic premise of the arguments and proposals presented in this book is that the general public alone is best equipped to evaluate effectively the actions of their public officials and to prevent corrupting influences from infecting the policy-making process. Thus, one should be skeptical of legislators who act contrary to public opinion for the same reasons that one should suspect a politician who contends that he or she is totally immune to influence generated by vast sums of money donated to an election campaign.

Such discrepancies are very difficult to detect because no one really knows the true sentiments of the voters in any given legislative district. There is relatively little information bearing on the connection between public opinion and the decisions of elected officials. As one careful review of the available research on this subject concluded, "Complete understanding of the frequency or infrequency of linkage between public opinion and policy is beyond the present knowledge of political scientists."[61]

While political polls have selected random samples of the national population to provide an accurate reflection of the sentiments of the entire country at a particular time, like samples seldom are drawn for legislative districts. As a result, a member of Congress who does not vote in accordance with the desires of the national population can easily reply, "But the people in my district feel differently about the question." The assessment may be correct in that probably no state or district is a valid microcosm of the nation. The legislator, therefore, cannot accurately determine from national surveys what the people in a particular constituency really want on most policy questions. Moreover, the questionnaires mailed to voters by representatives are usually biased and statistically unsound. They are sent for public reactions and campaign purposes rather than to elicit the desires of constituents.

Such problems, however, are statistical and technological, and can be overcome easily. One solution to the problems of learning the public's views would involve the installation of auxiliary equipment on radios, television sets, or telephones in every American home. This would permit citizens to express their preferences directly on major policy issues being considered by Congress or by other legislative assemblies.[62] In effect this is a proposal for "periodic plebiscites." At regular intervals, the proponents and opponents of a legislative measure would present their arguments on radio, television, and in newspapers. The time and space would be divided equally between the various sides of the issue. Immediately prior to an actual vote in a legislative assembly, the opposing sides would select spokesmen who would then agree on the wording of the question to be presented to the public. At the conclusion of the debate period, a key, for example, on the person's television set, would be opened for a specified period of time to give voters an opportunity to register their opinions by casting "yes" or "no" ballots on the proposal. The presentation of the issue, therefore, would resemble a legislative debate, except that participation would not be confined to elected officials. Most important, *all* citizens would have *an equal* opportunity to express their views on the issue.

Responses to the question then would be fed to computers, and the tallies could be made available extremely quickly. In this way, the total proportion of voters favoring and opposing an issue could be presented by state and legislative districts to permit the comparison of majority sentiment within a district and the legislative vote of the person representing that area. The votes could be cross-tabulated along such lines as age, sex, education, income, occupation, ethnic or racial attributes, organizational or interest-group affiliations, party identification, vote in preceding elections, and standardized measures of political efficacy or alienation. This would provide a detailed profile of the supporters and opponents of the proposal both within each legislative district and in the nation, state, or community as a whole. The transmission, of course, would be only one way. Careful safeguards would be employed to ensure that all information would be used solely for the purposes of analysis and to prevent invasions of privacy such as the retrieval of information for any other reason.

With this analysis, citizens would be able to compare their votes not only with the decisions of their elected representatives but also with the ballots cast by other groups. The institution of "periodic plebiscites" thus would provide a feasible method of guaranteeing that democratic values concerning the accountability of elected officials are adequately and realistically implemented.

The outcome of these plebiscites is not intended to be binding, nor would all citizens be required to participate. In fact, this plan is not proposed in the expectation that voters would necessarily compel their representatives to adhere strictly to the wishes of a majority of constituents. Some legislators might wish to give greater weight to their own consciences, to the people who voted for them, to persons affiliated with their own party, to the special needs of minority groups, or to the views of habitual nonvoters, as well as to the sentiments of the least efficacious and the alienated. Rather than demanding a slavish adherence to the views of the majority within a constituency, a more likely outcome of this system may be that legislators might adopt or even campaign for office on platforms that reflect different styles of representation. Some legislative districts might elect officials who act as instructed delegates of a majority of their constituents, while other legislators might wish to follow a more independent course. Still others might reflect the views of most party members, voters who supported them in the last election, or other critical sectors of society. Officeholders who ignored the opinions of cohesive minorities, of nonvoters, or of the alienated would at least have to assume the risk that those citizens would appear in the next election to punish them for their neglect. The processes of coalition-formation and reformation in a system with extensive access to essential facts could produce a dynamic and changing equilibrium that would constitute a strengthened defense against Madison's fear of the dominance of factions.[63]

The most important feature of the "periodic plebiscite," however, may be that it would help to ensure that the elected representatives of the people explain any obvious inconsistencies between their own voting records and the sentiments of either a majority or significant parts of their constituencies. At the present time, public officials are permitted to rationalize their decisions in any manner that they wish on grounds that are impossible either to verify or to refute. Such ambiguity offers abundant opportunity for politicians to use their votes to repay obligations to favored friends, political "angels," powerful pressure groups, and others who hold views that do not necessarily reflect the interests either of needy sectors of society or of the public as a whole. Plebiscites would help to correct this defect in existing political institutions.

By revealing constituent sentiments on key policy questions so that they can be used as one possible standard for evaluating political decisions, the plebiscite would help to accomplish several major long-range objectives. Initially, by permitting incumbent representatives to explain discrepancies between their positions and the views of constituents, it would provide voters with their first genuine opportunity to evaluate the motives of politicians who have long claimed they are uninfluenced by massive campaign contributions. Second, "periodic plebiscites" could form a basis for promoting or stimulating increased public confidence in governmental institutions and for facilitating a continuing involvement in political affairs among all segments of the population.

Obviously, a proposal of this nature will arouse extensive controversy and will require considerable experimentation. It might be appropriate to launch a pilot project for evaluation in selected constituencies. Although the plan has been discussed here primarily in reference to Congress, it could be implemented at any level. Eventually, consideration could be given to making some of the plebiscites binding or of using such a system to replace some conventional elections. Although plebiscites might not allow voters to record the intensity of their feelings on an issue, they would allow an equal opportunity for voters to express their opinions on crucial questions. Furthermore, they would provide a sustained foundation for political activity.

Critics of the plebiscitary process might focus on practical problems that obviously would arise in designing and implementing the system. Admittedly, the development, installation, and maintenance of the technological equipment required by "periodic plebiscites" would be a costly item in a government budget. Yet, the expense of this system must be compared to the vast sums of money and the unearned tax revenue currently supporting special interests. For average citizens who are concerned about the expenditure of their tax dollars, the implementation of the proposed plan could result in a major savings rather than an economic loss. Even more importantly, however, "periodic plebiscites" offer a valuable means of bridging the gap between the people and their government. The only enduring cure for corruption in the United States political system is an aroused and enlightened citizenry that is provided with the institutional means needed to impose its will upon government officials. The plan for "periodic plebiscites" is simply an additional means of achieving that critical objective.

There is some evidence that even the so-called reformers in Congress are frightened at the prospect of the people intruding on their inviolable domain. Robert Sherrill interviewed a number of members of Congress on the merits of a plan whereby the people would tell Congress directly what programs they wanted. The response was overwhelmingly negative. Comments from members of Congress ranged from, "That system doesn't contemplate intelligent consideration of the facts," offered by the old populist from Texas, Wright Patman, to liberal Phil Burton who stated, "The best votes I cast are those for bills that at first blush, my constituents would be against." Robert Kastenmeier, a reform Democrat from Wisconsin replied, "It's not that I don't have confidence in the electorate; I just like to think that they have confidence in me." And Sherrill added, "Further conversation indicated that he meant confidence the electorate would send a good man to Congress who then would have the strength to disregard the people who supported him."[64]

We concede that it would be difficult for the public to become informed on the many policy questions before the Congress. However, because neither the members nor the media have ever seriously attempted to provide adequate information for the mass of voters trying to "earn a living," we really do not have the basis for supporting the elitist views of those who mock the average citizen's intelligence. However, as Sherrill observed, "One suspects—and one suspects that Congress also suspects it—that the national electorate might make some rather sensible decisions on such questions as whether to subsidize corporations at the taxpayer's expense or whether to permit railroads to give up passenger service or whether to make wealthy agribusinessmen wealthier for doing nothing."[65] It seems reasonable to suggest that many members of Congress are fully aware of the fact that voters are far more willing than elected representatives to support proposed solutions to a number of pressing national problems. In terms of the nation's economic problems, former Senator Fred Harris was right when he observed that "Ordinary Americans understand better than do politicians that the real conflict over the distribution of income in our society is not between welfare mothers and auto workers; it is between poor working people and rich people."[66] Legislators also are fully aware of the fact that many of the solutions would disrupt their cozy mutual benefit society. For example, a 1974 Gallup poll reported that a clear majority—and in some cases an overwhelming majority—supported cuts in defense spending (56 percent), favored registration of all firearms (71 percent), restoration of wage-price controls (62 percent), public financing of all congressional campaigns (72 percent), providing financial aid to all schools (52 percent), and the legalization of abortion (52 percent).[67] Similar findings exist on many economic-related policy issues. In short, it may be that the public is more capable of making decisions on major policy questions than elected officials because *they* do not belong to the mutual benefit society.

The need for drastic and severe action is clear. Recent events are only indicative of a political system long steeped in corrupting influences. The crimes of those who violate the electoral process should be called exactly what they are, crimes against the people. As such, the punishment should be swift, certain, and costly enough to deter others from violating the public trust. No one should be allowed to steal government from the people, to use it for private gain. Democracy must be implemented, not just professed. If we fail to act, the penalty will be severe. For as the United States Court of Appeals stated in its ruling upholding the 1974 federal reform law, "The present situation cannot be tolerated by a government that professes to be a democracy."[68]

NOTES

1. Committee on Government Operations, United States Senate, *Confidence and Concern: Citizens View American Government* (Washington, D.C.: U.S. Government Printing Office, 1973), p. v.

2. Ibid.

3. Ibid., p. vi.

4. Delmar D. Dunn, "Contributors in the American Electoral Process," *American Politics Quarterly,* Vol. 2 (April 1974), pp. 221–230.

5. Joseph A. Schlesinger, *How They Became Governor* (East Lansing: Michigan State University Government Research Bureau, 1957).

6. "Was Justice Done?" *Newsweek,* September 16, 1974, p. 22.

7. *Des Moines Register,* September 10, 1974, p. 2.

8. "Was Justice Done?" p. 19.

9. Ibid., p. 22.

10. "Introduction" to the *Final Report of the United States Senate Select Committee on Presidential Campaign Activities* (Washington, D.C.: U.S. Government Printing Office, June 1974), p. xxiv.

11. "1974 Campaign Spending Law," *Congressional Quarterly Weekly Report,* October 12, 1974, p. 2865; see also *Congressional Quarterly Weekly Report,* June 14, 1975, p. 1241.

12. Ibid.

13. Ibid.

14. Jules Witcover, "Holes Found in Campaign Fund Law," *The Washington Post* and published in *The Los Angeles Times,* April 13, 1975, part 4, p. 5.

15. This discussion is from David S. Broder, "G.O.P. to Pour $20 Million into Campaign Loophole," *The Los Angeles Times,* September 15, 1975, part 2, p. 5. It is interesting to note that the so-called expert is Russell Hemenway, the director of the National Committee for a More Effective Congress.

16. *The Los Angeles Times,* October 11, 1974, part 1, p. 1.

17. Ibid., part 2, p. 6.

18. Jeff Fishel, *Party and Opposition* (New York: David McKay, 1973), p. 5.

19. Ibid., "Foreword" by Allard K. Lowenstein, p. x.

20. Warren Weaver, Jr., *Both Your Houses: The Truth About Congress* (New York: Praeger, 1972), p. 4.

21. James R. Polk, "On the Take," *The New Republic,* September 13, 1975, p. 14.

22. Ibid.

23. *The Los Angeles Herald Examiner,* June 17, 1974, p. A8.

24. *The Los Angeles Times,* October 19, 1974, part 1, p. 10.

25. Ibid.

26. John B. Anderson, "Public Campaign Funds Wouldn't Crush Interests," *The Washington Post,* June 16, 1974, p. C5. Reprinted with the permission of *The Washington Post.*

27. Harry V. Ball and Laurence Friedman, "The Use of Criminal Sanctions in the Enforcement of Economic Legislation: A Sociological View," *Stanford Law Review* 17 (1965):197–223.

28. Philip Hager, "Disclosure Laws Winning Acceptance," *The Los Angeles Times,* September 12, 1975, part 1, p. 1.

29. Ibid.

30. Robert Fairbanks, "Derby Club Is Going Dutch Treat," *The Los Angeles Times,* December 10, 1974, part 1, p. 3.

31. William Endicott, "Prop 9 Dries Up the Watering Holes," *The Los Angeles Times,* January 23, 1975, part 1, p. 1.

32. William Endicott, "Lobbyists' Fight on Tax Becomes a Beer Bust," *The Los Angeles Times,* August 28, 1975, part 1, p. 1.

33. Berg, one of the authors, has been involved in a project monitoring the implementations act in California since it went into effect in January 1975.

Interviews have been conducted with public officials, lobbyists, and members of reform groups, and this observation is based on that information.

34. Hager, "Disclosure Laws Winning Acceptance," p. 12.

35. Ralph K. Winter, "Money, Politics, and the First Amendment," *Campaign Finances* (Washington, D.C.: American Enterprise Institute for Public Policy Research, 1971), p. 60.

36. *Eastern Railroads Presidents Conference* v. *Noeer Motor Freight Co.*, 365 US 126 (1961).

37. Ibid., p. 127.

38. *Cranch* 290 (1813).

39. *Harper* v. *Board of Elections*, 383 US 663,668 (1966).

40. *Bolling* v. *Sharpe*, 347 US 497, 499 (1954).

41. *Shapiro* v. *Thompson*, 393 US 618, 642 (1969); *Schneider* v. *Rusk* 377 US 163, 168 (1964). See also *Colorado Anti-Discrimination Commission* v. *Continental Air Lines*, 373 US 714,721 (1963) (dictum).

42. *Shelly* v. *Kraemer*, 334 US 1 (1948).

43. See *Terry* v. *Adams*, 345 US 461 (1953).

44. *The Los Angeles Times*, August 16, 1975, part 1, p. 21.

45. Ibid.

46. Ibid.

47. Joel L. Fleishman, "Public Financing of Election Campaigns: Constitutional Constraints on Steps Toward Equality of Political Influence of Citizens," *North Carolina Law Review* 52 (1973):350–351.

48. Jim McClellan and David E. Anderson, "The Bipartisan Ballot Monopoly," *The Progressive*, March 1975, p. 18.

49. Ibid. See this article for an extensive discussion of such prejudiced laws, particularly pp. 19–20.

50. Ibid.

51. *The Sacramento Bee*, January 4, 1911, p. 11.

52. Quoted in Thomas W. Casstevens, "Reflections on the Initiative Process in California State Politics," *Public Affairs Reports* 6 (February 1965):1–3.

53. Gene Rebcock, "Local Government Referenda and Paid Advertising," *Journalism Quarterly* 43 (Autumn 1966):505–509.

54. Harlan Hahn and George M. Gillespie, "A Comparative Study of Attitudes on Fluoridation," *Journal of the Michigan State Dental Association* 58 (February 1966):89–92.

55. A somewhat different version of the discussion of recall can be found in

Larry L. Berg's "Putting the People in Charge: Recall is Needed Nationwide," *The Los Angeles Times,* August 25, 1974, part 8, p. 5.

56. People's Lobby, headquartered in Los Angeles, was founded in 1969. With a dues-paying membership of over 40,000 people, the group states that it was "formed to undertake the task of restoring public confidence in government by teaching citizens to use the tools of self-confidence in government and to make elected officials more responsive." As a citizens' action group, it spearheaded the drive for the reform initiative in California. Along with the Democratic nominee for Governor, Edmund G. Brown, Jr., it was the most important factor in securing voter approval for the measure. For an excellent description of the campaign for the reform initiative, see, *Proposition 9, the Political Reform Act: A Fact for California, A Proposal for America,* by the People's Lobby (Los Angeles: People's Lobby Press, 1974).

57. Karl R. Popper, "Plato as an Enemy of the Open Society" in Thomas L. Thorson, *Plato: Totalitarian or Democrat?* (Englewood Cliffs, N.J.: Prentice-Hall, 1963), p. 71.

58. For example, see David Nichols, *Financing Elections: The Politics of an American Ruling Class* (New York: New Viewpoints, 1974), pp. 25–26; and Michael Parenti, *Democracy for the Few* (New York: St. Martin's Press, 1974).

59. See Hager, "Disclosure Laws Winning Acceptance." Also, it should be pointed out that western states have led the move for reform laws, particularly those states with an initiative process.

60. Winston W. Crouch, *The Initiative and Referendum in California* (Los Angeles: The Haynes Foundation, 1950), p. 19.

61. Robert S. Erikson and Norman R. Luttbeg, *American Public Opinion* (New York: John Wiley, 1973), p. 282.

62. Robert Sherrill reports that General James Gavin suggested it might be a good idea to rig up an electronic device to permit referendum guidance. Robert Sherrill, *Why They Call It Politics,* 2nd ed. (New York: Harcourt Brace Jovanovich, 1974), p. 149.

63. See note 12, chapter 1, Supra.

64. Sherrill, *Why They Call It Politics,* pp. 149–150.

65. Ibid., p. 152.

66. Fred Harris, "The Real Populism Fights Unequal Wealth," *The New York Times,* May 25, 1972, p. 45. Also, for an interesting discussion of the divergence of views of the public and politicians on the economic system see Jeremy Rifkin, "The People Are Passing Us By," *The Progressive,* October 1975, pp. 13–14 and Michael Best and John Buell, "A New Democracy," *The Progressive,* October 1974, pp. 15–18.

67. *The Los Angeles Times,* November 4, 1974, part 1, p. 6.

68. *The Sacramento Bee,* August 31, 1975, Opinion Section, p. 3.

Index